THE FIFTEEN

THE FIFTEEN

The Lives and Times of the Women in India's Constituent Assembly

ANGELLICA ARIBAM
AKASH SATYAWALI

hachette INDIA

First published in 2024 by Hachette India
(Registered name: Hachette Book Publishing India Pvt. Ltd)
An Hachette UK company
www.hachetteindia.com

2

ISBN 978-93-91028-30-5

Hachette Book Publishing India Pvt. Ltd
4th & 5th Floors, Corporate Centre
Plot No. 94, Sector 44, Gurugram – 122003, India

Typeset in Dante MT Std 11/13.5
by Manmohan Kumar, Delhi

Printed and bound in India
by Manipal Technologies Limited

MIX
Paper | Supporting responsible forestry
FSC™ C043100
FSC www.fsc.org

To my nieces – Aria & Amaia, Likla & Leichal – for whom I want to shape a gender-just world.

ANGELLICA ARIBAM

To my parents, Champa and Hem Satyawali, for their love and encouragement of everything I do.

AKASH SATYAWALI

CONTENTS

INTRODUCTION

It has been more than seventy years since India became a democratic republic. Since the first official demand for women's suffrage in 1917 by a group of Indian women activists, the status of women has undergone massive improvements. However, in the male-dominated world of politics, the representation of women has seen only an incremental growth. The Constituent Assembly had fifteen women out of 299 members – a mere 5 per cent. As of January 2024, India ranks 142 out of 193 countries with just 15 per cent Lok Sabha members being women.[1]

In September 2023, the president of India gave assent to a law that provides 33 per cent reservation for women in the Lok Sabha and state legislative assemblies. At long last, there is hope that women will occupy a significant space in public offices. The women's reservation law is the culmination of three decades of intense activism. It is often said that we stand on the shoulders of giants. In this case, the right to representation can be viewed as part of the struggle from a century ago when Indian women leaders organized and advocated for women's right to vote. They won partial victories and persevered to demand their rightful share in all spheres – political, social, and economic.

The women leaders agitated to enact a child marriage restraint law, successfully advocated for expanding female education and health services, argued for a progressive personal law, adopted the Indian Woman's Charter of Rights and Duties which specifically made a case for women's economic empowerment, and marched on the frontlines of the freedom struggle.

The Indian Constitution, ambitious and idealistic in scope, was an acknowledgment of the aspirations of the freedom fighters and social reformers who had been striving for decades. The demands for a sovereign state, equal civic rights, safeguards for minorities, political and economic justice had been agitated upon for years. The Constituent Assembly comprised 299 members representing the provinces and princely states / groups. The lived experiences, struggles, and ideological moorings of the members influenced the Constitution.

Although the Constituent Assembly was meant to be a microcosm of India, certain sections of the population were not adequately represented. Only fifteen women were members of this distinguished body. The number further reduced to thirteen after the resignation of Leela Roy and Malati Choudhury. Like their male counterparts, the women members had been entrenched in the political and social spheres; their lives were intertwined with nation-building and their experiences shaped the republic. This book is an attempt to shed light on the remarkable lives of these fifteen women.

In the world's most populous country and the largest democracy, the Constitution is at the heart of every public discourse. The Constituent Assembly debates continue to reverberate in jurisprudence. A host of contemporary questions are sought to be answered by looking at the past. For example, there is intense contestation on whether or not India should adopt a Uniform Civil Code (UCC). Even those who agree that there must be a UCC differ widely on what form the civil code must take. Similar debates have arisen on the issue of citizenship that encompass within them how India defines secularism. Rights of detainees, state surveillance, ambit of executive power are key issues that are regularly debated in the public arena, including the parliament and the Supreme Court. Therefore, a holistic understanding of the different actors and groups behind the framing of the Constitution becomes vital.

This book is the culmination of a four-year-long journey that began with intrigue followed by curiosity and a keen sense of responsibility. As the conversation on gender has become more mainstream in the last decade, the consensus remains that women have often been invisibilized in our history. Prior to beginning research for this book, we, the authors, sporadically found mention of women leaders in our individual readings of Indian democracy in its nascent stage. Whenever we came across names like Annie Mascarene, Durgabai Deshmukh, or Hansa Mehta, it piqued our interest. We were eager to learn about the contributions of the women in the framing of the Indian Constitution. It soon became a rabbit hole.

As we delved deeper into the lives of the fifteen women, we experienced multifarious emotions – pride, reverence, shock, and inspiration. As no comprehensive literature is available on these women, our incredulity began to take the shape of a responsibility to tell their stories. It was daunting; yet an exciting task to undertake. The critical information had to be parsed through after looking at varied sources. Often, key events had to be pieced together from footnotes of other texts. The excitement came at the prospect of creating value for others who are interested in the subject and the lives of these women.

While neither of us, the authors, subscribe to superstitions and the notion of destiny, there was a powerful moment when we felt that this book was destined to be. This was brought upon by a passage in Renuka Ray's memoir. It felt like she had written a personal message to us ages ago as though she knew that someday we will be tracing the paths of the women leaders. The passage reads:

'Sixty years hence someone, perhaps a woman, looking back will tell the story of how a new movement arose and brought about a social revolution. Perhaps she will be kinder to my generation and times than I have been, as she will have the benefit of detachment, and a sense of perspective.'[2]

Throughout our work, we heeded Renuka Ray's words and remained as objective as possible.

We understand that the politics of these women was deeply shaped by their lived experiences and the world around them. Despite the differences in their social and economic status, the one cause that united them was the desire to leave a better India for future generations. Each of them approached this mission in their own way, some of which may not agree with present sensibilities.

These women had distinct ideologies. Leela Roy was a revolutionary at heart and in practice. Renuka Ray was often at the crossroads of armed and non-violent struggle. Sucheta Kripalani dabbled in subversive underground work but stayed clear of violent means. Sarojini Naidu, Hansa Mehta, Malati Choudhury, Rajkumari Amrit Kaur, Purnima Banerji, and Vijaya Lakshmi Pandit followed the Gandhian ideal of non-violence.

Based on our observations, we found that most of the challenges these women political leaders faced almost a century ago are still prevalent today. While the fifteen women came from diverse backgrounds across India, they battled patriarchy and misogyny. We also observed the fundamental role played by caste and class privilege. Except for a few, the women were all either born or married into affluent families. Begum Qudsia Aizaz Rasul and Rajkumari Amrit Kaur belonged to royal families of Punjab. Vijaya Lakshmi Pandit's and Hansa Mehta's families were political royalties. Sarojini Naidu, Malati Choudhury, and Renuka Ray hailed from influential Bengali families. Annie Mascarene (a Latin Christian) and Dakshayani Velayudhan (a Dalit) were exceptions to this norm. All fifteen women had supportive families who stood with them in their journeys.

Most of the women were actively involved in the social reform agenda. Perhaps conscious of their relative privilege, they actively contributed to social causes like education of women, abolition of untouchability, abolition of devadasi system and child marriages, women's right to property, etc. Actively involved in the freedom struggle, most of them spent considerable time in prisons. Many took on prominent leadership roles at the All India Women's Conference (AIWC). They even travelled to the League of Nations in Geneva to galvanize international support for Indian women's right to vote. Leela Roy started an organization that trained and nurtured young women to be capable political leaders. Malati Choudhury started schools for underserved communities. The women advocated for a progressive Hindu Code Bill to remove legal disabilities of women, and finally treat women at par with men.

Their contribution to politics didn't end with the adoption of the Constitution. They took on prominent roles in the newly independent democratic country. Vijaya Lakshmi Pandit scaled heights in diplomacy. Rajkumari Amrit Kaur was the first woman to become a union minister. Durgabai Deshmukh was a founding member of the Planning Commission. Annie Mascarene and Renuka Ray served as ministers in their respective state governments. Sarojini Naidu and Sucheta Kripalani went on to become the first female governor and chief minister, respectively.

The fifteen women contributed immensely to shape modern India. Each of their remarkable journeys not only tells us about law and polity but also presents a glimpse into the multiple Indias that existed – in their perfections and imperfections. Theirs are stories of resistance and hope.

Our attempt with this book is to provide the reader a comprehensive knowledge of the women behind India's Constitution and a window into the world wherein these women navigated extraordinary challenges and left lasting imprints. In tracing their history, we have exercised enormous caution and showed utmost respect to their individual ideological moorings. We tried our best to not let our personal beliefs and ideologies get in the way of analysing and telling their stories. We hope we have done justice to them and live in eternal hope that more people will remember these women as the giant leaders that they were.

AMMU SWAMINATHAN

'I know that the Constitution gives us in the Fundamental Rights, equal status, adult franchise and has also provided for the removal of untouchability [...] But all these things appearing on paper is not enough if we are to make this country happy and prosperous. We have to see that these ideas and ideals which are on paper in the Constitution are implemented by the people of this country.'

– On the adoption of the Constitution in the Constituent Assembly on 24 November 1949[1]

Captain Lakshmi Sahgal was the commander of Rani of Jhansi Regiment of the Indian National Army (INA), the country's first military regiment for women and also a close confidante of Subhas Chandra Bose. Lakshmi's name is etched in the pages of Indian history as a firebrand leader who was taken prisoner in Burma during World War II. But only a few know that Lakshmi's strength and courage came from a mother most extraordinary – Ammu Swaminathan.

Right from childhood, feisty Ammu did not hesitate to challenge authority. She had a mind of her own and wasn't one to conform. At every step of her life, she pushed the boundary. After marriage, Ammu used her growing privilege and clout as a socialite to advocate for gender reforms. She later joined the freedom struggle and spoke truth to power. As a mother, she supported the decisions of her sons and daughters even if she didn't agree with them. Illustrious in their own fields, each of her offsprings had much to credit their mother for their unconventional upbringing.

★★★

The story of Ammu began in a small town called Palghat (now Palakkad) near Kochi, Kerala. The youngest of thirteen children, A.V. Ammukutty was born to a Nair family on 22 April 1894.[2] Her father, P. Govinda Menon, was a local government official who struggled to provide for his large family. They could not afford sending her to school, so Ammu was taught to read and write Malayalam at home. She also learned to cook, in preparation for an early marriage like most girls of the time. Ammu, however, resented the idea of domesticity, leading her own mother to describe her as a 'tomboy'.[3]

Dr Subbarama Swaminathan, Ammu's husband, had entered the lives of the Menon family much before her birth. He came from a Tamil Brahmin family that settled in a village near Palghat, Ammu's hometown. Subbarama's father was an influential landowner and the Menons often sought his advice. During these visits, the Menons became closely acquainted with Subbarama. Soon after, tragedy struck the Swaminathan family with the sudden death of Subbarama's father.[4]

His father's death was quickly followed by the demise of his mother. Young Subbarama was now left to support his grandmother, a brother, and two sisters. They were, according to his daughter Lakshmi, 'very, very poor'. The Menons stepped in and persuaded him to enter the provincial college in Calicut (present-day Kozhikode) on a scholarship. However, the scholarship money wasn't enough for him to support his family. So he made ends meet by tutoring boys, some even older than him.[5] Though he loved physics he chose to pursue law instead, in the hope of making a lucrative career in it. Soon after, he joined the Madras Law College, where he won the Gilchrist Scholarship for the University of Edinburgh.[6] Around this time, the Menons had just given birth to Ammu.

During the nineteenth century, the Hindus considered it taboo to cross the seas. Subbarama's relatives were against his plans of going to the United Kingdom on the grounds that crossing the oceans meant that he would lose his 'upper-caste' status. But Subbarama paid no heed to the superstitions. Determined, he left for the UK and made the most of the opportunity by pursuing his passion for both science and law – he received his LLB from Edinburgh in 1898, and a BSc a year later.[7]

After obtaining two degrees, the ambitious double graduate decided to use his remaining scholarship money to obtain a PhD from the University of Harvard, USA. He submitted his thesis in just six months, much to the bewilderment of the faculty. His daughter Lakshmi narrated the amusing exchange: 'when he submitted it, Harvard said, "but you have two and a half years to go!" "I'm sorry," he replied, "If I stay I'll be wasting your money and my time, especially my time. I've got to get back and start earning my living. Here's your thesis."'[8] University records confirm that he was awarded the PhD in 1900.[9]

A progressive Subbarama continued to reject the diktats of the caste system. One story goes that upon his return to Madras (now Chennai), Subbarama's Brahmin relatives insisted that he perform purification rituals because he had travelled across the seas. Subbarama, however, refused to oblige and quipped that if he had to, he would perform them holding beef in one hand and alcohol in the other![10]

He channelized his whole energy into his legal practice, becoming one of the luminaries of the Madras High Court.[11] He was now well into his thirties and decided to look for a bride. His irreverence towards his community made it difficult for him to find an alliance among the Brahmins of Madras.[12] He then turned to the Menon family for help. At the time, even though most Brahmins wed within their community, marriages between Brahmin men and Nair women were acceptable in Kerala.[13]

Ammu was just stepping into her teens when Subbarama showed up at their doorstep. By then, Ammu's father had passed away and all her sisters were married.[14] Ammu's mother informed Subbarama that her 'tomboy' daughter knew only one language – Malayalam.[15] Undeterred, he requested to see her and was fully taken by her. Despite an age difference of twenty-three years, Subbarama proposed marriage.[16] Ammu was not opposed to the match but had a few conditions[17] – she wanted to move to Madras, learn English from an Englishwoman, and not be asked 'what time she would reach home', a question that her brothers were never asked.[18] Subbarama was moved by Ammu's free-spiritedness and readily agreed to all her conditions.

The wedding took place soon after, at the end of 1908, when Ammu was just fourteen years old.[19] Child marriage was prevalent across India then. In fact, two decades later, the Child Marriage Restraint Act (also known as Sarda Act) fixed the minimum age of girls for marriage at 14.[20]

Many communities in Kerala, including the Nairs, were matrilineal and followed the *sambandam* system, a kind of contractual marriage that could be dissolved by either party at will. Children born of *sambandam* marriages belonged to the mother. This meant that succession was traced through the female line and the children could not inherit their father's property. It was also matrilocal in nature, where the bride continued living in her maternal home.[21]

However, Ammu's family and Subbarama chose to have a conventional Hindu wedding. Unfortunately, Subbarama's family disapproved of his marriage to a non-Brahmin partner and did not attend the ceremony.[22] Later, the couple renewed their vows at the registry office in London in order to officially sever ties from the *sambandam* system. After this, Ammu and her children adopted the last name – Swaminathan.

The couple moved to Madras immediately after their wedding. Subbarama was doing well in his career. They named their residence Gilchrist Gardens after the scholarship that gave Subbarama a new lease of life. It was here that Ammu fully came into her own and flourished. Her wish to live a life unhindered by conservative stereotypes of gender as well as financial limitations came true. Subbarama kept his promise and hired an English governess, he even took Ammu to England to stay with a British family so that she could learn the language better.[23] He also introduced her to theatre and tennis. Ammu also began acting in amateur plays and learnt to drive. It was a rare sight to have a woman drive around Madras in the early twentieth century.

Ammu and Subbarama had four children – two sons and two daughters. The first was Govinda.[24] Lakshmi was born five years later in 1914, followed by another son Subbarama Krishna. The youngest daughter, born in 1918, was named after family friend Mrinalini Chattopadhyay, sister of political activist Sarojini Naidu. The four children had a very British upbringing. They grew up with governesses, talked in English, and were even trained in British etiquettes. Ammu gave her children a strict upbringing without showing overt affection, but she also gave them the freedom to experience life in their own way.[25]

Education was of prime importance in their household, and Subbarama wanted all four children to be educated in England.[26] Govinda went to a boarding school in Darjeeling and then left for a public school in England at the age of twelve.[27] He read law at the University of Oxford and later served as standing counsel of the Government of India and then as advocate general of Tamil Nadu.

Lakshmi wanted to be a doctor in the spirit of serving people.[28] Instead of going to England like her brothers, she pursued medicine at Madras Medical College,[29] specializing in obstetrics and gynaecology. Later, she joined the freedom movement as one of Bose's closest aides in Singapore and came to be known as Captain Lakshmi Sahgal of the INA.

Subbarama Krishna went to England when he was seven.[30] Mrinalini, the youngest, attended school in Switzerland, where she developed a passion for dance. Like her sister, she elected not to study in England, and decided to pursue a career in dance. She went to Santiniketan in present-day West Bengal, for dance training while completing her higher education.[31] Mrinalini blossomed into a fine performer of classical dance forms such as Bharatanatyam, Kathakali, and Mohiniattam. She married renowned physicist Vikram Sarabhai and came to be known as Mrinalini Sarabhai. She even received the Padma Bhushan, India's third-highest civilian award, for her contribution to Indian classical dances.

Despite a liberal upbringing and their father's high status in legal circles, the Swaminathan children faced caste discrimination from the paternal family.[32] Subbarama and Ammu were shocked when they came to know that their daughters were not allowed to eat inside their Brahmin grandparents' house on visits and had to eat their meals seated on the floor of a verandah.[33]

Such instances did not affect the relationship that Ammu shared with her husband. Her life transformed for the better with his love, support, and resources. She was full of dreams and aspirations, and wanted to carve her own identity in society. She rejected conservatism and lived as a socialite – wearing expensive clothes and jewels, throwing lavish parties, and serving Western cuisine to her friends. The who's who of society, including poets, freedom fighters, and British aristocrats were all regulars at Ammu's soirées. While this led to resentment in the tradition-bound community, the Swaminathans were unconcerned and enjoyed their lifestyle.[34]

Mrinalini attested to her mother's popularity, calling her the 'Queen of Madras'.[35] The children enjoyed the privileges of growing up in the exhilarating environment at Gilchrist Gardens, and were exposed to a variety of people and the politics of the time.[36]

In spite of the flurry of activities at home, Subbarama remained consumed with work. He even took time off from family vacations and worked. But this did not mean he neglected his wife. According to Mrinalini, her father 'indulged' Ammu, and she even recalled how he would make her coffee in the morning.[37]

In the midst of her hectic and eclectic social life, Ammu developed an interest in both politics and the women's movement. This was 1914, and she was all of twenty. Perhaps her exposure to Madras' high society and invigorating conversations on the status of women awakened her desire to crush gender stereotypes. Seeing her own mother as a widow, Ammu strongly detested the practices that compelled women to shave their heads, wear white saris, and renounce jewellery upon the death of their husbands.[38]

Three years later, in 1917, she joined hands with prominent leaders such as Annie Besant, Malathi Patwardhan, Kamaladevi Chattopadhyay, Margaret Cousins, Jeena Raja Dasa, and Ambujammal to set up the Women's Indian Association (WIA).[39] Their aim was to address the many socio-economic challenges faced by women including child marriage, the devadasi system, widow remarriage, divorce, and inheritance, while also working towards expanding equal educational and economic opportunities.[40] WIA was one of the first organizations that boldly connected Indian women's social and sexual subjugation with patriarchy, poverty, and political disenfranchisement.[41] It was also India's first national body to advocate for female suffrage.

The Montagu-Chelmsford Commission was formed in 1917 to formulate a report on how to introduce self-governing institutions in India. It was to prepare a list of reforms which would form the basis of the Government of India Act 1919. The WIA was part of a combined women's delegation led by Sarojini Naidu that met the commission and demanded for the Indian women's right to vote.[42]

In 1918, the WIA made a similar request in front of the Southborough Franchise Committee, one of the bodies tasked with figuring out who gets the right to vote, in favour of enfranchising women in the expanded provincial legislatures as part of the Government of India Act 1919.

Unfortunately, their request wasn't accepted. In response, General Secretary of WIA Margaret Cousins wrote an angry letter to a newspaper, 'On behalf of the members of the 46 Branches of the Women's Indian Association, all of which have signed requisitions in favour of women suffrage, I protest vigorously against the decision of the Southborough Committee that the franchise shall not be extended to women because, forsooth, "the social conditions of India make it premature".'[43]

The Government of India Act 1919 allowed provincial legislatures to enfranchise women. Instead of a national campaign, women's groups started demanding the right to vote provincially. The Madras Presidency gave women the right to vote in 1919 at the municipal level, but they were restricted from contesting elections. This was widely criticized. In 1921, the sex criterion was removed for anyone contesting elections at the local level.

Ammu would later serve as the vice president and president of the WIA.[44] In 1927, the WIA moved to form the All India Women's Conference (AIWC) alongside other organizations under the leadership of Margaret Cousins. Ammu was a prominent member. She was one of the fiercest advocates who fought for a legislation to end child marriage, popularly known as the Sarda Bill,[45] a stance only made stronger by the fact that she herself was a child bride.

When Mahatma Gandhi called for the mass burning of foreign clothes during the Swadeshi movement in the 1920s, Ammu couldn't resist the pull of his message.[46] This also influenced her children. It was Ammu who introduced Lakshmi to politics. According to Lakshmi, her mother was committed to social revolution, and 'wanted to change society totally, for she believed it was most unjust to women and to the poor.'[47] Subbarama too made changes. He wore only khadi later in life but didn't join the Indian National Congress (INC). According to his son, Govinda, Subbarama was suspicious of politicians.[48] But he didn't try to stop his wife from entering politics.

Subbarama died in 1930 when Ammu was only thirty-six.[49] True to his character, Subbarama had Ammu taken care of even in death. He didn't want her to follow the customs of widowhood.[50] He also left a will that ensured neither his wife nor his daughters were deprived of inheritances. He bequeathed their family home in Ammu's name. His daughters were to have an equal share in property as his sons. Lakshmi said, 'If he hadn't made a will, my brothers would have got everything and we wouldn't have got a thing.'[51]

Months after her husband's death, Ammu took full plunge into active politics. It was 1930 – the historic year of the Civil Disobedience Movement and Dandi March.[52] She signed up housewives for the membership of the Congress.[53] Other than donating time and money, she also put Gilchrist Gardens at the complete disposal of the Congress.[54] Many stalwarts of the freedom movement passed through the gates of the residence. The list included C. Rajagopalachari of the Madras Congress, Aruna Asaf Ali, Harindranath Chattopadhyay, and his three sisters – Sarojini Naidu, Suhasini Nambiar, and Mrinalini Chattopadhyay; his wife Kamaladevi Chattopadhyay, and Vijaya Lakshmi Pandit.[55]

Ammu's children had different reactions to their mother's participation in the freedom struggle. While Lakshmi was deeply involved in her mother's activities, Govinda was sceptical of the 'Gandhi-cap-toting Congress flock'.[56] Comrade Suhasini Nambiar, the most radical of the three Chattopadhyay sisters and the first Indian woman to be a member of the Communist Party, spent a couple of years at Gilchrist Gardens evading police arrest.[57] Teenager Lakshmi was profoundly influenced by her thoughts. While the whole house slept, Lakshmi would sit up all night and listen to Suhasini's stories of her earlier life in Berlin, the Russian Revolution, and her observations of the German communists. Lakshmi was also inspired by Edgar Snow's 1937 book *Red Star Over China*.[58] However, she didn't turn her back on the Congress yet and invited heavyweight political leaders visiting Madras to give speeches in different colleges.[59]

Ammu continued to divide her time between the Congress and the AIWC. She used the platforms to fight for women's suffrage and argued for equality of women in all spheres, including politics. In 1933, Ammu's future Constituent Assembly colleague Amrit Kaur campaigned with advocate and political figure Shareefa Hamid Ali in London for women's suffrage and then headed to Geneva to lobby the League of Nations and the International Labour Office. Ammu also joined the delegation as an AIWC member. The AIWC made an official submission to the League of Nations, which read: 'We constitute one-fifth of the world's women; we are keenly alive to the vital importance of the Council's work; we are systematically studying the problems connected with the position, rights and duties of women and could, therefore, co-operate to international advantage.' This was the first time that representatives of the all-India women's movement were claiming an independent space for Indian women in an international setting. Their Geneva campaign was highly publicized and garnered a lot of attention and support.[60]

After her return, Ammu contested the Madras Corporation civic polls. She won the election and served from 1934–39.[61] The Government of India Act 1935 was passed soon after and granted women aged 21 years and above the right to vote across the country. This law enabled as many as six million Indian women to vote and stand for elections to both general seats and the seats reserved for women.[62]

The next step for Ammu was to take the battle for women's political rights home to the Congress. On 22 August 1936, Ammu wrote to then Congress president Jawaharlal Nehru, along with a copy of the AIWC manifesto *Candidates for the Coming Election*. In her letter, she pointed out that 'Women make a special contribution to the general welfare and progress of the country.' She requested for the list of candidates that were to represent the party in the elections of 1937. In her letter she drew attention to the lack of women members in the Congress Working Committee (CWC) – the highest decision-making body of the Congress. Ammu demanded that Nehru appoint at least one woman in the CWC with immediate effect.[63]

In his response, Nehru wrote that women will be naturally fielded from the seats reserved for them. However, he didn't make any commitment to field women from the general seats. Nehru further stated that the Congress was devoting thought and energy towards the political independence of women. He also subtly hinted at the lack of electability of women.[64]

Undeterred by such disappointing responses to their pleas in favour of women, Ammu and many other women leaders of the time continued their work. When her tenure at the Madras Corporation ended in 1939, Ammu decided to spend time with her family. She took Mrinalini on a world tour – Java, Bali, and the USA. While Mrinalini studied drama in New York for six months, Ammu headed to Chicago to catch up with Margaret Sanger.[65] At this time, Lakshmi headed off to Singapore in 1940 following the failure of her first marriage.[66] On their way back from the USA, Ammu and Mrinalini met Lakshmi. Unlike most mothers of that era, Ammu didn't give Lakshmi a difficult time for either her failed love marriage or the blossoming romance with another man. Seeing Lakshmi unhappy with the judgments and patriarchy of the Indian diaspora in Singapore, she suggested that they return to Madras together.[67] Lakshmi, however, chose to stay on and the rest is history. The mother-daughter met years later after Lakshmi's release from a Burmese prison in 1946.

After the world tour, Ammu immersed herself in the freedom struggle again. She participated actively in the Quit India Movement of 1942. With most of its senior leaders in jail, Ammu donated large sums of money to the Congress to keep the movement going. Using her platform as the president of the AIWC

Madras chapter, she also organized strikes and demonstrations. Her friend S. Manjubhashini, president of the Madras Women Students' Organization, joined her in these activities. Both of them also organized the printing and distribution of anonymous pamphlets to instigate nationalist sentiments. On 19 February 1943, Ammu was arrested and jailed in Vellore for a year.[68]

Like her husband, Ammu had zero tolerance for casteist beliefs, perhaps influenced by the discrimination meted out to her and her children at the hands of her in-laws. An incident from her time at Vellore's Presidency Jail for women sheds light on Ammu's indignation at caste supremacy. One day, she witnessed a fellow inmate use a casteist slur, *Shudrachi,* to address a female sanitation worker. Annoyed by this, Ammu walked up to the inmate and said, 'Yes, tell me.' The confused inmate explained that she was calling the sanitation worker, to which Ammu replied, 'I am a *Shudrachi* too. Now say what do you want.'[69]

In a similar vein, she once criticized Jawaharlal Nehru for adopting the title of 'Pandit' because she believed it to be an assertion and endorsement of caste superiority. Nehru pointed out that he had never asked anyone to address him this way. She retorted that he still chose to respond to it, so it was still an endorsement of caste assertion.[70] This showed that Ammu recognized the subtle nature in which the caste discourse played out.

Coming back to her political career, Ammu contested the election for Central Legislative Assembly (equivalent to the present-day Lok Sabha) of 1945 as a Congress candidate. She won from Madras City with 10,883 votes as opposed to 2,154 of her closest rivals.[71] She became a member of the Constituent Assembly in 1946.

A few years before this, in 1937, there had been a major turning point in the Indian women's movement. Dr G.V. Deshmukh, a member of the Central Legislative Assembly, introduced a reformist bill – the Hindu Women's Right to Property Bill 1937. This Bill gave Hindu widows a right to intestate succession, or the right to inherit property if their husbands died without a will, which had thus far been granted only to sons. It also gave the women the same rights as the deceased husbands in undivided joint families. The legislation was opposed by many orthodox groups. It was sent to a select committee called the Rau Committee for review.

While Ammu was glad that the Bill would bring some relief to Hindu widows,[72] she was also aware that this central legislation did not apply to the devolution of agricultural land, since agricultural property fell in the 'jurisdiction of provincial legislation'. In a majority agrarian society, it was important to grant these inheritance rights too, but these needed provincial reforms[73]. Ammu took on the mantle and, alongside members of the AIWC and Madras Legislative Assembly, urged the Madras government to include agricultural lands within the domain of property.[74] The campaign was successful, and the reforms were passed in Madras in November 1946.[75]

In February 1948, Dr B.R. Ambedkar introduced a draft Hindu Code Bill in the Constituent Assembly based on the recommendations of the Rau Committee to remove the legal disabilities that Hindu women suffered. It was met with widespread criticism from the male members as they saw it as the breakdown of the Hindu family and culture. Most of the opposition was based on the idea that daughters shouldn't be allowed to inherit property. Dr Ambedkar constituted a select committee of twenty people to go through the draft Bill in order to amend and codify the Hindu Laws.[76] Ammu was appointed to the committee headed by Dr Ambedkar.[77] When the body submitted its deliberations after a year, it was again greeted with stiff opposition. Nehru then decided to shelve it until the first parliamentary elections.

When the motion to adopt the Constitution was being discussed on 24 November 1949, Ammu called the Indian Constitution the realization of a great dream of four hundred million people. She reminded the members of the Constituent Assembly that all the rights, ideas, and ideals meant nothing if not implemented. Ammu also complained about how long and bulky the Constitution was, having envisioned it as a 'small volume which one could carry in one's purse or pocket'. She was deeply committed to the subject of women's rights and was proud of the fact that this was now enshrined in the country's law: 'People outside have been saying that India did not give equal rights to her women. Now we can say that when the Indian people themselves framed their Constitution they have given rights to women equal with every other citizen of the country. That in itself is a great achievement and it is going to help our women not only to realize their responsibilities but to come forward and fully shoulder their responsibilities to make India a great country that she had been.'[78]

No matter what the Constitution says, the fight for women's rights continued to be an unending journey even in the provisional parliament. Once when the Minister of Law, Dr Ambedkar announced the formation of an advisory committee for the Hindu Code Bill, Ammu took the House by storm. She openly questioned if any representatives of women's organizations were to be taken on the non-official Advisory Committee to advise on the Hindu Code Bill. When she mentioned that the Bill affects the women of the country more than the men, the male-dominant House erupted into laughter. Not one to mince her words, she called out the blatant display of sexism in the country's highest law-making body. Instead of backing off, she reiterated her question showing everyone that she meant business. 'Every time that any question of women's rights comes up in that House, there is general laughter, as if it is a joke. I do not mean it as a joke. I would like the Hon. Law Minister to tell us whether in view of the fact that the Hindu Code really affects women very largely and there are several women's organizations in India, they have been asked to send representatives to this Advisory Committee that is going to be called very soon.'[79] She didn't drop the questions till Dr Ambedkar informed her that women's organizations have been invited. All the frivolous laughter of men could not deter the feisty Ammu from seeking representation of women.

In the first Lok Sabha elections of independent India, Ammu was one of the twenty-four women elected out of 489 members.[80] Representing the Congress in Dindigul, a city in modern-day Tamil Nadu, she secured 77,285 votes and defeated Communist Party of India's (CPI's) candidate by a margin of more than 10,000.[81] She was nominated to the panel of chairmen of the Lok Sabha in 1953.[82] While some reports suggest that she was nominated to the Rajya Sabha in 1954, Rajya Sabha records reflect that she was a member from 9 November 1957 until her retirement on 2 April 1960.[83]

Ammu also served as India's goodwill ambassador to Russia, China, the USA, and Ethiopia.[84] Her interest in arts and movies, developed when she dabbled in amateur theatre in her youth, never waned. When the Federation of Film Societies of India was formed in 1959, with filmmaker Satyajit Ray as president, she served as its vice president.[85] During 1960–65, she was also the president of the Bharat Scouts and Guides, a voluntary, non-political education movement for the youth. She remains the only woman to hold that position in the history of the organization.

Ammu breathed her last on 4 July 1978, at the age of 84. She lived a rich life with myriad experiences – from poverty to opulence, from travelling the world to being confined in jail, and from being a child bride to a leader of the women's movement in India. But the essence of her life was her keen desire to change the status of women in the country, which guided her in her personal choices as well as political ones, fighting for reforms in marriage, succession, and inheritance laws. Her life was a true example of recognizing one's privilege and using it to advance the causes of those bereft of the same.

Subhashini Ali, her granddaughter and politburo member of the Communist Party of India (Marxist), reminisced about Ammu in *The Indian Express*, 'My mother (Lakshmi Sahgal) stayed beside her during her last moments, before she died'.

She also shared a striking memory she has of Ammu. Once when Subhashini sought her husband's opinion on what sari to wear, she was strongly rebuked by Ammu: 'What kind of a granddaughter of mine are you?' Subhashini proudly remembers Ammu's feisty spirit, 'I have never seen a woman like her – so independent and so fierce.'[86]

ANNIE MASCARENE

> 'We are here laying down principles – rudimentary principles – of democracy, not for the coming election but for days to come, for generations, for the nation. Therefore principles of ethics are more suitable to be considered now than principles of expediency. I am a believer in politics as nothing but ethics writ large.'[1]
>
> – Against the Centre's role in managing the Election Commission in the Constituent Assembly on 16 June 1949

After years of standing up to social deprivation and discrimination, Annie Mascarene was elected as a Member of Parliament from Thiruvananthapuram as an independent candidate in 1951. Additionally, she also holds the record of being the only woman ever to win from the Thiruvananthapuram Lok Sabha constituency in Kerala till date.

★★★

Annie Mascarene's struggle for equality was a lifelong quest. She was from a marginalized Latin Catholic community in the princely state of Travancore, in modern-day Kerala.[2] For years Annie's fisherfolk community remained on the fringes of the cosmopolitan and progressive Travancore society. At the beginning of the first century AD, St. Thomas the Apostle set foot in erstwhile Calicut (present-day Kozhikode) and converted many upper-caste families – including Brahmins – to Christianity.[3] They came to be known as Syrian Christians and retained their caste privileges.[4] The society remained deeply divided on caste lines. When the Portuguese arrived and introduced the Latin rite in the sixteenth century, many Dalits and other marginalized communities – such as the fisherfolk and coconut gatherers – too converted to Christianity.

The elite and the powerful frowned upon these conversions because the Latin Christians – people who were at the lowest rungs of the caste system – were no longer obligated to serve the upper castes. But the royals of Travancore had no objection to the conversions and the Portuguese carried on. The conversions did not erase the caste divisions, though.[5]

Gabriel Mascarene, Annie's father, was a low-ranking official in the government of Travancore. Annie, born on 6 June 1902, and her two siblings (a brother and a sister) spent their childhood under financial constraints.

A brilliant student, Annie secured admission into the Maharaja's College in Trivandrum,[6] considered the best for higher education in the region. Impressed by the quality of education at the institution, the Government of Travancore decided to fund the education of 80 of its 500-odd students. Only the brightest could find a seat at Maharaja's College; therefore, the public held its students and teachers in high esteem. Annie's academic brilliance became her ticket to the coveted institution, making her one of the few women of the time to pursue higher education. Unlike many other students of the college, Annie's chances of landing a cushy government job were slim. Up until 1921, the Travancore government did not employ women.[7] Being a Latin Christian didn't help her job prospects either as she was a part of a deeply communal society where the minorities – such as the Ezhavas (a 'lower caste' Hindu community), Christians, and Muslims – were kept away from employment in certain government departments.

Luckily for Annie and the people of Travancore, the 1920s saw a progressive era under Maharani Sethu Lakshmi Bayi, who assumed power in 1924 as Queen Regent on behalf of her nephew

Chithira Thirunal Balarama Varma. She introduced several social reforms, such as allowing all castes to access hitherto restricted roads, and recruitments on the basis of merit with preference to historically underprivileged groups. The Maharani also promoted the education of girls and women. As an incentive, women who attended college at the time were invited to have tea with the Maharani at her palace.[8] Annie was one of the students.

In 1925, at the age of twenty-three, Annie earned a double MA in history and economics. Immediately after this, she moved to Ceylon (now Sri Lanka) to become a lecturer instead of languishing in a patriarchal and casteist work environment in Travancore. In 1927, the Maharani opened up legal studies for female students despite stiff opposition from men.[9] Annie decided to grab the opportunity and returned home. She went back to her alma mater to read law. After graduation, Annie transitioned to teaching law in the same institution.[10]

Annie's political career began soon after, driven by the political upheavals in Travancore. The reign of Sethu Lakshmi Bayi ended in 1931 when her nephew assumed power as the Maharaja of Travancore. In 1932, the Maharaja inaugurated a bicameral legislature in Travancore, a revolutionary reform intended to smoothen communal rivalries.[11] Earlier, the right to vote was enjoyed by only those who paid land revenue of at least ₹50 or those with a minimum annual income of ₹2,000.[12] Now, the right to vote was extended to landowners and landholders paying at least ₹5 in tax per annum.[13] Though the qualification was lowered, the policy made only 2.5 per cent of the population eligible to vote.[14] It excluded the peasants who indulged in farming on tenured lands and those who paid taxes in the name of landowners who were mostly upper-caste Hindus, especially the Nairs.[15]

The Maharaja's supposed reformist policy strengthened the Nair dominance as more lower-income Nair landowners were now eligible to vote while continuing to leave out the poor from marginalized communities. It galvanized the communities of

Ezhavas, Christians, and Muslims into action, and they came together to form the All Travancore Joint Political Congress (ATJPC).[16] Annie too joined the party and was an active member. The ATJPC's decision to boycott the 1933 elections went down in history as the Nivarthana Agitation or the Abstention Movement. The ATJPC also demanded reforms in public services, where Tamil Brahmins (who were not natives of the area) held most of the important posts. It had caused the minorities to feel overlooked despite having the required qualifications.

The 1933 elections were proof that the concerns of the ATJPC were justified: the Christians, with a population of 16.04 lakh, won 10 seats; Ezhavas, with 8.09 lakh, won three, and the Nairs with a strength of 8.68 lakh, won 35 seats.[17] It is to be noted here that the candidates from minority communities were proxies fielded by the government to save their face so that the ATJPC boycott would fail. However, despite their attempt, the Nairs won a thumping majority in spite of being just one-fourth of the total population validating the concerns of the ATJPC.

The Maharaja saw the error in his policy and made amends in 1935. The ₹5 tax payment criterion was reduced to ₹1 and seats in the Assembly were reserved for Ezhavas, socially backward Christian sects as well as Muslims.[18] The Nairs, unhappy with the success of the ATJPC, tried to break the Ezhavas away from the outfit by calling it a 'Christian movement'. The age-old demand of the Ezhavas to be allowed entry into temples was fulfilled in 1936, in an attempt to form a united bloc with 'lower-caste' and 'higher-caste' Hindus. But the ATJPC persevered and soon became the single largest party in the legislature in the 1937 elections.

Gradually, on seeing the success of the ATJPC, a group of prominent Nair leaders proceeded to join the party. Collectively, they formed the Travancore State Congress (TSC) in February 1938, and Annie was one of its founder-leaders.[19] The work of the TSC was divided into two departments – the Working Committee and the Publicity Committee. Annie was the only woman elected to the Working Committee and was also a member of the Publicity Committee, for which she regularly wrote articles in newspapers and made speeches.[20]

The main objective of the newly formed TSC was establishing a responsible government based on universal adult franchise.[21] The previous experience of the ATJPC influenced this goal – though the party had won a majority in both the Upper and Lower Houses, it had no real authority in a government still under the autocratic control of Maharaja Chithira Thirunal and Dewan C.P. Ramaswami Iyer.[22] The TSC presented a memorandum to the Maharaja to sack the Dewan for various improprieties, and to also conduct an enquiry into all the appointments, financial transactions, and administrative decisions made by him. This memorandum was signed by all the members of the Working Committee of the TSC including Annie.[23] The Dewan, however, viewed the memorandum as a personal affront.

Subsequently, the TSC intensified its mass campaign for the removal of the Dewan and demanded a responsible government. In their agitations and protests, frequent disruptions were caused by 'unknown persons' who resorted to stone pelting and heckling the leaders of the TSC. In the name of maintaining law and order, the police often disbursed the crowd with the use of lathis and bullets.[24]

As a crucial voice of the TSC, Annie made several speeches that were critical of the government. Because of this, she faced intimidation and harassment, and multiple attempts were made on her life and property. The first attack, in April 1938, was in the form of a warning – the house where she lived with her mother was pelted with stones. In another instance, a constable rammed his bicycle into her.[25] Three weeks later, intruders broke into her house at night, assaulted her and made away with her valuables, not even sparing her clothes and utensils.

Concerned about her mother's safety as well as her own, Annie reported the matter at the Palayam police station. Despite the police inspector's assurance of swift action, no efforts were made to nab the culprits. She then submitted a memorandum to the Maharaja requesting protection.[26] That, too, failed to yield results.

Rather than getting discouraged, Annie, brave as ever, published a pamphlet in May 1938 in which she lambasted the police for its inaction. The then Commissioner of Police threatened to charge her with defamation if she did not tender an apology but Annie refused.[27] The Commissioner informed the chief secretary that she was a dangerous agitator propagating inflammatory ideas against the state. In his regular report to the Maharaja, the Dewan stated that Annie was critical of the government in her writings and speeches and that she exhorted people to not pay taxes and school fees. Subsequently, Annie was booked for sedition and brought to trial. But the court granted her bail.[28]

In the meantime, the TSC became interested in being a part of a greater India that unitedly fights against the British rule.[29] Majority of the people now aspired to self-rule instead of monarchy. In August 1938, in order to suppress the nationalist movement, the Dewan banned the TSC using his discretionary powers.[30] The government also censored all news and press communiqué to hide the facts about the goings-on in the state. Realizing that it was important for the movement to shed light on the truth for the rest of British India, the TSC sent its leaders to different parts of the country. Annie, who went to Mysore and Bombay, addressed several meetings, and her powerful oratorial skills drew huge crowds as well as the media.[31]

Upon her return, Annie was arrested in Chengannur by the Travancore government, at midnight on 13 November 1938. Based on speeches she had delivered earlier in Travancore, Annie was tried for sedition in two separate cases. The sessions judge of Trivandrum sentenced her to eighteen months in jail and fined her ₹1,000. She served the sentence.[32] This was Annie's first prison term, but it certainly wasn't her last.

Meanwhile, Gandhi sent Rajkumari Amrit Kaur to Travancore to negotiate with the TSC, urging them to focus on the demand for responsible government and withdraw the allegations on the Dewan as it was distracting from their main goal.[33] The leaders of the movement heeded Gandhi's advice. Subsequently the ban on the TSC was revoked.

Annie, after her release from jail, chose to remain with the TSC and carried on with her activism. In 1942, the TSC held meetings and protested the arrest of Gandhi and other leaders during the Quit India Movement. The government of Travancore prohibited the agitations and protests,[34] but a determined Annie and other TSC leaders challenged the ban. One of the speeches she gave at a party meeting in Trivandrum was considered inflammatory. Once again, she was packed off to prison, this time with a two-year term and a fine of ₹500.[35]

Even after her second stint in jail, Annie's work with the TSC carried on uninterrupted in its demand for a responsible government in Travancore. The party aligned itself with the Indian National Congress (INC) and the idea of uniting with India post-Independence. To learn more about and immerse herself in the freedom struggle outside of Travancore, Annie travelled across western India and spent time in Gandhi's ashram at Wardha, in modern-day Maharashtra as well as the Sabarmati Ashram in Ahmedabad.[36]

Her relationship with Gandhi, however, became strained soon after. Annie made his sister and niece, who were on a pilgrimage in Rameswaram, speak at a political gathering. Gandhi considered it a fraud because both the speakers had no interest in public matters. An unhappy Gandhi wrote to Annie on 28 October 1945: 'Why did you drag my sister and her daughter? My sister is wholly illiterate. Her daughter can with difficulty read or write something... Neither takes any interest in public matters. It is fraud upon the public to put such ignorant persons on the platform and make them repeat things parrot-like, leading the public to believe that some good work has been done.'[37]

In another instance, Gandhi chastised Annie for a speech she made in Bombay, now Mumbai. In a letter dated 21 February

1946, he wrote: 'A report of the speech you made at Bombay has appeared in the newspapers. If it is correct, what you said is not right. Even otherwise, I know that you have no control over your tongue and when you stand up to speak, you blab anything that comes to your mind... Such indiscreet talk can do good neither to you nor to the poor people of Travancore. Besides, by your act you put the whole fair sex to shame.'[38] Gandhi also wrote to the TSC president Pattom Thanu Pillai informing him that Annie was unfit to be his co-minister of the TSC party.[39] In spite of the harsh criticism from Gandhi, Annie persevered in her fight for the people of Travancore.

Meanwhile, the ongoing protests for a responsible government led by the Communist Party compelled the Dewan to grant some constitutional reforms. On 16 January 1946, he proclaimed reforms to share power between the monarchy and the elected representatives.[40] Though universal adult franchise was guaranteed, the head of government would be appointed by the Maharaja rather than being elected by the people. Additionally, the reforms also cancelled reservations.[41] This was a huge blow to the disenfranchised communities. Almost all community-led organizations erupted in protests against the proposed reforms. Over the next couple of months, hundreds of lives were lost in the agitation. On 31 October, the strikes were called off and more than 60 organizations were banned by the state.[42]

A few weeks after the unrest, Annie was arrested again, this time on charges of inciting violence. Spreading rumours to incite hatred, contempt, and acts of violence were punishable by detention of up to six months, of which Annie was found guilty. She was promptly sent to Trivandrum's Central Prison on 20 November 1946.[43]

In June 1947, the Dewan announced that Travancore would be an independent country once the British left India. The news didn't go down well with the masses. There was even an attempt on the Dewan's life on 25 July, which scared both him and the Maharaja. The Maharaja immediately cabled the Viceroy, Louis Mountbatten, his consent to accede to India. On 19 August 1947, the Dewan resigned his office[44] and a fortnight after his departure, the Maharaja announced the establishment of a responsible government on the basis of universal adult franchise, the first province in India to do so. This was a victory for the people of Travancore.

After the release of the TSC leaders, including Annie, and the completion of negotiations, Travancore's first popular-elected government came to power on 24 March 1948.[45] By then, the TSC was split, with a faction joining the INC and the others either vanished or went on to form their own parties.

Annie was amongst three elected women in an Assembly of 120 representatives, the other two were Accamma Cherian and Devaki Gopidas.[46] Together these three trailblazers advocated for a variety of issues including – colleges for women, expansion of public libraries, improvement of food and agricultural production, and development of the coastal area of the Travancore State.

As freedom fighters who were jailed several times, all three of them had experienced horrid conditions in the prisons for women. It moved them to strive for better facilities for female inmates. Annie also argued for the security of jobs and emoluments in order to check corruption among employees of public service.[47]

As a representative of the Travancore Assembly, Annie was sworn in as a member of the Constituent Assembly on 29 December 1948, two years after the proceedings of the framing of the Constitution had started. Given her legal expertise, Annie was nominated to the select committee on the Hindu Code Bill, alongside other prominent members such as Hansa Mehta, Ammu Swaminathan, Renuka Ray, Durgabai Deshmukh, and Begum Qudsia Aizaz Rasul.

Most of Annie's arguments as a member of the Constituent Assembly stemmed from her political experience in the TSC and the Travancore Legislative Assembly. She channelized her learnings from her activism years, which was aided by the legal grounding received while reading and teaching law at Maharaja's College.

While discussing the powers given to the Centre to manage the functions of the Election Commission, Annie stressed that a true democracy required giving power to the people: 'I am a believer in the right of the people of the province to elect their representatives independent of any control, supervision and direction of any power on earth. I believe that to be democracy. If the Centre is to think that expediency demands that they should supervise and control the election, as one sitting in the Provincial Legislature I can see in the Centre as many delinquencies as they see in us.'[48]

When another member, K.M. Munshi reasoned that the power given to the Central government was a matter of 'efficiency', Annie pointed out the follies made by other countries on such ground. She argued, 'May I remind [Mr Munshi] of the expediency and reality of nations in days long gone by – of the Parliament of Rome, of the Long Parliament of England? Cromwell thought that it was expedient to run the administration by a unicameral legislature. The Napoleonic heroes thought that it was expedient to run the administration by a unicameral legislature. But time has proved the effect of those expediencies.'[49]

She was keenly aware of the Assembly's role in shaping the nation, and was unwilling to sacrifice the future for convenience in the present. She was determined in ensuring that the 'rudimentary principles of democracy' they were working on were for the 'days to come, for generations, for the nation.'

Annie dwelled on the subject of amendments even in her final speech before the adoption of the Constitution. She suggested amending the Constitution, if needed, after attaining the full stature of a nation. Tapping into her extensive knowledge of legalities, Annie drew parallels with various countries. She spoke about the US constitution and how long it took to frame to get it to its 'final shape'. Even Australia's was revised repeatedly.

She mentioned in parliament, 'Look at the Constitution of Australia. Had it not to go through many changes and wait till the Convention at Sydney? It had to be shaped and reshaped, modelled and remodelled in the cauldron of public opinion at Sydney.'[50]

Annie also talked about the need for a strong Centre, especially during the early days of founding a country: 'If at the beginning of a state, a nation is faced with so many political, economic and social problems, there should be a strong Centre, so that power could radiate through all the parts. The Centre should not be so strong as to kill the autonomy of the local governments. But we have not got any such power concentrated in the Centre to kill the autonomy in the States.'[51] To the members who criticized the Constitution for giving too much power to the Centre, she said, 'There are provisions in the Constitution to amend it and if the Centre is too strong we need not fear because when the nation has attained full stature and we can stand on our own legs, we can amend the Constitution and distribute powers equally.'[52]

While Annie participated in the proceedings of the Constituent Assembly with total commitment, she also multi-tasked as the minister of health and power in the new Travancore–Cochin government headed by Chief Minister T.K. Narayana Pillai. She was the first woman minister in the Travancore–Cochin Legislative Assembly after the merger of the two provinces in July 1949.

Unfortunately, six months later, Annie and two other colleagues were made to resign in order to make room for new members in the Cabinet.[53] In an unexpected move, Annie accused her Cabinet colleague and state Congress leader E. John Philipose of corruption. She levelled charges of appropriating funds in the purchase of bus chassis as the transport minister.[54] This led to factionalism within the state Congress and Philipose offered to resign. Ultimately, the government fell, and the entire Cabinet resigned on 24 February 1951.[55] Philipose subsequently won a defamation suit against Annie in the Madras High Court.[56]

Following this debacle, Annie parted ways with the Congress and contested the first Lok Sabha election as an independent candidate from Thiruvananthapuram. Despite losing the defamation case, Annie still commanded respect among the people. They supported her formidable stance against corruption, fighting even her own political colleagues, as evidenced by the overwhelming number of votes she received. Her closest rival was her former boss and former chief minister T.K. Narayana Pillai, a candidate of the Socialist Party.[57] Annie bagged 1,16,617 votes, winning by a margin of 68,117 votes.[58] The crushing defeat forced a demoralized Pillai out of politics.

While congratulating the Speaker of the House on the first day of parliament in May 1952, Annie drew attention to the handful of women in the House, precisely saying, 'On behalf of those few ladies here, I hope that you will give us sufficient protection and opportunities for expressing our opinion in this House.'[59] She believed that women had not been given their political due in independent India.[60] Only around 5 per cent members elected to the House of 489 members were women.[61]

In 1952, Annie advocated strongly against the Preventive Detention Act in parliament. This was a colonial law that gave power to the police to arrest anyone on the vague premise that they might commit a crime in the future. Her time in prison had shaped her views on individual freedom. When she pointed out that the discussions in the House were dominated solely by male speakers, she was met with ridicule, with some members questioning the existence of female detenus.

Bent on being heard, Annie then brought up her own extensive experience in detention. 'If I had known anything in life, if I am familiar with anything in life it is detention, detenus, detention camps, police and lock-up. That is why, Sir, I said that this Act and deliberations on this Act should not be the monopoly of men.' In her fiery speech, she used her considerable knowledge of the law to support her argument, 'We have law based on equity, justice and good conscience and we want to have a law that will command obedience to the fundamental canons of justice. I wish to say… this Detention Act violates all these rules of equity, conscience, justice and obedience to law.'[62]

She reminded the government of the day about the need to reform the law. 'People who have been kept down by detention acts, have in course of time succeeded in getting rid of them either by legislation or revolution. Let us not have the latter. We are willing to live as law-abiding citizens, if the Congress Administration can give us justice and can remedy the evils that exist and not create disturbance in our minds,' she said. Despite her strong remarks, no reforms were made.

Annie stood tall throughout her life on an edifice of ethics and idealism. She was uncompromising in her beliefs and did not shy away from doing what was right, irrespective of the price she paid for it. Despite her exemplary work, she lost the 1957 Lok Sabha election. She came fourth and secured only 18,471 votes whereas the winner got more than one lakh votes.[63] The earth-shattering loss marked the end of her public life as a politician.

Six years later on 19 July 1963, Annie breathed her last. This bold and uninhibited firebrand leader was buried in the Pattoor Cemetery in Thiruvananthapuram.[64] A leader who fought for a just world, Annie put a high premium on the need for the rule of law and ethics. Harassment and threats to her life could not deter her from her chosen path. In 2013, vice president of India Hamid Ansari unveiled a full-sized statue of Annie Mascarene in Vazhuthacaud. Chief minister of Kerala Oommen Chandy paid homage to the courageous personality 'in the forefront of the historical freedom struggle in Travancore'.[65]

BEGUM QUDSIA AIZAZ RASUL

> 'I look forward to the day when individuals will cease to regard themselves as members of religious minorities. But this can only be done if and when the majority also cease to be conscious of their majority and members of all communities, big or small, sincerely and simultaneously begin to consider themselves and one another as full and equal citizens of a Secular State.'
>
> – On the status of minorities during a debate in the Constituent Assembly on 22 November 1949

In November 1946, as the members of the Constituent Assembly gathered in New Delhi, British India was in the throes of an upheaval. Britain had decided to split India along religious lines, leading to large-scale violence and arguably the largest forced migration in history. The Partition was the culmination of the British Empire's 'divide and rule policy', institutionalized in the wake of the Revolt of 1857, which united Indian soldiers and several Hindu and Muslim rulers against colonial rule. German philosopher Karl Marx wrote about how the 'Mussulmans and Hindoos, renouncing their mutual antipathies, have combined against their common masters.'[1] This religious unity for a common cause posed a serious threat to the colonizers.

To break this unity, W.R. Mansfield, the chief of staff of British forces in India, suggested creating communal divisions to strengthen British control. 'I am strongly of the opinion that Mussalmans should not be in the same company or troop with Hindoos or Sikhs, and that the two latter should not be mingled together,' he said. By 1862, the reorganization of the armed forces along caste and religious lines was initiated.[2]

Nearly fifty years after the revolt, in October 1906, a Shimla meeting between Lord Minto, the then Viceroy of India, and a deputation of Muslim leaders took Britain's divisive policy several notches higher. In their address to the Viceroy, the deputation appealed for safeguards to ensure a fair Muslim representation in legislative and executive bodies. Lord Minto lent enthusiastic support to the demand, assuring the Muslim leaders 'that their political rights and interests as a community will be safeguarded in any administrative reorganization.'[3] This was the genesis of separate electorates, which was based on the premise that 'only a Muslim could represent Muslims, or protect Muslims' interests'. In December 1906, 'a handful of landed and aristocratic elites' founded the All-India Muslim League (AIML) in Dhaka, with the objective of 'advancing the interests of all Muslims'.[4] Some of the prominent founding members of the Muslim League had been part of the Shimla meeting.

Apart from electoral changes, the British tried to drive a wedge between religious communities by announcing the partition of Bengal in 1905. Indians responded to the move by launching the Swadeshi movement. The government tried to crush the resistance with the arrests of leaders and their followers. The nationalist fervour was on the rise, as were anxieties amongst the minorities.

Begum Qudsia Aizaz Rasul was born against this backdrop of unrest and uncertainty, in either 1908 or 1909.[5] An adroit politician, she was able to harness her environment and would go on to challenge patriarchy and champion secular and liberal ideas at a time when bigotry and communal passions ran high. Although elected to the Constituent Assembly as a representative of the Muslim League, she was vocal against having separate electorates, one of the principal causes her party advocated. On her way to charting a successful career in public service, Qudsia broke many norms, including discarding the purdah.

Born to Nawab Sir Zulfiqar Ali Khan and Mahmuda Sultana, she was named Qudsia, Arabic for 'sacred' and 'pure'. Her birth coincided with the enactment of the Indian Council Act 1909, popularly known as the Minto-Morley Reforms, which introduced elections to provincial and an all-India Imperial Legislative Council based on a limited franchise, allowing entry of Indians into minor decision-making positions. Along with it came separate electorates and 'weightage' in representation in the councils, the latter suggested by the Muslim League.[6]

Qudsia's father Zulfiqar was an accomplished politician. He hailed from the royal family of Malerkotla in Punjab and was chief minister of Patiala state from 1911–1913. Many years later, in 1930, he was the Indian delegate to the League of Nations.[7] He was also a beneficiary of the Minto-Morley Reforms, having been elected to the Imperial Legislative Council from a reserved seat in Punjab.[8] Mahmuda Sultana, her mother, belonged to the ruling family of Loharu, located in present-day Haryana.[9]

Malerkotla boasts of a rich history. In 1704, a Mughal commander, Wazir Khan, put two minor sons of Guru Gobind Singh to death. The then Nawab of Malerkotla, a distant relative of Wazir Khan, went against his ilk and protested the killings. He had appealed to Aurangzeb, the reigning Mughal emperor, to spare the boys. The Sikh guru later thanked the Nawab for his intervention and blessed his house. More than two centuries later, the Muslim-majority Malerkotla saw little violence during the partition. Communal amity was maintained even during some of the darkest hours in the country's history.[10]

The state of Loharu, too, had its share of intriguing tales. In 1835, the reigning nawab was executed for the murder of William Frazer, a British civil servant living in Delhi. The family's land was confiscated and members put under house arrest.[11] The heirs were released, and their titles restored only after the

Revolt of 1857. Urdu poet Mirza Ghalib and noted educationist Sir Syed Ahmad Khan, an advocate of separate electorates, were connected to the Loharu family by marriage. Nawab Amir-ud-din Ahmad Khan of Loharu served as advisor of the state of Malerkotla between 1893 and 1903.[12] The professional ties between members of the two houses probably led to the marriage of Zulfiqar and Mahmuda in 1903.

The rich legacies of Malerkotla and Loharu accorded Qudsia an advantage few in India could dream of. She had access to formal education at a time when India's female literacy ratio was 1.05 per cent.[13] Qudsia received her primary education at home, with 'Urdu and Persian teachers and an English governess'.[14] She started attending school only when she was eleven. She went to Jesus and Mary Convent in Shimla and later attended the Queen Mary College in Lahore, a girls-only academic institution for the elite. Qudsia enjoyed her time at school, making many friends and actively participating in sports.[15] The convent education invited objections from Zulfiqar's contemporaries and his family. A fatwa, a formal Islamic ruling, 'condemning convent education as anti-Islamic' was issued by an *ulema*, a religious scholar. But Qudsia's father stood his ground. However, in a contrast to this progressive stance, he 'insisted on her wearing a burqa'.[16]

Zulfiqar had a conditional appetite for progressive values. The women of the house enjoyed a great degree of freedom. They would attend concerts, host parties, and indulge in political discussions. But all this was done behind the veil.[17] Despite the exposure to the modern world owing to their social standing, Qudsia and the women of her household were expected to observe purdah. She continued this practice and only discarded it after she was married.[18]

Qudsia's interest in politics began at a young age. She acted as her father's secretary, thereby getting an opportunity to observe national politics and prominent public figures from close quarters.

Zulfiqar's political career was on the rise since the Minto-Morley reforms. In 1927, the British announced the appointment of the Simon Commission to review the working of the Government of India Act 1919 and propose further reforms. The Congress decided to boycott it because it had no Indian representative – Muhammad Ali Jinnah, the leader of the Muslim League, too, found the omission objectionable. This led to the convening of an All Parties Conference (APC) where a committee was formed for drafting a Constitution. The committee was chaired by renowned lawyer and activist Motilal Nehru with his son, Jawaharlal, as secretary.

In 1927, an eighteen-year-old Qudsia accompanied her mother to visit Mahatma Gandhi in Shimla.[19] At around that time, Sarojini Naidu wrote to Zulfiqar suggesting he allow his daughter to attend an All India Women's Conference (AIWC) session in Delhi.[20] The AIWC, founded the same year, aimed at promoting the education of girls and women. The 1928 Delhi session was presided by Sultan Jahan, the begum of Bhopal. At the conference, Sultan Jahan called upon women to 'avoid the religious divisions and bickering which had affected Indian political life.' She sought support for the Sarda Bill, an anti–child marriage legislation, and decried the practice of purdah as being harmful to the cause of women's education. Sultan Jahan was a highly regarded ruler and patron of India's women's movement. She ascended to the throne in 1901 and continued observing purdah. It was in later years she came out of the veil and urged other women to follow suit.[21] Her landmark speech at Delhi perhaps influenced Qudsia to discard purdah later in life.

Meanwhile, in 1928, the APC's committee submitted what came to be known as the 'Nehru Report'. The 'Nehru Report' made far-reaching constitutional demands, with many provisions finding their way into the Indian Constitution two decades later. The document did not mention separate electorates, indicating an end to the provision.

In Punjab, the decision to boycott the Simon Commission caused a rift in the Muslim League. Zulfiqar was part of the group that welcomed the Commission – he was later appointed to the All-India Committee for Cooperation with Simon Commission. When the 'Nehru Report' was published, a group of Muslim League leaders, including Zulfiqar, placed on record their disagreement, especially with regard to the issue of separate electorates.[22] Years later, Qudsia followed her father's footsteps in standing diametrically opposite to the official party line, but against separate electorates.

In 1929, she married Nawab Aizaz Rasul, a *taluqdar*, a landowning aristocrat from Sandila in the Hardoi district of the United Provinces, now known as Uttar Pradesh. She was now known as Begum Aizaz Rasul. The match was said to have been arranged by Malcolm Hailey, the governor of Punjab. Qudsia's first glimpse of the prospective groom was from behind a curtain when she was in Lucknow to assist her father with work related to the Simon Commission.[23]

Her marital home was mired in orthodoxy; Qudsia had a very traditional mother-in-law who favoured a strict adherence to purdah. It was only when the couple left Rasul's ancestral home for a smaller accommodation that Qudsia gained a degree of personal freedom. This was when she decided to discard the purdah.[24] It was not an easy decision, as Rasul was not pleased with her initially but came around later.[25]

Rasul, a leader from the Awadh region, was part of the 1931 United Provinces Muslim Conference[26]. It was attended by distinguished men from the province who later joined the Muslim League. In 1935, Britain enacted the Government of India Act, a new constitutional scheme that gave Indians limited autonomy in governance matters. The Act retained separate electorates and reserved seats for women in legislatures. When elections to the provincial assemblies and councils were announced in 1936, Qudsia and her husband decided to take the plunge into electoral politics. Rasul contested for the United Provinces Assembly from Hardoi district on the ticket of the newly formed National Agriculturalist Party (NAP), a coalition of 'Hindu and Muslim landlords along with sections of business capital.'[27] Qudsia on the other hand, contested as an independent on a seat reserved for Muslims representing Hardoi, Sitapur, and Kheri districts in the Legislative Council.[28] Both Rasul and Qudsia emerged winners. However, it was Qudsia who faced an eventful and tumultuous campaign.

The religious leaders were not amused by her candidature and issued a fatwa, the second recorded incident in Qudsia's case. They declared that voting for a non-purdah Muslim woman was un-Islamic.[29] The anger amongst the conservatives was not only due to her disregard for purdah but that a woman had dared to openly compete with men. Qudsia ran a spirited campaign, receiving unstinted support from Rasul. She won the election with a thumping majority. Her victory was significant as she was contesting for a general seat (seat not reserved for women). Across the country, only ten women had won the general seats, one of them was Hansa Mehta. The fact that voters were often from a similar social standing as hers contributed to her victory. Qudsia later pointed out that her win was an indication that Muslims were 'not really as orthodox as they were made out to be'.[30]

Qudsia called the 1937 election her 'political baptism' and claimed that she had been goaded to contest by friends. She herself was keen to do 'something to ameliorate the condition of Indian women'.[31]

By this time, Qudsia had formally given up purdah for public gatherings, maintaining the practice only during her meetings with her orthodox mother-in-law. In fact, her mother-in-law once sent a curtained palanquin to pick up Qudsia from a railway station. This was much to the amusement of the public and press who called her the 'two-faced Begum' – one-moment observing purdah and the other discarding it. The name-calling did not deter the young politician. She decided to be pragmatic about the purdah and chose her battles wisely. She wrote, 'Revolution, be it political or economic, must have strong roots; otherwise it will be wiped out by a counter revolution. And so I blended orthodoxy and modernism harmoniously, yielding without compromise and uncompromising with rancour.'[32]

Qudsia was the Leader of the Opposition in the United Provinces Council between 1937 and 1940[33] and also served as the Deputy Speaker.[34] Her time in the legislature invited further wrath from the conservative sections of society, whose feathers she continued to ruffle, as she raised the issue of birth control and asked for more women police officers, subjects that were not considered appropriate for public discussion.[35] A staunch advocate for female education, she sought more expenditure for the cause. Commenting on the budget, she said, 'On the education of women depends the progress and welfare of the people of any country. The real cause of mass illiteracy in India… is due to the ignorance of Indian women.'[36] In 1940, she was re-elected to the council with an increased vote share.[37]

Her term coincided with intense debate on *zamindari* abolition, a contentious issue in the feudal United Provinces. Qudsia maintained duality on the issue. She supported the abolition, exhorting the zamindars to 'see the writing on the wall and graciously give these rights to the tenants who toil and sweat. If they did not, their lands would be forcibly taken away from them'.[38] The fact that she was married to a *taluqdar* made her stance all the more impressive. However, there is also evidence of Qudsia being sympathetic to the zamindars. Qudsia believed that it was 'in their [zamindars'] best interests' to effect a compromise with the government.[39] The United Provinces Zamindari Abolition Committee's report of 1948 also has a note of dissent from Qudsia where she states, 'I do not agree that the proposal to abolish *zamindari* is either just or advantageous to the State or to the mass of the people, since in this Province at least, a considerable portion of the "mass of the people" about one-fourth are zamindars and they are to be made paupers.' Qudsia spoke of the zamindars' contribution to the political struggle and blamed Congress for turning against them. She warned, 'The abolition of *zamindari* on the payment of a wholly inadequate compensation and without the provision of an alternative source of livelihood is bound to create anarchy and chaos and will, probably lead to increase of crime.'[40] Qudsia also raised the issue of compensation during the Constituent Assembly debates, warning the United Provinces government that it was inviting trouble for itself by 'depriving the zamindars of their source of livelihood'.[41]

Post the provincial elections, both Rasul and Qudsia joined the Muslim League. Rasul became secretary of the United Provinces Muslim League in 1937. The following year, Qudsia was appointed to the newly formed All-India Muslim Women Sub-Committee of the Muslim League.[42] The couple's 'modern ways' did not sit well with some members of the League. In 1944, Raghib Ahsan, an advisor to Jinnah, wrote to him about a cocktail party Qudsia and Rasul had hosted and how such actions were damaging the reputation of the Muslim League. He requested an enquiry and penal action.[43]

Qudsia was not to be intimidated, and deftly questioned the hypocrisy of such complaints. She described the incident in her autobiography, 'One rather serious charge brought against my husband and myself was that we had given a cocktail party for Sir Maurice Hallett, the governor of UP, in which alcohol was served. A resolution condemning us for this lapse was sought to be brought against us. When I heard about this, I sought an interview with the Secretary, AIML, Nawabzada Liaquat Ali Khan and did some plain speaking with him. Everyone knew that some of our leaders were not averse to indulging in mild drinking so I told him, I would be obliged to defend myself by hitting back. The resolution never saw the light of day.'[44]

Qudsia's association with the Muslim League brought her into conflict with the AIWC, of which she had been an active participant since its inception. In the early years, Qudsia often advocated secular policies. At the 1937 Nagpur session of the AIWC, she moved a resolution proposing that all 'primary education should be imparted on a non-communal basis'. The resolution was adopted unanimously.[45] At the same session, the AIWC reaffirmed its opposition to separate electorates of all kinds.

In the 1930s, the AIWC had broadened its agenda and was focused on effectively contributing to the freedom movement. Its policies mirrored the Congress's opinion – which led to alienation amongst several Muslim members. At the 1939 session, an idea of a separate conference for Muslims was mooted. During a session, Muslim women led by Qudsia 'staged a walkout in protest of AIWC policies.' The situation escalated at the 1940 session – Qudsia was then the President of AIWC's Awadh branch – over the use of the word 'swaraj' in a resolution calling for communal unity. Some delegates and Muslim leaders had objected to the word 'swaraj' citing its association with the Congress party. Aruna Asaf Ali moved an amendment and suggested using the word 'freedom' instead of 'swaraj'. In her intervention in the debate, Qudsia called for going beyond 'fighting over words' and 'that the problem was one of communal unity and not a question of words and she was certain that if there was no unity there could be neither progress nor freedom nor swaraj.'[46] The 1940 session ended with the AIWC reiterating its opposition to separate electorates.[47] Qudsia was one of the lone voices amongst the Muslim activists who supported joint electorates.[48] Unlike separate electorates, where candidates and voters must be from the same community, in the joint electorates, seats are reserved for a particular community but voters from all communities are allowed to vote. Qudsia had been elected to the Legislative Council on a Muslim seat. Without separate electorates, she was going to find it tougher to sail through in an election. Despite that, she aligned with AIWC's majority opinion on the issue. However, as the political atmosphere got communally charged, she chose to be firmly ensconced in the Muslim League. Two months after the 1940 AIWC session, the Muslim League adopted a resolution that finalized Qudsia's departure from the organization.

In March 1940 at Lahore, the Muslim League called the administrative framework as provided in the Government of India

Act 1935 'totally unsuited to and unworkable' and 'unacceptable to Muslim India'.[49] This was the clarion call for a separate nation. Jinnah concluded his presidential address with the following remarks, 'Friends, I therefore want you to make up your mind definitely, and then think of devices and organize your people, strengthen your organization, and consolidate the Mussalmans all over India. I think that the masses are wide awake. They only want your guidance and your lead. Come forward as servants of Islam. Organize the people economically, socially, educationally, and politically, and I am sure that you will be a power that will be accepted by everybody.'[50]

Qudsia enthusiastically supported this call for a separate Muslim country. In November 1941, a resolution of the Muslim League's Women's Sub-Committee, of which she was a secretary, concluded, 'The Committee wants to point out that the struggle for the emancipation of the Muslim women in India is bound up with the struggle of the Muslim nation for the achievement of Pakistan.'[51] In 1943, she supported another Muslim League resolution that said, 'That this Session of the AIML is convinced that the attainment of the cherished goal of Pakistan is only possible by the untiring effort, willing sacrifices and grim determination of the Muslims, and they should therefore do their utmost to acquire the strength requisite for such an undertaking.'[52] Qudsia did extensive work for the League, travelling to different cities to bolster the party organization and election campaigning.

At the League's Legislators' Convention in April 1946, Qudsia, speaking on behalf of women delegates, said, 'Every child in every Muslim home is being brought up in the spirit of Pakistan and women will make their share of sacrifices if bloodshed comes. They are no longer sleeping, and are just as impatient as their menfolk to discharge their responsibilities to the nation to which they belong.'[53] Despite these brave words, Qudsia was also deeply affected by injustice meted out to the common Muslim woman. In February 1947, she wrote to Jinnah expressing concern over the 'bestial violence' and 'forced conversion' that women in Bihar and Garhmukteshwar (a town in the United Provinces) had to face. 'Who knows how many more trying situations you may have to confront and cope with before attaining the goal of Pakistan,' she said in the letter.[54]

Qudsia's support for the idea of Pakistan was complicated – she knew Jinnah wanted 'Muslims to stand on their own feet and be economically well-off'[55] – but she herself had doubts over the financial viability of a separate nation. She believed 'communal business' in the form of rioting and looting had started and she also felt a partition was the right decision in light of the then-prevailing circumstances.[56]

However, she realized that the Muslims in the United Provinces would be at a disadvantage should the country be divided along religious lines. When she apprised Jinnah of her anxieties, he is said to have replied that they (Muslims in provinces where they were in a minority) would have to make that sacrifice. After Partition, many towering Muslim League leaders decided to leave for Pakistan, including members of the Loharu state. In a 1997 interview, Qudsia recalled the Urdu press questioning the United Provinces politicians who left the 'poor' Muslims behind, with no one 'to look up to or look after their interests'. Despite her initial support of the idea of Pakistan, Qudsia and Rasul felt they had a 'moral responsibility' 'to stay on and help the Muslims'.[57]

When Liaquat Ali Khan, Pakistan's first prime minister, born in the United Provinces, said that his government was 'absolutely opposed to the migration of Muslims', it led to resentment and disillusionment among members of the Muslim League in India.[58]

The scale of the violence and devastation that accompanied the Partition was a woeful indictment of communal politics. In November 1947, Muslim leaders, including Qudsia, had requested security in the wake of the prevailing situation.[59] The following weeks saw a realignment of national priorities. Having borne the brunt of Partition, Indian leaders were firm on the need to uphold secular values.

Qudsia was elected to the Constituent Assembly in 1946, when she was secretary of the Muslim League. The only Muslim woman at the Assembly 'found herself thrust forward as spokesman for the Muslim community'.[60] She was a member of the Advisory Committee on Fundamental Rights, Minorities, and Tribal and Excluded Areas. The Committee, headed by Sardar Patel, submitted its report in April 1947 and recommended doing away with separate electorates. As an alternative, it suggested reservation of seats for minorities under joint electorates.

When the issue of separate electorates came up before the Assembly, Qudsia was vocal about abolishing what she now considered a self-destructive weapon. She spoke after another Muslim League member, Mohammad Ismail, had moved an amendment to retain separate electorates.[61] Incidentally, after Partition, the Muslim League had been split into Pakistan's Muslim League and the Indian Union Muslim League (IUML). Ismail, a leader from Madras (now Chennai), had been appointed president of IUML, inviting derision from Qudsia who said 'Muslims in the U.P. who are 14 per cent of the population certainly do not like to be guided by Madras where Muslims are only 4 per cent of the population'.[62] Disagreeing with the amendments, she said, 'For my part, I have from the beginning felt that in a secular state separate electorates have no place'. Qudsia also spoke against reservation of seats for minorities, calling them 'meaningless and useless'. She added 'To my mind reservation is a self-destructive weapon which separates the minorities from the majority for all time. It gives no chance to the minorities to win the good-will of the majority. It keeps up the spirit of separatism and communalism alive which should be done away once and for all.' Qudsia suggested that Muslims 'should throw themselves entirely upon the good-will of the majority community' and pave the way for establishing a secular democratic state.[63]

At the same time, she exhorted the Hindus to make sure that the minorities did not feel left out and to instil feelings of 'confidence, good-will and security'. 'Then only can loyalty accrue, because it is the condition of people's minds that creates loyalty. It is not the asking for it that makes for it' mentioned Qudsia. Her impassioned appeal in the Assembly was successful in building support for the abolition of the separate electorates and reservation for minorities. Muhammad Saadulla from Assam, rued that reservation of seats had been given away 'on the solitary support of Begum Aizaz Rasul'.[64] Qudsia's support for the abolition of separate electorates and her disagreement with her party leadership stood in stark contrast to the actions of her own father, Zulfiqar, who decades ago had joined other Muslim League leaders to oppose the Nehru Report – which had omitted separate electorates – and even welcomed Simon Commission despite Jinnah's objection.

With respect to her stance on separate electorates, there is more to her claim than what meets the eye. As part of AIWC, she had opposed separate electorates but supported reservation under joint electorates. Later, she had gone a step further and thrown her weight behind the idea of a separate nation. Post-partition, political exigencies forced her to do a volte-face, perhaps in a bid to curry favour with the Congress leadership. The prevailing sentiment was against separate electorates and the Congress enjoyed an absolute majority in the Assembly. Any opposition to the abolition to separate electorates was destined to achieve little. During the debate, when she was urging Muslims to give up any special privileges, she commended Congress for standing 'for the protection of minorities'.[65]

As the deliberations of the Assembly progressed, Qudsia's support for the causes that were primarily associated with the Congress grew stronger. In 1949, she even sought to name the Parliament of India as Indian National Congress. Her rationale was, 'If the words "Indian National Congress" are substituted for the word "Parliament", the participation of the Congress in the national struggle will be permanently commemorated. This will also save the Congress from degenerating in course of time as all political parties are bound to do. It will liberate the Indian people from the glamour of the Congress and make it possible for them to exercise their vote democratically for otherwise the name of the Congress will unduly influence their emotions.'[66]

Recognizing the need for preserving minority languages and cultures, she moved an amendment that would entitle 'any minority residing in the territory of India or any part thereof having a distinct language and script' to 'primary education imparted to its children through the medium of that language and script'.[67] The amendment was defeated. In her later years, Qudsia took up the advocacy of educating children in their mother tongues. She wrote to Prime Minister Jawaharlal Nehru who agreed with her proposal and forwarded the same to the chief ministers.[68] The 'fundamental rights' chapter in the Nehru Report (1928) proposed free elementary education with the provision of imparting education to minorities in their own language. This proposal did not become an official policy in independent India. Recently, the New Education Policy (NEP) 2020 has recommended the use of the mother tongue or local language as the medium of instruction for primary classes.

Qudsia was also a staunch believer in fundamental rights and criticized what she considered were too many exceptions to freedom. She argued, 'I find that what has been given with one hand has been taken away by the other. Fundamental rights should be such that they should not be liable to reservations and to changes by Acts of legislature.'[69]

When the framers of the Constitution accepted the policy of no discrimination, Qudsia welcomed the decision with these words, 'The women of India are happy to step into their rightful heritage of complete equality with men in all spheres of life and activity. I say so because I am convinced that this is no new concept which has been postulated for the purposes of this Constitution, but is an ideal that has long been cherished by India, though social conditions for some time had tragically debased it in practice.'[70]

In 1950, she formally joined the Congress. Subsequently, she was elected to the Rajya Sabha from Uttar Pradesh and went on to serve as a member from 1952 to 1956. Qudsia was also the first woman to be nominated to the panel of vice chairmen in the Rajya Sabha, or the Upper House. In the Rajya Sabha, she underlined the importance of equal status and equality of opportunity for women as given in the Constitution of India.[71] More than a decade after her time in the Rajya Sabha, Qudsia was elected to the Uttar Pradesh Legislative Council in 1969. Her career in the state legislature spanned twenty years. Between 1969 and 1971, she was the minister for social welfare and minorities in the state. Qudsia was also instrumental in the promotion of women's hockey in India. She was the president of the All India Women's Hockey Association for two decades.[72]

Though she campaigned against separate electorates at the Constituent Assembly, by the end of the century she felt a need for reviewing the official policy. In a message sent to a convention to discuss the status of Muslims in April 1999, she said, 'As communal feelings have grown and the concept of Hindutva has gained popularity, it is time now to think anew of how to improve the educational and socio-economic conditions of Muslims.'[73]

In 2000, she was awarded the Padma Bhushan for her contribution to social work.[74] She died in 2001 and was buried in Sandila, her husband's hometown. Begum Qudsia Aizaz Rasul was a consummate politician. Realpolitik and not ideology influenced her decisions. She seamlessly straddled different worlds, braving severe odds and carving for herself a place in public life. The only Muslim woman in the Constituent Assembly, Begum Rasul made her voice count, leaving behind a rich legacy of service and an indelible mark on Indian polity.

DAKSHAYANI VELAYUDHAN

'I refuse to believe that the 70 million Harijans are to be considered as a minority… What we want is the removal, immediate removal, of our social disabilities. Only an Independent Socialist Indian Republic can give freedom and equality of status to the Harijans. Our freedom can be obtained only from Indians and not from the British Government.'

– On the rights of citizens in the Constituent Assembly on 19 December 1946[1]

Dakshayani Velayudhan achieved many firsts in her life – the first Dalit woman to graduate in science in Cochin, the first Dalit woman in the Cochin Legislative Council, and the lone Dalit woman in the Constituent Assembly.[2] *She dedicated herself to the upliftment of the Dalit community, and used the pulpit of the Constituent Assembly to demand that historically disadvantaged caste groups be given the same liberties and freedoms as every other Indian. She was an ardent follower of Mahatma Gandhi. The oppression she faced since childhood in Cochin's, now Kochi, deeply caste-entrenched society shaped her worldview and politics.*

***

Dakshayani belonged to the Pulaya caste, an untouchable or 'slave' caste in the princely states of Cochin and Travancore. The untouchables in those regions comprised various caste groups: Nadar, Ezhava, Pulaya, and Paraya.[3] Within this group, the Pulayas were considered to be highly polluted and impure by the dominant groups. However, the status of the Pulayas was not always so. Up until 700 CE, they were an influential community.[4] Even as their overall caste status deteriorated in the later centuries, community chiefs who were thought to be descendants of Pulaya kings were commonly known as Aikkara Yajamana.[5] In the early nineteenth century, the Pulayas were bought and sold as slaves to members of higher castes.[6] Treated as untouchables, they were behind other caste groups in every sphere of life – social, political, religious, and economical.

Even the Parayas, who were considered lower than the Pulayas, had a better literacy rate in the 1901 census, that is 1 per cent compared to 0.2 per cent of the Pulayas.[7] They mainly performed agricultural work and were not paid for their labour. Not only were the Pulayas to maintain distance from the higher castes, but they also could not even go within thirty feet of the Ezhavas who were also categorized as a lower caste group.[8] They were not allowed to draw water from public wells or walk on the same roads as the upper caste people. In fact, in order to prevent any chance of crossing paths, Pulayas had to announce their presence every four or five steps. If this call was answered by an 'upper-caste' person approaching that way, the Pulayas had to clear the path by either hiding in the fields next to the road or taking a detour.[9]

The abhorrent oppression of the Pulayas was not restricted to just public areas. Their social status didn't give them the right to clean clothes. They couldn't wear ornaments, carry umbrellas or even tile the roof of the huts they lived in.[10]

The Pulaya women could wear only beaded necklaces to cover their upper body.[11] Anyone who dared wear an upper cloth could be raped or have their breasts chopped off as punishment by higher caste men.[12] Their children were barred from government schools.[13] Despite the abolition of slavery in the latter half of the nineteenth century, the Pulayas were forced into bonded labour due to the absence of economic or welfare schemes that could help elevate their overall status.[14]

At the turn of the century, Christian missionaries established schools allowing the Pulaya children to access free education.[15] This was also when the social reform movement took a concrete shape under the leadership of Sree Narayana Guru, an Ezhava spiritual figure, who used simple religious idioms to debunk caste hegemony.[16] At around the same time, Ayyankali, a Pulaya man, fought for the right to walk on the public roads as well as the right to education. Between 1905 and 1907, Ayyankali also founded the Sadhu Jana Paripalana Sangham (SJPS), which was an umbrella body of various Dalit sub-caste organizations.[17] Under SJPS, agricultural labourers organized mass agitations to demand that their children be allowed in government schools, without the fear of being subjected to physical assault from the upper castes.[18] The movement, which was greeted with both success and stiff resistance in different pockets, lasted till around 1914.[19]

This was the socio-political background when Dakshayani was born to Kunjan and Maani on 4 July 1912 in Mulavukad, Bolghatty, a small island off the coast of Cochin.[20,21] She was the fourth child, after two sons and a daughter. Dakshayani, meaning the daughter of Durga, was an unusual name in a community that didn't name their children after gods and goddesses.[22]

But it wasn't just Dakshayani's name that was unconventional. Her family had broken many social moulds. According to her unpublished autobiography, Dakshayani's 'two elder brothers were the first in the community in the state to crop their long-knotted hair and wear shirts'.[23] This was significant as most Pulaya men had wild, matted hair, and wore nothing more than areca palm tree's bark or a piece of cloth that covered only parts of their lower body for decency.[24] However, people from other castes showered Dakshayani's brothers with abuse and stones for defying caste rules.[25]

Dakshayani's family was not typically poor, as they owned their home. They also owned more than an acre of land with coconut and other fruit trees, which served as a source of income for the family.[26] Her father had acquired this property from his maternal uncle who had the title Aikkara Yajamana, meaning the descendent of kings, granted by the then maharaja of Cochin.[27] Dakshayani's father used the family residence as a school for the children of the village. Even though he was a granite construction worker, he took out time to teach the children.[28] Her mother was a daily wager in the fields who also traded in dried fish. Tragedy struck the family when Dakshayani was only three years old as her beloved father passed away.[29] With Kunjan's untimely death, the family's financial condition worsened, and their house was mortgaged.[30]

Their personal struggles aside, the family was deeply involved with the reformist wave that had washed ashore in Cochin. Dakshayani's brothers and uncle were founding members of the Pulaya Mahajana Sabha (PJS).[31]

The dramatic circumstances that surrounded the birth of the organization present a telling picture of the deep caste divisions of the time, as well as the innovative approaches the Dalits adopted in their resistance. The year was 1913 and Dalits were barred from assembling on land owned by the Maharaja, so the Pulayas decided to take the matter offshore. According to Dakshayani, the PJS members met on 'country boats tied together in the sea at Bolghatty – the sea did not have a caste'. She added, 'The raft was made by joining together a large number of bamboo catamarans with the help and support of the fisherfolks'.[32] Through songs and poems, the PJS kept its fight for equality and dignity going.[33]

When most of the village converted to Christianity, three members of her family – Dakshayani, her mother and her brother refused to follow suit.[34] In those days, it was rare to have a family following two different faiths.[35] However, it wasn't long before Dakshayani's mother converted to Christianity due to pressure from the prospective in-laws of Dakshayani's sister. The conversion gave her and the other new Protestant Christians the right to draw water from wells and walk uninhibited on public roads.[36]

At this time, Dakshayani started attending St. Mary's School in Mulavukad, Kerala.[37] She was a bright student who often answered questions that others in her class couldn't.[38] When it was time to move to senior school, Dakshayani was enrolled at MLCC High School in Chathyathu, which was so far that it took a ferry ride and a three-four-hour walk to reach.[39]

'I had a brilliant educational career,' she wrote in her book. 'The education was free beginning to end.' Further, both she and her younger brother started receiving a stipend from the state government after the fifth grade.[40] This helped improve the family's finances and the children eventually stopped their mother from taking up daily wage jobs. As they entered college, the duo ended their dependency on their eldest brother, paid monthly instalments towards the mortgage on the house that they took on years ago, and formed their own family unit.[41]

Dakshayani's college education was remarkable in a number of aspects. She chose to study BSc Chemistry at Maharaja's College in Cochin, where she was the only female student in the sciences.[42]

Dakshayani was one of the first Dalit women to go to college in Cochin. The news created quite a stir and a large number of people assembled at the college gate to get a glimpse of the woman who had made history.[43] She wrote, 'There was media frenzy to get my photograph as I entered college – as first from the community,' she said. Regardless of the commotion, she 'entered without being noticed' as the media gathered 'had a stereotypical notion' of what Dakshayani looked like. Perhaps the media presumed Dakshayani would be unkempt with wild hair as the Pulayas were traditionally expected to be.

Inside the college the reception was not so warm. Discrimination followed her within the classroom, as one of her upper-caste teachers would not show her any of the practical experiments. Instead, she learnt by observing from a distance and ended up with a second-class division in 1935.[44]

Despite the odds, a purposeful Dakshayani completed graduation and applied for the post of a schoolteacher. In

July 1935, she was posted to the government high school in a village in Trichur, now Thrissur, district.[45] The Ezhavas were the majority caste in the area. While Dakshayani found them to be friendly and welcoming on most fronts, she was forbidden to draw water from their wells.[46] The long shadow of caste inequity tailed Dakshayani here too. On her way to work one day, she found herself on the same road as a Nair woman. 'All along the road… there were paddy fields on both sides. The Nair woman asked me to make way for her to pass as she was observing unapproachability. I told her directly to her face, if you want to go, you may go down in the field. The field was four [or] five feet below the road level. As I didn't concede to her demand, she had to do as I said,' she wrote. The Nair woman later remarked that she had to walk on faeces because the fields were used for open defecation.[47] Dakshayani, quite literally, stood her ground.

In the school where she was a science teacher, she wasn't allowed to forget her caste identity. Her students, who were from class 6 to class 10, took time to warm up to her.[48] Once, at a conference for teachers, the Nair women sat away from Dakshayani. This led her to boycott meetings where Pulaya and Ezhava teachers were made to sit separately from other attendees.[49]

Dakshayani was a follower of Mahatma Gandhi, but her job didn't allow her the time for full-fledged participation in the freedom movement.[50] The financial obligation towards her family kept her from giving up her job. Though she intensely wanted to boycott classes during the Quit India Movement, she couldn't do so due to the restrictions imposed by the school. But she also didn't hide her allegiance to the leader – she expressed her solidarity with the movement and made it clear to her students that she was a Gandhian.[51]

Dakshayani was invited to speak at meetings for Aikya Kerala also known as Aikya Keralam, a movement for a unified Kerala comprising Cochin, Travancore, and British Malabar.[52] In one of the meetings, Dakshayani believed that Malayali speakers should be under one state and strongly spoke in support of Kerala as a state. In the meeting she said, 'Like in language, the Malayalees were once united under a single political authority and when this history took its natural course, the land of the Malayalees was split into three segments. It is sure that the state of Kerala will take shape in the future... Aikya Keralam is a psychological need of the Malayalees. How will we be able to establish a strong administration in Keralam, which is a geographically distinct unit, without the state of Keralam?'[53]

After working as a teacher for over five years, Dakshayani married R. Velayudhan, a social worker who later became a politician, on 6 September 1940, at the Sevagram Ashram in Wardha, Maharashtra.[54]

Kasturba Gandhi, freedom fighter and wife of Mahatma Gandhi wove a white sari with a red border for the bride.[55] The wedding was officiated by a leprosy-afflicted person in the presence of Gandhi and Kasturba.[56]

The food served at the wedding was vegetarian, something Dakshayani was not used to. In fact, before the wedding, Gandhi observed her discomfort with the 'chapatti and jaggery' that was served in the Ashram kitchens. Amused Gandhi asked her 'did you expect fish here?' Dakshayani recalled, 'He added that we could cook non-vegetarian in our own hut.' However, 'cooking with firewood in an *angithi* made of mud was a hassle', so Dakshayani stuck with the Ashram menu.[57]

Dakshayani and Velayudhan went on to have five children – four sons and a daughter. Velayudhan was an alumnus of C.M.S. College, Kottayam Arts College, Trivandrum, and the Tata Institute of Social Sciences, Bombay (now Mumbai). From 1941–1945, he worked at Tata Oil Mills in Ernakulam as a labour welfare officer. In 1945, he worked as an information officer at the Press Information Bureau (PIB), Government of India, in Madras. He held the post till 1948. In 1952, he was elected to the

Lok Sabha.[58] He was also uncle to K.R. Narayanan, India's first Dalit president.[59]

Marriage with Velayudhan remarkably reduced the financial burden on Dakshayani's shoulders.[60] Her next posting was in a high school in an upper-caste-dominated village in Ernakulam district. The couple lived in different towns due to their respective jobs, but they spent time whenever there were holidays or vacations. At this point, Dakshayani's interest was no longer limited to just teaching. She wanted to contribute to social reform.[61]

Dakshayani was also keen to file the nomination for one of the three reserved seats for the Scheduled Castes (SCs) in the Cochin Legislative Council.[62] The other two aspirants were K. Kochukuttan and K.K. Kannan Master. The Council had a total of 58 seats, out of which 20 were to be nominated and 38 were to be elected. As per the rules, government employees could not be nominated for the Council, but all three aspirants for the SC reserved seats including Dakshayani were government employees. She received the news about her nomination via telegram, while she was in Madras where her husband was stationed due to his job at the PIB.[63] So she and the other two aspirants resigned from their respective jobs to join the Council.[64] Dakshayani yet again broke another barrier by becoming the first Dalit woman in the Cochin Legislative Council.

Elated Dakshayani gave her maiden speech at the Council on 2 August 1945 in English, a choice that surprised many.[65] She pointed out that the funds meant for the upliftment of the depressed classes were used by the ministers with undue liberty and 'at the expense of the helpless Depressed Class people'.[66] She passionately added that the one lakh rupees allocated for the welfare of the community was insufficient, and it should be at least three times the figure.

Dakshayani also drew attention to the lack of representation of Depressed Classes in local governance such as panchayats and municipalities. Calling for a proportionate representation, she suggested that '[s]eats may be reserved for the Depressed Classes in the Panchayats on the basis of the population in the Panchayat area. In any case, one seat may be allotted by reservation in every Panchayat. The same may be done in the case of representation in the Municipalities'.[67]

Dakshayani also dwelled on the inhumane nature of untouchability and said, 'Untouchability is a sin against humanity and it stands in our way to progress... If Hinduism is to survive, untouchability has to be wiped out from the face of the Earth.' She ended the speech with the following resounding words: 'Our state can never claim to be enlightened as long as even a single individual is considered as an untouchable.'[68]

In 1946, thirty-four-year-old Dakshayani was elected to the Constituent Assembly from Malabar in the Madras Presidency.[69] It was a close contest and Dakshayani won the election in the second round of counting.[70]

Dakshayani remained committed to highlighting the plight of the Dalits in the Constituent Assembly debates. She delivered her first speech on 19 December 1946, and it expressed hope for a casteless society. She said, 'In the Indian Republic there will be no barriers based on caste or community. The *Harijans* will be safe in a Republican State of the Indian Union. I visualize that the underdogs will be the rulers of the Indian Republic.'[71]

Dakshayani was against separate electorates, and she appealed to the Dalit members of the Assembly to not insist on them. She said, 'We should not make ourselves the laughing stock of our future generations by harping on separatism. Communalism, whether Harijan, Christian, Muslim or Sikh, is opposed to nationalism.'[72]

In the next sentence, she called on Dr Ambedkar urging him to place his service to the nation by joining the nationalist forces. 'He is the only leader of the Harijan community and his non-co-operation with the nationalist forces is a great tragedy to the Harijans; his co-operation with the nationalist forces will enhance the emancipation of the Harijans. Here is a unique occasion for you Sir, (Dr Ambedkar) to place your services before the country.'[73]

Cautious about aligning with the Communist Party, she accused them of exploiting the Harijans by promising pieces of land. She commented, 'They promise pieces of land to the *Harijans* and in that way they try to take them away from the nationalist forces... We cannot depend on such a party for our emancipation and our emancipation lies in the national forces which are represented in this Assembly.'[74]

Dakshayani's vision of upliftment wasn't based on special safeguards but on a mindset change that can be achieved by the removal of social disabilities and granting every citizen the same freedoms.[75]

In a discussion regarding elections for the advisory committee, Dakshayani noticed the absence of Dalit representation in the Hindu candidates' list in the Muslim provinces. Again, she made a strong argument for the members to recognize the intersectionality – caste and religion – of their identity. She said, 'I find that no Harijan's name is included among the Hindus. We, Harijans, consider ourselves one with the Hindu community and we have every right to represent the Hindus in the Muslim provinces.'[76] When another member pointed out that there are already seven members from the Harijan community in the overall list, Dakshayani explained, 'That doesn't mean that the Harijans have no right to represent the Hindus in the Muslim majority provinces. So, I simply wanted to bring to the notice of this House that they should not go with the impression that the Harijans here have come only to represent the Harijans of India. We claim that we belong to the Hindu fold.'[77]

A daughter of the Pulaya community who was traditionally meant to be enslaved, Dakshayani was happy to see the proposal for the prohibition of forced labour. She felt that it would be beneficial to the 'underdogs' of India that will finally, 'have a voice when India gets her independence'.[78] With the prohibition, these forced labourers had the right to demand wages and would get financial independence. She believed such a law would 'bring about an economic revolution'.[79]

When the matter of separate electorates came up in the House on 28 August 1947, Dakshayani demonstrated that she was an astute observer as well as a great orator. Four members submitted their names for an amendment stating an SC individual who wins an election from a reserved seat will also have to secure at least 35 per cent of the SC votes to be declared a winner.[80] Though Dr Ambedkar's name was first on the list, it was S. Nagappa who moved the amendment. Incidentally, Nagappa came from a joint electorate seat and Dr Ambedkar wasn't present in the House. Using these facts to assert her argument, Dakshayani said, 'I am surprised to find that a member [Nagappa] who came in as result of a joint electorate came forward to move this amendment whereas a member [Dr Ambedkar] who, was all the while standing, for separate electorates and for the so-called percentage is not to be seen in the House today. If there was any sincerity in moving this amendment, we could have found the person who headed the list, and I do not know why another member [Nagappa] took up that responsibility.'[81]

Attacking the rationale behind Nagappa's amendment, Dakshayani said, 'If we analyse the demand for a percentage of the votes of the community, we will come to the conclusion that it is nothing but unadulterated separate electorates.' She found a fundamental flaw in the amendment and believed such a system rendered no value to the votes cast by members of the other communities.[82] She further spoke on how the Harijans could be exploited for votes as they were 'not in a position to withstand the attractions that they will have to face at the time of elections'.

Her politics regarding reservation was clear in the next few sentences. She said, 'As long as the SCs, or the Harijans, or by whatever name they may be called, are economic slaves of other people, there is no meaning demanding either separate electorates or joint electorates or any other kind of electorates with this kind of percentage.' She added, 'Personally speaking, I am not in favour of any kind of reservation in any place whatsoever' and the House cheered.[83] The amendment was dropped. However, the Assembly approved reservation for SCs and Scheduled Tribes (STs) in legislative bodies.

In the debate on the abolition of untouchability (Article 17), Dakshayani began with, 'We cannot expect a Constitution without a clause relating to untouchability.' She put the onus of changing the status quo on the oppressors by sharing an anecdote from her time as a college student when a classmate asked her to contribute to a fund for the abolition of untouchability. Her response to her classmate was, 'You people are responsible for this and therefore it is for you to raise the money and it is not proper that you should ask me for money.'[84]

She credited Gandhi for the mindset change amongst upper-caste Hindus. 'The change of heart that we find in the people today is only due to the work that has been done by Mahatma Gandhi and by him alone. We find that there is a vast change in the outlook and attitude of the people today towards the untouchables.'[85] However, she cautioned that the existence of the law is not the end of the road because its success depends on the mindset of the people. She hoped that 'in course of time, there will not be such a community known as Untouchables'.

When the draft Constitution was discussed, Dakshayani criticized it for its lack of originality. She termed it as 'totally foreign to us'. She accused the members of the Assembly of not bringing their best in the Constitution. She argued, 'We hear daily speeches made by our great leaders and their ideals and principles but in the Constitution, we find that it is barren of their ideas and principles… it is a great tragedy to find such a draft has been placed before us.'[86] She strongly felt that the Constitution was a reproduction of the Government of India Act 1935, and said, 'We have not left out even a comma from it.'

Dakshayani suggested that the draft Constitution should be put through a litmus test as an election issue for the people to vote on. Ending her speech, she said, 'If the majority of the electorates accept the Constitution, then we can take it that the whole country has accepted it. If the majority of the electorates reject it then we must take it that the whole country has rejected it, and the party that comes into power, and the Legislature that will be formed thereafter, can take up the Constitution and make the amendments that are necessary.'[87] Her unique suggestion was not taken into consideration.

While Dakshayani didn't see eye to eye with many of her colleagues on official matters, she was close friends with others like Annie Mascarene and Durgabai Deshmukh.[88] She also gave birth to her youngest child, a son during this period.[89] Despite the mounting family expenses and a growing family, Dakshayani sent money from her salary as a Constituent Assembly member to K.R. Narayanan, her nephew by marriage, for his education at the London School of Economics (LSE).[90]

After the Constitution was adopted on 26 November 1949, the Constituent Assembly came to be known as the Provisional Parliament.[91] New members were added to the body and it functioned until a new Parliament was elected in the first general elections.[92] Dakshayani was an active participant herein too.[93] She was often told by many members that she asked many questions.[94] It is not surprising that an opinionated and dynamic woman member was rebuked in this manner, given that male politicians are often known to subjugate their women peers.

Dakshayani's husband was also nominated by the Congress to the Provisional Parliament.[95] With it, the husband–wife duo became India's first Dalit couple in parliament. After three months, Velayudhan resigned and joined the Socialist Party led by Ram Manohar Lohia.[96] His decision to leave the Congress put Dakshayani in a tough spot with the party leadership. Nehru is said to have remarked, 'He [Velayudhan] could have said the government is corrupt but why did he say the Congress is corrupt?'[97]

In the 1952 general elections, Velayudhan got elected to the Lok Sabha as an independent candidate from Quilon Cum Mavelikkara (now Kollam) constituency in Kerala.[98] With five growing children, their household expenditure was increasing, and managing it all with their meagre income as politicians proved difficult. Politics as full-time jobs also left them with little time for their children. It was time to take a hard decision. Dakshayani quit politics and took up a job as a publicity officer at an insurance company.[99] For twenty-one years, she held the same job in New Delhi.[100] Carrying ahead the Gandhian thought of service, she took part in social activities such as the resettlement of partition and Tibetan refugees.[101]

In the 1957 general elections, Velayudhan contested as a candidate of the Praja Socialist Party (PSP) from Kottayam, Kerala. He suffered a great loss and got only 4.9 per cent votes and stood last.[102] As they struggled with the loss of his income, their eldest son helped stabilize the family's economic situation with his earnings as a doctor.[103] A couple of years later, Dakshayani returned to politics. In 1971, she contested the Lok Sabha elections from Adoor as an independent candidate.[104] She secured 3,930 votes and finished fourth.[105] This was her last foray into electoral politics.

Unlike many of the other women politicians of the time such as Ammu Swaminathan, Sarojini Naidu, and Renuka Ray mentioned in this book, Dakshayani never joined the All India Women's Conference (AIWC). According to her daughter Meera, her mother considered it to be an elitist organization.[106] She was not entirely wrong. Dakshayani's trajectory to the Constituent Assembly was very different from the rest of the women – she had neither been in the women's movement nor a part of the mainstream freedom struggle. This could be grounded in the fact that Dakshayani wasn't privileged like the others. She had to fight everyday battles of survival – financially and socially. Despite her desire to join the freedom movement, she couldn't due to the dependency of her family on her government salary which she would have lost if she participated in the resistance movement. She quit her job only after she was nominated to the Cochin Legislative Council.

However, when she retired from politics, she started getting involved with the social movement. The 1970s saw a rise in Dalit consciousness.[107] Dakshayani channelled her energy towards contributing to the rising Ambedkarite movement. In 1977, she joined forces with a few Ambedkarite middle-class women to organize a national conference for Dalit women and subsequently, formed the Mahila Jagriti Parishad (MJP), of which she became the president.[108] Describing the atmosphere of the conference and the importance of such a platform, Meera said, 'The lively conference, with over 200 Dalit women participating from different states, with their own stories, poems, speeches and songs, reflected their attempt to create a space of their own.'[109] The organization worked to upskill Dalit women in the slums and also provided them with adult literacy.[110]

Meera also mentioned that at around this time, Dakshayani was invited by the students of the prestigious Jawaharlal Nehru University to speak on the birth anniversary of Dr Ambedkar.[111] The speech read, 'When Manu declared there should be no freedom for women, it was Dr Ambedkar who brought revolutionary changes in Hindu society through the Hindu Code Bill. He gave Hindu women the right to her father's property. He made changes in the adoption laws.'[112]

Despite their differences in the Constituent Assembly, Dakshayani considered it to be her honour to have worked with Ambedkar.[113] 'It was my good fortune that I could see one of the greatest sons of India and the greatest untouchable leader of India.' She also mentioned to the students that in 1945–1946, she was managing editor of *Jai Bheem*, an Ambedkarite publication in Madras.[114]

After a brief illness, Dakshayani passed away on 20 July 1978 when she was sixty-six years old.[115] On reflecting on her mother's life, Meera believed that Dakshayani 'always regretted leaving

Kerala'.[116] However, her home state of Kerala did not forget the illustrious daughter who descended from the 'slaves' and earned her rightful place in the highest law-making body in the country. To honour her contributions, the Kerala government instituted the annual Dakshayani Velayudhan Award in 2019, to recognize women who contribute to empowering other women in the state. The Department of Women and Child Development earmarked a fund of ₹2 crores, with every honoree getting ₹1 lakh.[117] Even decades after her death, Dakshayani acts as a vehicle for the upliftment of marginalized communities.

DURGABAI DESHMUKH

> 'I firmly believe that millions and billions of rupees cannot create what sincere, honest, and devoted workers can. Millions and billions come running after a devoted worker. That is why I believe that dedicated workers are the backbone of an institution or a country.' [1]
>
> – On creating a prosperous country in her memoir *Chintaman and I*

At the turn of the twentieth century, the role of women in Indian society began to change. Once restricted to homes and performing domestic duties, women and girls were now being encouraged to pursue education by social reformers and missionaries. Most women were for the first time interacting with others outside their families.[2] This step was imperative in helping expand their horizons. Soon, women's organizations sprung up across the country, becoming the platforms where girls and women were able to voice their opinions in all spheres of life, ranging from child marriage, the devadasi system, suffrage, legal inequities and so on. Indian women were now forming their own groups, discovering their interests, and figuring out avenues to pursue them.[3]

With a mission to improve the condition of women, the Women's Indian Association (WIA) was formed in 1917 with prominent leaders such as Annie Besant, Margaret Cousins, Ammu Swaminathan, and many others at the forefront.[4] This was the first national women's body in the country, headquartered in Madras (now Chennai).[5] WIA's main objective was to educate women across a variety of subjects from politics and religion to life skills such as first-aid and sewing. The organization challenged patriarchal norms and aimed to abolish child marriage, raise the age of consent, win female suffrage, promote women's education, and much more. Though in its infancy, the WIA even sent a delegation to the British Secretary of State to urge for women's enfranchisement.

However, while reformist agenda was espoused in the urban elite circles, there wasn't any change in the plight of girls and women in rural areas. In the same year that the WIA was founded, in a remote corner of the Madras Presidency a spirited eight-year-old Durga was being married off. Decades later, that very girl served in the Constituent Assembly beside Ammu Swaminathan, one of the WIA co-founders. Durga, or Durgabai would go on to become a leading light of women's rights and causes.

***

Durga was born on 15 July 1909, to a middle-class Brahmin family in Kakinada, in coastal Rajahmundry (currently in Andhra Pradesh).[6] She later came to be known as Durgabai, a name given to her by those who admired her.[7] Her father B.V.N. Rama Rao and mother Krishnavenamma were social workers.[8] Their work inspired Durgabai. Her father tended to those suffering from the plague and cholera, risking his own life in the process. He even took Durgabai along on several occasions and she observed her father tending to the needy first-hand. This was a very unconventional childhood for the times. According to Durgabai, 'Though the streets of Kakinada were deserted, my father would take my mother and the two children – I had a younger brother, Narayana Rao – to the church, the mosque or the burning ghat to show us how the bodies were disposed of, perhaps with a view to making us courageous enough to face the inevitable event of death.'[9]

Her father helped her see the problems that people faced every day. Durgabai adored him, but she also blamed him for her early marriage calling it his 'only mistake'.[10]As a child she was married to Gummidithala Subba Rao, the son of a wealthy zamindar.[11] When she was fifteen, it was time for them to live together as a couple. But by that time, Durgabai was already an established social activist and was reluctant to accept Subba Rao as her husband. So, she told her father, and even convinced Subba Rao to marry someone else. Then Durgabai was free to continue to serve those who were not able to voice their issues. Many years later, after Subba Rao's death in 1941, Durgabai, a staunch defender and protector of women's rights, took his widow under her wing and put her up in her household until her final days.[12]

Durgabai's foray into activism and social work started when she was very young.[13] Apart from her parents, she was also influenced by Mahatma Gandhi. She took Gandhi's call for non-cooperation very seriously. In protest during the Swadeshi movement, she quit school after completing fifth standard because English was a part of the curriculum from sixth standard onwards.[14] Along with her mother and brother, she decided to wear only handwoven and hand-spun khadi. She even threw all the mill-made clothes into a bonfire.[15]

Durgabai was a keen observer of the world around her, and was sensitive to the social inequities between men and women. The devadasi system – the practice of dedicating women to a deity and their exploitation by men perturbed her. In Kakinada, devadasis were made to perform the *Bhogamelam* dance (an art form known for its sexual depictions and raunchiness) at wedding processions, which was seen as a 'status symbol'. Durgabai found this practice to be a 'reprehensible custom'.[16]

The twelve-year-old Durgabai decided to do something about it. On hearing about Gandhi's visit, she wanted to make the most of it and raise awareness of the social evils that women faced.

She first went to the devadasis and discussed Gandhi's work with them to pique their interest in meeting him. She also spoke to Muslim women who observed purdah, hoping that meeting Gandhi might inspire them to change this custom.[17]

The task of organizing the meeting came with various hurdles for Durgabai. While the women were open to the idea of meeting Gandhi, they could not attend a public programme with men. Durgabai had to think on her feet and assured them that she would arrange an exclusive women-only meeting.

The next problem for the twelve-year-old was convincing the local hosts of Gandhi's visit to agree to a women's gathering. Durgabai requested them to 'spare Gandhiji for at least ten minutes to address a gathering exclusively of women,' but they countered with the condition that they would agree only if she collected five thousand rupees for a purse, which they wanted to gift Gandhi.[18]

The young Durgabai took it as a challenge and raised the sum in just three days with the help of the devadasis.[19] Despite fulfilling the precondition, the hosts continued to be unhelpful. They refused to find an appropriate venue for the gathering. A determined Durgabai looked for alternatives. After doing some groundwork, Durgabai decided that the girls' school where she studied would be the best option for the gathering and secured her headmaster's approval to hold the meeting.[20]

Now that the venue was decided, Durgabai still struggled to get the hosts to give her the allotted ten minutes with Gandhi. Finally, after repeated pleas, they decided to reserve a mere two minutes of the leader's time for the programme. On the day of the event, according to Durgabai, 'more than one thousand women were waiting for his *darshan*. I made one of the elderly women present the purse. They touched Gandhiji's feet and felt so inspired that even before he started to address them they gave the jewels, bangles, necklaces, gold chains, and whatever they had on their person as additional offerings for his cause.' The total value of the collection, including the purse, was ₹25,000.[21]

The two-minute *darshan* stretched to over half an hour. Gandhi emphasized the need for the abolition of the devadasi system as well as reforms among Muslim women. Durgabai translated Gandhi's speech from Hindustani into Telugu for the audience.[22]

Unsurprisingly, Gandhi was thoroughly impressed with young Durgabai. 'When I was bidding goodbye to him, he said, "Durga, get into my car."' She got into his car and sat next to his wife Kasturba Gandhi.[23]

At the main public meeting, Gandhi told the organizers that he wanted Durgabai to translate his speech as she had done a splendid job in the earlier meeting. She seamlessly translated his speech, impressing him even more. From that day, Durgabai 'was his translator whenever he visited the South, not only Andhra but also Madras (though [she] could only speak a smattering of Tamil)'.[24]

Gandhi's visit also led to changes in the lives of the devadasis. According to Durgabai, some of them started to get their 'daughters married to boys who were bold enough to face the social censure'.[25] Many more successes orchestrated by her were to follow.

Two years after Durgabai's first meeting with Gandhi, the Congress decided to hold its annual session in Kakinada. At this time, Gandhi was running a campaign to popularize the use of Hindi in south India through the Dakshina Bharata Hindi Prachar Samiti in Madras.[26] The first Hindi Sahitya Sammelan was to be held along the Congress session, which paved the way for the Hindi Prachar Samiti to move to Kakinada.[27] This gave Durgabai the chance to learn the language systematically. She also learned patriotic songs in Hindi.

In 1922, there was a need for Hindi speakers to coach the women volunteers at the Congress session, the Hindi Sahitya Sammelan, and at a khadi exhibition. Durgabai stepped up to the task. Her parents spared a few rooms in their home, and there, young Durgabai single-handedly taught hundreds of women how to speak Hindi.[28] This was how Durgabai's Balika Hindi Pathasala came to be.[29]

Most of the 400 women Durgabai taught were recruited for the Congress session. Unfortunately, Durgabai was rejected because she was only fourteen at the time. Durgabai was slightly disheartened. But her enthusiasm was rekindled when she was accepted as a volunteer both at the Hindi Sahitya Sammelan and the khadi exhibition.[30]

At the exhibit, Durgabai was given the job of a ticket checker, under strict instructions that only those with tickets to be allowed entry. A young man tried to enter, but he neither had the ticket nor the money to buy one.[31] A stickler for rules, Durgabai denied him entry. When the organizers saw that Durgabai was turning away Jawaharlal Nehru, distinguished leader of the Congress, they came running and twisted her ears. They asked her if she knew the man. In her response, she said, 'I knew it was Jawaharlal Nehru but that I was only following my instructions and doing my duty.' The organizers bought a ticket for Nehru and chided Durgabai again. Nehru intervened and applauded the young girl's dedication to her work. According to him 'the country required such girls who could discharge their duties with courage and conviction.'[32]

Even after the Congress session, Durgabai's Balika Hindi Pathasala continued to draw a large number of women. To accommodate them, she shifted the classes to a bigger house donated by a family. The women were also taught to spin the *charkha* and sing patriotic songs in Hindi. It became one of the two organizations in Kakinada that was designated as a national institution. In her memoir, Durgabai recounted that industrialist Jamnalal Bajaj was very impressed with seeing hundreds of women weaving and singing. He couldn't believe that a young teenager was the founder of the mammoth institution. He even offered Durgabai money to help run the organization, but Durgabai politely declined the generous offer, saying there was no need for money at the moment and that if ever there were a need, she would ask him herself.[33]

Many eminent personalities visited the Balika Hindi Pathasala and made similar offers. Instead of financial contributions, she only accepted books as donations for the libraries. Durgabai held onto this trait throughout her life. She never used her position or fame to enrich herself, and chose to lead an austere life.

As more students joined the institute, the stature of the Pathasala grew over the years. The school soon began training students for Hindi certification.[34] The graduates then went on to spread their knowledge to others. Unfortunately, the school had to shut in the crackdown on organizations in the wake of Civil Disobedience Movement in 1930.

During the same time, Durgabai was also one of the foremost leaders of the Salt March in southern India in 1930, and was arrested along with her mother.[35] In fact, between 1930 and 1933, she had been arrested three times.[36]

Durgabai was imprisoned in jails in Kakinada, Vellore, and Madurai.[37] Her time in prison changed her and her perspectives. In Vellore, she witnessed how innocent women were often coerced into confessing to crimes they did not commit due to their lack of understanding of their rights.[38]

Once she was out of prison, Durgabai resolved to study law to help women convicts. She also observed the difference in the treatment of political prisoners based on their stature. According to law, prisoners were divided into three categories – Class A, B, and C. The more prominent the prisoner in question, the more access to facilities they had. She found this to be a horrid practice. In protest, Durgabai who was an A class prisoner requested that she be transferred to C class as she 'found hundreds of women, very old and sick, suffering in C class.'[39] The jail authorities denied her request on the grounds that she should have made the request to the magistrate at the time of the trial.

The next time she was arrested, Durgabai urged the magistrate to send her to C class. The magistrate hesitated but

Durgabai ultimately got her way. The authorities put her in solitary confinement for almost a year. 'As I was locked up in Madurai jail in a cell next to the death cells and gallows, I used to hear the agonizing cries of the prisoners to be hanged early next morning. This has greatly upset me and I began to get fits of hysteria,' she recounted. Her physical appearance changed drastically and because of poor nutrition, she had become quite frail. Durgabai even suspected the jail administration of trying to poison her. After her release, her physician strongly advised her to stay away from politics owing to both her declining physical and mental health.[40] The year was 1933, and Durgabai was in her early twenties.

During her time away from politics, she decided to study law to be of service to women convicts who weren't aware of their rights. But before law, she had to complete her high school and learn English too. At twenty-four, Durgabai learned the English alphabet with the help of a tutor. Impressed with her learning abilities, her tutor made her appear for the matriculation examination of Banaras Hindu University (BHU) in 1934. After that, she applied for the intermediate examination at BHU. She lived on campus and learned about the functioning of the university under the tutelage of politician and education reformist Madan Mohan Malviya who extended his support to her.[41]

Durgabai wanted to major in political science. Unfortunately, Malaviya was conservative in his beliefs and against women studying a subject he considered the domain of men. Determined to study politics, Durgabai decided to continue her education at Andhra University in Vishakhapatnam.[42]

In 1939, she took the special BA Honours examination in Political Science. She secured a first-class division along with a scholarship at the London School of Economics (LSE). In addition, Durgabai got a seat at the prestigious Inner Temple to read law. Unfortunately, the outbreak of World War II came in the way of her plans, so she enrolled at Madras University to complete her LLB degree in 1941.[43] In just four years, she was on the way to becoming one of Madras's leading names in criminal law.[44]

She had also established the Andhra Mahila Sabha in Madras. While a student at Andhra University, Durgabai often visited her family who were living in Madras. On her visits, she would give Hindi lessons to the neighbourhood children with her mother. As more students joined, their mothers came for Hindi classes too. Just like the Balika Hindi Pathasala, this initiative soon took the shape of an institution known as Andhra Mahila Sabha. Founded in 1937, the organization's main objectives were to empower women by providing adult education and skilling them to generate incomes.[45] A women's hostel for those who came from out of town was also opened.

Almost a decade later in 1946, under her leadership, Andhra Mahila Sabha became a full-fledged institution with around 800 members and with various activities such as Hindi classes, classes for BHU admission entrance tests, music and dance as well as an industrial production unit.[46] Later in 1948, she also founded the Andhra Education Society for the children of the Telugu-speaking community living in Delhi.[47]

Towards the end of 1946, Durgabai now aged thirty-seven, was elected to the Constituent Assembly, A dutiful Durgabai attended every single sitting of the Constituent Assembly.[48] She was a member of the Steering Committee where Vallabhbhai Patel, freedom fighter and Congress leader, entrusted her with the responsibility of reviewing the amendments proposed by others. Durgabai moved more than 750 amendments, both individually and in collaboration with other members.[49]

Durgabai was also the only woman to be included on the Panel of Chairmen of the Provisional Parliament. This meant that in the absence of the Speaker, she could preside over the House and conduct its business. As the name 'Panel of Chairmen' suggests, the position was held by men so far, therefore Durgabai faced some sexism. She recounted, 'Once when I was in the chair and a member addressed me "Sir", several members protested and said I should be addressed "Madam Chairman". I, however, said it did not matter how I was addressed.' She added that they should 'not bother' about 'differences in the matter'.[50]

In the Constituent Assembly, Durgabai spoke on numerous subjects. Some of her most memorable arguments were on the subject of language, religious freedom, age criteria in the Rajya Sabha, the role of courts, the appointment of judges, and judicial autonomy.

The current eligible age to become a member of the Rajya Sabha is 30 years, but it was originally proposed to be set at 35 years. Durgabai moved an amendment that it should be brought down to 30. She argued that being older doesn't particularly mean wiser. In one of her speeches she cited examples to add weight to her argument, 'Our present Prime Minister became President of the Congress before he was 40 and [William] Pitt was 24 when he became prime minister of England. Therefore we have no reason to fear that because a man is only 30 he will not be able to perform his functions in relation to the State.'[51] Various other members spoke in support of her amendment. Eventually, Dr B.R. Ambedkar, the chairperson of the Drafting Committee, accepted Durgabai's amendment and set the eligibility age limit at 30.

The debate on Hindi as the national language saw the most impassioned speeches from all speakers, including Durgabai. Though she had been a Hindi teacher for decades, Durgabai argued in favour of Hindustani as the national language instead of Hindi. She said, 'The National language of India should not be and cannot be any other than Hindustani which is Hindi *plus* Urdu.' She called out the authoritarian attitude of the native-Hindi speakers in the House and highlighted strong opposition to the imposition of Hindi in southern India. She considered the propaganda for Hindi 'a serious obstacle to the growth of the provincial languages and provincial culture.' She cautioned that the narrative to turn Hindi above all other languages was 'embittering the feelings of the non-Hindi speaking people' and would be responsible for 'losing the support of people who know and who are supporters of Hindi' like herself.[52]

Apart from being vocal on the subject of languages, Durgabai used her legal knowledge to propose multiple amendments to the judicial system. While discussing the eligibility of judges, Durgabai moved an amendment that every judge should be a citizen of India.[53] It was adopted.

Durgabai supported the article to provide constitutional remedies for fundamental rights. To her, 'a right without an expeditious and effective remedy serves no purpose at all.' She went to the extent of calling such a right unworthy of the paper on which it is written. She was certain that constitutional remedies would 'ensure effective enforcement of the fundamental rights guaranteed to a person.'[54]

On the other hand, Durgabai also believed that rights should not be absolute and was in support of restrictions on fundamental rights.[55] Durgabai stressed that the nation comes above all when discussing individual freedom during arrests. To the champions of individual freedom, she said, 'I know that in my love and enthusiasm for individual freedom, I only stand for myself, and my interests; and the State is far superior, because it stands for the freedom and liberty of several individuals like myself.'[56]

One of Durgabai's most memorable speeches was an appeal to safeguard children and the youth from exploitation and abandonment.[57] She was concerned that the abandoned children would 'take to beggary and also to many vices such as stealing and they would cultivate very bad habits.' She pleaded to the Drafting Committee to give protection to these children as it was the duty of the nation to protect them.[58]

Following India's independence, while working for the Constituent Assembly, Durgabai was pleased to be a part of the debate on the Hindu Code Bill.[59] She was modest, as she wasn't just a part of the discussions, but a member of the Select Committee on the Hindu Code Bill.[60] The Bill aimed to codify and reform Hindu personal law in favour of a common law code. Along with her friend, Renuka Ray, activist and politician, they participated in debates, and often spoke up against the majority of male members who opposed the bill.

Durgabai remarked that the passage of the bill would 'be a great landmark in the social history' of India. The bill was to provide Hindus – both men and women – the freedom to live a life which they wish to live without in any way affecting or infringing their liberty to adhere to the old ways.

Still a voice to protect women's rights, Durgabai was determined to shut down critiques of those opposed to daughters inheriting a share of the father's property. She said that the daughter 'should enjoy her property in her full right… as an heir to the father.'[61] Durgabai debunked rumours that the law was against Indian culture, and explained, 'the *smritis* themselves have recognized the share of the daughter and there is nothing revolutionary about it'. She staunchly believed that the failure to enact the Hindu Code Bill would be a 'great misfortune'.[62]

Durgabai and Ray were disappointed with the attempts to delay the passage of the bill.[63] Nehru, now the prime minister of India, asked them to have faith in him and be patient until the first elected government is formed. He assured them that there won't be impediments to the passage of the vital legislation.

Nehru kept his word after the 1952 general elections. However, neither Durgabai nor Ray were elected from their respective parliamentary constituencies. Alternatively, Nehru offered them both seats in the Rajya Sabha, in doing so, he was making an exception to his policy that no one should be sent to Rajya Sabha after losing Lok Sabha elections. But both Durgabai and Renuka declined the offer.[64]

Durgabai's work and contribution to the Constituent Assembly had earned her appreciation and admiration from all quarters. One of her admirers was Chintaman Dwarakanath Deshmukh, the first Indian governor of the Reserve Bank of India. Chintaman had served in the Indian Civil Services for

26 years.[65] Unbeknownst to each other, Durgabai had also heard a great deal about him from mutual friends.[66] However, they had not had the opportunity to meet each other until he joined Nehru's Cabinet as the union Finance Minister in 1950. Durgabai voraciously criticized the budget presented by Chintaman in 1951 as 'a rich man's budget with no provisions of the poor'. To her surprise, she was appointed as a member of the Select Committee on the Finance Bill.[67] They were now acquainted and worked together from time to time.[68]

After losing the 1952 elections, Durgabai decided to move to Madras. She wanted to resume her legal practice and also devote time to the Andhra Mahila Sabha. But Nehru had other plans for her, and her fate changed again. First, he gave her financial support to carry out relief work in the drought- and famine-hit areas of Rayalaseema (now in Andhra Pradesh). After that, Nehru sent her on a goodwill delegation to China in 1952, which was led by politician and diplomat, Vijaya Lakshmi Pandit. During her visit, Durgabai was deeply impressed by the concept of family courts in the Chinese judicial system and sent reports to both the prime minister and Chintaman, the finance minister.[69]

Upon her return, she learned from Nehru's personal secretary that she was appointed as the governor of Madhya Pradesh. Her appointment letter was just waiting for the prime minister's signature. However, Chintaman convinced Nehru that Durgabai be made a member of the Planning Commission and given charge of social services. Given her background as a social activist, Nehru liked this idea better and appointed Durgabai to the commission in June 1952. She served alongside Chintaman, Nehru, and three others.[70] It was during this period that Chintaman and Durgabai became a couple, even though they were poles apart in personality.

Chintaman proposed to Durgabai in November 1952 in his garden.[71] Recollecting that day, Durgabai wrote, 'I told him that I was almost a rustic, not in the least a socialite, and that I did not even know how to wear fashionable footwear or go to those parties in the evening; did he still want to marry me?' He took her to a eucalyptus tree and 'inscribed two Sanskrit shlokas on its bark: it was a proposal of marriage. I accepted, and he kissed me.'[72]

The couple had a registered wedding at Durgabai's residence on 22 January 1953.[73] Nehru, along with Sucheta Kripalani, the first female chief minister of Uttar Pradesh, and Durgabai's brother signed as witnesses.[74] This was not the first marriage for either the bride or the groom. Chintaman also had been married for twenty-nine years to his British wife who died in 1949. He also had a daughter from his first marriage.[75]

The couple, though workaholics, made time for each other. Durgabai loved cooking and also took to growing wheat, vegetables, and mangoes in the gardens of their official residence.[76] The differences in their personalities often came up in conversations with friends and family. While Durgabai was 'blunt and outspoken', Chintaman was suave and 'westernized'. Durgabai often wondered if her friends thought, 'would I, who had no social graces or cared for them, got along with Chintaman, who was the very embodiment of style and grace.'[77]

Their relationship was built on a foundation of patience and mutual respect. They were intellectuals in their own right. After more than two decades of marriage, Durgabai reflected, 'When I look back at the 26 years of our married life, I cannot find even a single instance where we differed significantly. Thus, there was no question of adjustment because adjustment and compromise arise only when one differs basically from the other on a significant matter. We are happy that we have been happy to keep up this affection and understanding during all this period.'[78]

On the work front, after the first five-year plan was finalized in 1952, Durgabai wanted to resign from the Planning Commission and focus on her family life. But like the rest of her plans, this was not to be. Nehru asked her to be the first chairperson of the Central Social Welfare Board (CSWB), an organization that was to provide services to women and children for their empowerment and protection. Durgabai gladly accepted the position and began work in 1954.[79] She paid special attention to skilling and educating rural women. The Board set up 30,000 welfare centres across more than 1,50,000 villages.[80] She was able to unite thousands of voluntary organizations across India working for social development. Crèches, health centres, and care centres for abandoned women were formed in villages, and district committees were formed to oversee and decentralize their activities.[81,82] Durgabai served in the position till 1962.

Chintaman stepped down as finance minister in 1956.[83] Soon after, he became the chairman of the University Grants Commission, the statutory body of higher education in India. But just two days into his new role, Nehru offered to nominate him as the director-general of the International Monetary Fund. Chintaman declined as he preferred to serve his country instead.[84]

Durgabai and her husband had a pact that only one among them would draw a salary.[85] For them, service to their people came before personal wealth. So, Chintaman drew a token salary of only ₹1 since Durgabai was earning as a full-time chairperson of the CSWB. After the end of her tenure, Chintaman became the vice-chancellor of Delhi University.[86] This was when Durgabai took up a pro bono legal practice at the Supreme Court.[87]

The couple moved to Hyderabad in 1967, to focus on social development activities.[88] They travelled across India and the world on invitations from international organizations and governments. In 1975, Durgabai and Chintaman received the Padma Vibhushan for their individual contributions to the country.[89]

The country was independent, and Durgabai got to do the work that she set out to do next to a man to match her vision. Unfortunately, health problems were to follow. In 1976, Durgabai lost her eyesight to chronic diabetes.[90] In the first few months of 1981, Durgabai's health began to deteriorate steadily. In the early hours of the morning on 9 May 1981, at the age of 71 Durgabai died in her husband's arms.

A devastated Chintaman in a memoir dedicated to his wife wrote: 'Durgabai had often said to me, "when the time comes I should like to pass away in your arms" [...] Returning to the day of the tragedy, there she lay within my arms without any of us saying a word, the doctor standing by.' Her wish was fulfilled.[91]

A child bride who learned the English alphabet in her early twenties, Durgabai dedicated her life to the cause of education and upliftment of every Indian citizen. She received national and international awards in recognition of her service – including the UNESCO World Peace Medal, Paul G Hauffman Award, Nehru Literacy Award, Padma Vibhushan, and many others.[92] She headed many firsts too – Durgabai prepared the first report of the National Education Policy for Women,[93] and even established the National Council for Women in 1958 and was its first chairperson among many others.[94] Several universities awarded her honorary doctorates for her work in social welfare.[95] She used her skillset and made government bodies to implement best practices that benefitted millions. Durgabai was a spirited woman who lived life on her own terms without a care about material gains or personal wealth. She rejected offers for financial assistance from industrialists like Jamnalal Bajaj and also gave up government salaries. To her, nothing came before service to the country.

Chintaman described her best in *My Durgabai*, his heartfelt tribute to the love of his life, 'She was so good, gentle, unassuming; her heart was full of compassion. She was the finest human being within my ken and flawless like the most perfect gem... Her capacity for affection was boundless. To know her was to love her. Of censure she had no fear. She was fearless. Pride she had none. Her desire to do good to others was altruism incarnate. She and I were integrated into an inseparable whole.'[96]

HANSA MEHTA

> 'We have too many personal laws in this country and these personal laws are dividing the nation today. It is therefore very essential if we want to build up one nation to have one Civil Code. It must, however, be remembered that the Civil Code that we wish to have must be on a par with, or in advance of, the most progressive of the personal laws in the country. Otherwise, it will be a retrograde step and it will not be acceptable to all.'
>
> – An appeal for enactment of a uniform civil code in the Constituent Assembly on 22 November 1949

'All men are created equal' – proclaims the Preamble to the American Declaration of Independence. The Declaration inspired the Constitution of the United States of America, one of the most important documents in history. While it asserted that 'all men are created equal', the Declaration had nothing to say about women. In the absence of an explicit proclamation of equality, women were relegated to secondary status. After the American Civil War ended in 1865, the Constitution was amended to abolish slavery (13th Amendment) and grant citizens equal protection of laws (14th Amendment). The words 'male inhabitants' were categorically inserted in the 14th Amendment to define voters. The 15th Amendment granted African-American men the right to vote in 1870, but American women had to wait another five decades to exercise the same right.

In 1947, the United Nations Commission on Human Rights (UNCHR) set about drafting the Universal Declaration of Human Rights (UDHR) in the aftermath of World War II. Eleanor Roosevelt, the former first lady of the USA, was the chairperson of the commission. The Draft Article 1 of the UDHR said, 'all men are born free and equal'.[1] Hansa Mehta, reformist and activist, who was also the Indian delegate to the commission, stood strongly against the exclusionary language. Her years of feminist activism had imbibed in her the importance of equality in all spheres and forms. She argued that the words 'all men' could be used to restrict the rights of women. She prevailed upon her colleagues to choose a gender-neutral international human rights framework that proclaims, 'all human beings are born free and equal'.

Hansa Mehta's intervention came from the progressive values she was brought up with. She was born to a privileged family on 3 July 1897 to Sir Manubhai Mehta and Harshadagauri Mehta. Her paternal grandfather Nandshankar Mehta[2] was a renowned administrator, social worker, and the author of the popular Gujarati novel *Karan Ghelo*. Nandshankar was an advocate for women's education and widow remarriage, and openly criticized caste-based discrimination. He was also associated with the Prathana Samaj, a religious reform movement that was similar to the Bhakti movement.[3]

Manubhai, Hansa's father taught law, philosophy, and logic to undergraduate students at Baroda College, now known as The Maharaja Sayajirao University of Baroda. In 1916, he was appointed the dewan of Baroda, where he served under Baroda's progressive ruler, Maharaja Sayajirao Gaekwad III (r.1875–1939). He held the post for eleven years, before moving to the princely state of Bikaner. During Sayajirao's reign, Baroda witnessed major governance and social reforms, including a ban on child marriage and legislation to abolish untouchability.[4]

Manubhai's interest in social reforms and the family's progressive values and background ensured Hansa got a formal education. In fact, she attended a girls' high school established by Sayajirao. In an interview, she reiterated, 'My father inherited the liberal ideas of his father and we were educated in the same way'.[5] Between 1913 and 1917, Hansa studied philosophy at Baroda College. She was one of the three women enrolled in her batch. The college atmosphere was hostile and unfriendly towards the three young women, as the male students and faculty weren't used to having women students around.

During her college years, Hansa and her friends were isolated and forced to keep to themselves. Writing for the college's golden jubilee commemorative volume, Hansa noted the palpable alienation she underwent and how the institution was designed for men alone. The women constantly faced an additional burden of remaining 'in dignity', which meant that they had to self-censor in terms of appearance and mannerisms. They could not assert or be themselves.

The men at Baroda College let them down and often took them for granted. Once, they called a strike without consulting or informing the women. On another occasion, a student read out a paper on 'Duties of Indian Women'. The women were angry, and Hansa had thought of getting back at the men and speaking on the duties of Indian men. However, sensing the futility of the exercise, she chose not to respond. Later, determined to have her voice heard, Hansa issued a rejoinder and spoke of what the women perceived to be their duties. Seething at the patronizing ideas of her fellow male classmates and keen on making a mark, Hansa was nervous before the speech. She placed an immense burden upon herself knowing that if she faltered, it would be seen as a 'failure of all women in general'. The speech, though, concluded without hiccups. Emboldened by her successful defence, Hansa decided to try her hands at writing for the college magazine.[6] She turned out to be a prolific writer, authoring several children's books over the years and contributing incisive articles in leading publications on diverse subjects.

After completing her undergraduate degree in India, Hansa took up a course in journalism at the London School of Economics and Political Science.[7] In London, she became acquainted with Sarojini Naidu, who had already argued for women's suffrage before the Montagu-Chelmsford Committee in 1917. The London years were sort of a political baptism for Hansa. She 'lived in a political atmosphere', interacting with senior leaders of India's freedom movement such as Bal Gangadhar Tilak, Lala Lajpat Rai, and Annie Besant.[8]

Hansa found a mentor in Naidu, who took her under her wing. Naidu took her along to different events. In 1920, Hansa accompanied Naidu to the Eighth Conference of the International Woman Suffrage Alliance held in Geneva. The exposure made this shy college student become an assertive activist. Newly recruited to the feminist movement, Hansa travelled to the USA to take a closer look at the educational systems there. Keen on founding a college in India 'along the lines of America's colleges for women', Hansa visited several American universities 'and colleges interested in offering full scholarships to Indian women'.[9] Her visit to the USA coincided with a period of intense political activity around the issue of women's suffrage.

By June 1919, the US House of Representatives and the Senate passed a proposal to grant women the right to vote. The proposal, now known as the 19th Amendment, was ratified in 1920.[10] Finally, American women had constitutional protection with respect to the right to vote. The 19th Amendment inspired women leaders in the USA to also advocate for the 'Equal Rights Amendment' – a proposal to amend the Constitution. The text of the resolution which was introduced in the House of Representatives read, 'Men and women shall have equal rights throughout the United States and every place subject to its jurisdiction'.[11] The years of struggle for something as basic as voting rights had been a bitter lesson for feminist leaders. They knew that real progress would be evasive until 'equality' was explicitly enshrined in the Constitution. The proposal was not ratified and remains a key concern to this day.

The demand for women's right to vote found a parallel audience in India, where it was a subject of activism and intense discussion. In December 1917, Naidu led a delegation of women that met Edwin Montagu, the secretary of state for India, and Lord Chelmsford, the viceroy. In their address to Montagu and Chelmsford, the delegation highlighted that women in India had 'awakened to their responsibilities in the public life'. They wanted women to be recognized as 'people', specifying that 'it may be worded in such terms as will not disqualify our sex' and allowed the right to vote and 'same opportunities of representation' as the men.[12] The hectic advocacy, however, met with limited success. Britain enacted the Government of India Act 1919 (based on a report by Montagu and Chelmsford), which listed being a woman as a disqualification to the right to vote. However, it allowed provincial legislatures to enfranchise them. Hansa's meeting with Naidu in London was in the course of the latter's efforts towards acquiring voting rights for women.

After her tour of the USA, Hansa returned to India where nationalist sentiments were rising after Mahatma Gandhi's active involvement with the Congress. Incidentally, Gandhi's first detention in India was in Baroda, while Hansa's father Manubhai was the dewan.[13]

Hansa's first meeting with Gandhi was at the Sabarmati Jail when she accompanied Naidu and a group of women from Bombay (now Mumbai). Before this meeting, Hansa had previously seen him from afar on two occasions. At first, she was left unimpressed, but after the second sighting, she was intrigued. Personally meeting Gandhi 'visibly moved' her. In later years, she maintained a close working relationship with him. Hansa held him in high regard, but unlike others, did not revere him. She believed that one must 'learn and think for oneself… instead of taking shelter behind Gandhiji's words in everything'.[14]

Around the same time, Hansa met Dr Jivraj Mehta, her future husband, who was, briefly, Gandhi's personal physician. The doctor had been invited to work in Baroda by Sayajirao. Jivraj worked as the state's chief medical officer between 1923–24, when Manubhai was the dewan. Interestingly, Jivraj, following the steps of his father-in-law, too went on to become dewan of Baroda between 1948–49.[15]

Hansa and Jivraj's proposed union met with stiff resistance from the conservative members in her family, especially on her mother's side. The objections to the marriage were mainly based on caste as Hansa was a Nagar Brahmin and Jivraj a Vaishya. Hansa was threatened with excommunication from her community, but she was defiant and refused to bow down. 'I told them I was going out of the caste myself, as I did not believe in caste,' shared Hansa in an interview. Their marriage found support from the king, Sayajirao, who attended their wedding, a very public endorsement of inter-caste marriages.[16] Hansa and Jivraj's journey as a couple was also entwined with their role in the struggle for India's independence. They were Gandhi's trusted aides in Bombay and later, members of the Constituent Assembly. Post-Independence, Jivraj served as the prohibition minister of the then Bombay state between 1952 to 1960 and was also the first chief minister of Gujarat in 1960.[17]

Hansa did not take to the freedom movement immediately and was more focused on education and women's rights issues at first. She was a member of the Bombay Municipal School's Committee as well as the Bhagini Samaj, a women's welfare organization founded in the memory of social reformer and activist Gopal Krishna Gokhale. Very soon, Hansa established herself as the voice of the young Indian feminists who were not content with piecemeal reforms. She articulated a vision that was audacious for the times and struck at the roots of inequities. This brought her into conflict with some of the senior leaders of the women's movement.

In January 1927, the All India Women's Conference (AIWC) held its first meeting in Poona (now Pune) where representatives from different women's organizations convened to discuss educational reforms. The conversation moved to child marriages as the activists felt that early marriages were impeding female education. In its resolution, AIWC called for the promotion of female education and implored the government to set the age of consent at sixteen. A second resolution condemned the practice of child marriage and sought to penalize such marriages. Hansa, representing Bhagini Samaj, moved an amendment that called for declaring child marriages invalid. There was a lot of opposition to this. Some delegates opposed the move as they believed it would affect the legitimacy of children born of such marriages. The other concern was of the state infringing upon personal laws. The amendment was ultimately defeated because it was seen as an attack on the sacramental nature of marriage under Hindu law. Hansa's arguments, however, were a precursor to the debate on the Uniform Civil Code (UCC), a common law for all citizens irrespective of religion. [18] Two decades later, Hansa made an impassioned appeal for the implementation of the same code before the Constituent Assembly.

Within weeks of the 1927 conference, Rai Sahib Harbilas Sharda introduced the Hindu Child Marriage Bill (also known as Sarda Bill) in the Central Legislative Assembly. The Bill was second in line of progressive legislations, the first being Hari Singh Gour's 'Age of Consent' Bill. There was deep scepticism among women leaders with respect to both the Bills. This is because, while the legislations were a step forward, they failed to adequately address the problems at hand and conflicted with the demands of the AIWC. The Sarda Bill proposed setting the minimum age for marriage of girls at 12 while AIWC had demanded it be set at 16. In addition, Hansa wanted marriage to be defined as a 'strictly monogamous and equal contract'.[19] The Sarda Bill was eventually enacted as Child Marriage Restraint Act 1929. The nomenclature was important as it now covered child marriages across religions.

At this time, the AIWC was going through a churn of its own. It had started as an umbrella organization of different women's groups and called itself a non-political entity that focused on education. In 1927, when Britain announced setting up the Simon Commission to study constitutional reforms in India, huge protests broke out around the country. Kamaladevi Chattopadhyay, the then honorary secretary of AIWC, joined the demonstrations. This irked Lady Dorothy Irwin, the wife of the then viceroy Lord Irwin, who was scheduled to preside over the AIWC's 1928 conference in Delhi.

Over time, the growing political nature of the organization led some delegates to fear the withdrawal of official support for its educational activities. Others, like Hansa, were in favour of expanding the AIWC mandate. They believed that problems women faced had been instituted with the support of the government; to hope for positive change with official support was bound to lead to disappointment. Hansa also strongly opposed giving Lady Irwin an expanded role in the organization, in order to protect the conference's newly expanded social reform agenda. Following the dissent, a compromise was affected through which Lady Irwin's role was limited to educational activities.[20] While the AIWC retained its non-political character for another decade, Hansa's bold stance made her a name to be reckoned with. As time passed, Hansa became sceptical of AIWC's methods. Writing on the conference's ninth session, she wondered if AIWC was having an impact or was it 'merely echoing parrot-like' the Western women?[21] AIWC's agenda and policy prescription ignored the ground realities. Hansa was therefore keen on affecting a positive material change in the lives of Indian women from the grassroots up.

While AIWC had decided to stay away from politics, Hansa plunged into the freedom movement in 1930, with the launch of the Civil Disobedience Movement. In March 1930, on his way to Dandi to break the salt laws, Gandhi met a group of women in Karadi, a village in Gujarat, and 'talked about picketing of foreign goods and liquor'.[22] There were apprehensions amongst the women about breaking the law, which would inevitably lead to their arrest. Hansa, for instance was unwilling to go to prison as she had young children.[23]

In April 1930, Gandhi sent her a message, asking her to campaign against liquor consumption in Bombay. He added, 'India expects every woman to do her duty at this moment in the fight for freedom'.[24] Gandhi's message inspired Hansa and a group of women from Bombay to form the Desh Sevika Sangh and mount a strong picketing campaign. Their efforts proved effective, forcing the government to declare the Sangh illegal and outlaw picketing, putting the volunteers at risk of arrest.[25] Faced with growing difficulties, some women left the organization. Hansa decided to stay put as she was 'the captain' and her leaving would disrupt the activities.[26] The opposition against alcohol found its way to her Constituent Assembly speeches in which she criticized the way the states had implemented prohibition.[27]

In the 1930s, with the launch of the Civil Disobedience Movement, Hansa, like many Indians of the time, resigned from her post in government office. She stepped down as the Justice of the Peace,[28] a role that was appointed by the British to preside over criminal matters. Soon after, she was invited to join the Bombay Provincial Congress Committee. Back then, the committee had a war council to coordinate the activities of the Civil Disobedience Movement. The president of the council was called the 'dictator of Bombay'. The 'dictator's' role was thrust on her within weeks of her joining the independence movement.

The reluctant freedom fighter took to politics like a duck to water. While the government tried to crush the spirit of the historic movement by arresting leaders, Hansa mobilized the masses against imperial rule. Under her leadership, the Congress promoted swadeshi by organizing *prabhat pheris*, early morning processions where the participants walk around singing devotional and patriotic songs, around Bombay and picketing shops selling foreign goods. Hansa was an adept organizer.

Under her leadership, the Bombay Congress held large meetings to propagate the message of the Civil Disobedience Movement.

On 1 August, she led a huge procession to mark the tenth death anniversary of Bal Gangadhar Tilak. When the police restricted their movement, Hansa and other Congress leaders, many of whom were in Bombay for a working committee meeting, sat on the road through the night despite heavy rains.[29] The government responded to the defiance by arresting several prominent members of the party. An undeterred Hansa managed to organize another procession within a week's time, with police permission.[30] Her tenacity earned her a place in the Congress Working Committee, the highest decision-making body of the party. Her first time attending a working committee meeting in Delhi was eventful. The meeting was declared unlawful[31] and all its members, barring Kamala Nehru and Hansa, were put behind bars.

Upon her return to Bombay, Hansa, too, was arrested, but not before a show of strength by Congress supporters while she was still at New Delhi railway station. Records say that railway engines were made to hoot non-stop by the authorities to drown out the cries of 'inquilab zindabad' by supporters of Kamala and Hansa who were at the station to greet them.[32] After her arrest, Hansa spent three months in prison on the charge of publishing the *Congress Bulletin*.[33] In 1932, she was arrested again, but this time with her husband. A weekly publication explained the cause of Jivraj's arrest, 'Dr Mehta is not known to be an active politician and his detention in jail can be explained only on the ground of his harbouring a Congress worker in the person of his wife.'[34]

Between leading the Congress party in Bombay and her two incarcerations, Hansa managed to make time for her educational as well as social reform agenda. She was elected to the Bombay University Senate in 1931 and 1936 and was also a member of the Senate of the Indian Women's University. While she authored several books in Gujarati, she also translated works by Shakespeare and other Western writers. She was also the organizing secretary of the National Council of Women in India in 1930 and elected as its vice president in 1936.[35]

In 1936, elections to the provincial assemblies and councils were announced under the Government of India Act 1935. As a committed member of the AIWC, which was against reservation, Hansa refused to contest a seat earmarked for women in Bombay.

In December 1931, the British had formed the Indian Franchise Committee to suggest a new constitutional framework for India. AIWC placed before the Committee a memorandum that called for equal rights for all citizens, non-discrimination, adult suffrage and, most importantly, no reservation of seats for women.[36] AIWC's stand against reservations was a contentious one and a corollary to the larger debate that had engulfed the political circles.

Congress leaders had been opposing separate electorates on the premise that it would widen the gulf between Hindus and Muslims. In August 1932, the British Prime Minister Ramsay MacDonald announced the Communal Award. The Communal Award ensured continuance of separate electorates for Muslims, Sikhs, Europeans, Anglo-Indians and Indian Christians. The British also announced the extension of separate electorates to the Depressed Classes, taking India by storm.

In September 1932, Gandhi went on a fast demanding its withdrawal. He feared that the Communal Award was going to deepen divisions among the Hindus and weaken the national struggle. Dr B.R. Ambedkar had supported the Award, but Gandhi's fast forced him to negotiate an alternate governance framework. Gandhi broke his fast with the signing of the Poona Pact, an agreement between leaders of the Depressed Classes and the rest of the community; Hansa was a signatory to the Pact. Under the Poona Pact, separate electorate for Depressed Classes were replaced with joint electorates. Unlike separate electorates, where candidates and voters must be from the same community, in the joint electorates, seats are reserved for a particular community but voters from all communities are allowed to vote. A day after signing the Poona Pact, a conference of Hindu leaders constituted a Harijan Sevak Sangh, which sought to abolish untouchability and work towards opening public spaces and temples to the marginalized classes. Hansa served as the vice president of the Sangh.[37]

The storm raised by the Communal Award reached AIWC. In December 1932, AIWC passed a resolution denouncing the Communal Award. Aruna Asaf Ali, a prominent Congress leader and sister of Purnima Banerji, proclaimed that the 'difference which separated men did not exist' among women.[38]

It has been argued that over time the AIWC had changed their position, to align itself with the nationalist movement. It had initially supported reservations but opposed them later 'due to the broader context of the nationalist movement'.[39] The Congress wanted to do away with separate electorates as it saw them as reinforcing communal and caste identities. While condemning reservations was easier for upper-caste leaders, it fuelled alienation among other minority members, especially the Muslim leaders in AIWC. Hansa emphasized her opposition to reservations in the Constituent Assembly, where she said, 'We have never asked for privileges. The women's organization to which I have the honour to belong has never asked for reserved seats, for quotas, or for separate electorates. What we have asked for is social justice, economic justice, and political justice.'[40]

Eventually, Hansa successfully contested the 1936 elections from a general seat in the Legislative Council. She was appointed a parliamentary secretary for education and health. Hansa worked on some far-reaching reforms that the government initiated. A few notable initiatives were starting vocational schools, creating a secondary education examination board, and reserving fifty per cent seats in teacher training colleges for women.[41] However, in September 1939, the Congress chose to resign from the ministries in protest against Britain's decision to make India a part of World War II without consulting the provincial governments. The following year, Congress launched the individual Satyagraha. As the war was raging, plans to organize a mass movement were replaced with an advocacy programme. Under the individual Satyagraha plan, Congress workers would go to the people and preach against the war. Hansa was one such *satyagrahi* and was imprisoned for five months.[42]

While the war raged on, Britain continued to dither on its promises to India, leading the Congress to launch the Quit India Movement in 1942. This time Hansa did not court arrest. To aid the families of those arrested she helped form the prisoner's relief committee to raise funds.[43]

By 1945, the victory of the Allied Forces was inevitable and Indian independence was finally on the horizon. Women activists were hopeful that their aspirations of equality were going to be realized in an independent India. They had stood against the colonial rule and were now keen on forging a republic that would elevate their status.

Hansa presided over the annual conference of AIWC in December 1945. At the conference 'members were instructed to collect the relevant clauses dealing with women's rights from various constitutions'.[44] In her presidential address, Hansa talked about crystallizing their demands through a women's charter of rights. Hansa also spoke of raising the economic status of women. 'It is in the economic sphere that woman will have to fight hard to establish her position,' she said. Hansa then broached a subject that remains unresolved – the issue of unpaid household work, which she felt had not been recognized yet and wanted to highlight. Hansa passionately voiced, 'It is the work of the housewife. She works from early morning till late at night ... It is time that the importance of this work was recognized and conditions of work improved.' She then enumerated another essential but ignored right – the right to leisure. Hansa had put her privilege to good use. She was well-travelled and informed of the advancements around the world. The progressive thinking on display was a testament to her commitment to feminist causes.[45]

The AIWC session of 1945 was in many ways redemption for Hansa. In the 1927 session, she had caused some flutter when she sought to outlaw child marriages and recognize marriages as a 'strictly monogamous and equal contract'. Now at the helm of affairs, Hansa made it known that the charter of women's rights would advocate holistic changes to personal laws vis-a-vis succession, divorce, polygamy, and guardianship. She also made it clear that a woman 'shall have a right to limit her family'.[46] At its 1946 session, the AIWC adopted the Indian Woman's Charter of Rights and Duties. In presenting the 'Charter of Rights and Duties' of women, life had come full circle for Hansa since her college days when an errant male classmate thought he could decide the duties of Indian women. The charter was 'forwarded to the Central and provincial governments, strongly urging that the fundamental rights and economic and social directives embodied in it form "an integral part of the Constitution"'.[47] Hansa was elected to the Constituent Assembly from Bombay on a Congress ticket in 1946.[48]

On the eve of Independence, 14 August 1947, Hansa presented to the Constituent Assembly the national flag 'on behalf of the women of India'. In her short speech, she said, 'It is in the fitness of things that this first flag that will fly over this august House should be a gift from the women of India. We have donned the saffron colour, we have fought, suffered and sacrificed in the cause of our country's freedom... We pledge ourselves for working for a greater cause, to maintain the freedom that we have attained. We have great traditions to maintain, traditions that made India so great in the past. It is the duty of every man and woman to preserve these traditions so that India may hold her spiritual supremacy over the world.'[49]

Hansa's role in the Constituent Assembly was greatly helped by her work in moulding the international rights regime. In 1945, the UN adopted its charter. The preamble to the charter 'determined to save succeeding generations from the scourge of war', reaffirming its faith 'in fundamental human rights'.[50] It also laid out the contours of the newly formed organization.

In February 1946, the Economic and Social Council, established under the UN Charter, resolved to establish a Commission on Human Rights (HRC) and a Sub-Commission on the Status of Women. The key responsibility before the HRC was to instruct and 'submit proposals, recommendations and reports regarding, inter alia, an international bill of human rights'. Effectively, it was charged with preparing the International Bill of Human Rights of which the UDHR formed a crucial component.

Hansa was not the first choice to represent the country. India was represented by Kshitish Chandra Neogy, a politician from West Bengal. Nehru nominated Hansa to the HRC after Neogy's withdrawal from the body. The Sub-Commission on Status of Women, which was to be a supporting arm of the HRC,[51] was eventually conferred the status of a full commission and is now known as the Commission on the Status of Women (CSW). Hansa sat on the Sub-Commission and shared with the delegates the Indian Woman's Charter of Rights and Duties prepared by the AIWC. Impressed with the document, the UN Sub-Commission adopted verbatim the first three paragraphs of its preamble when reporting on its mandate and guiding philosophy.[52]

At the first HRC session held in New York in January–February 1947, Hansa proposed Eleanor Roosevelt's name as chairman. She advocated for cooperation with the CSW in drafting the International Bill of Rights.[53] At the next meeting, Hansa argued for the bill to be a simple document easily understood by the common people. She wanted the bill to be supplemented with an adequate implementation machinery that would kick in whenever a human rights violation took place. Hansa was of the opinion that the proposed bill 'would be meaningless unless an unequivocal definition were given of the relationship which ought to exist between the individual, the community, the state, and the international organization.' She also spoke of South Africa's mistreatment of Indian-origin indentured labourers, an issue previously raised at the UN by diplomat and politician Vijaya Lakshmi Pandit.[54]

The second session of the HRC was held in Geneva in December 1947, a few months after India gained independence. At the meeting, Hansa again spoke of the International Bill of Rights forming part of both international and domestic law. She apprised the delegates of India's commitment to incorporate fundamental human rights into its Constitution. When the matter of implementation of the Bill of Rights came up, she said that the UDHR must not contain anything 'which would not be implemented'.[55] Subsequently, she was made part of the Working Group of Implementation and elected 'chairman'.

Hansa proposed that individuals must have the right to petition for violation of their human rights. Her working group asked the UN Secretariat 'to draw up a full and detailed scheme of regulations and procedures regarding the right of petition'. The move was scuttled by the USA which was sceptical about the implementation.[56]

At its thirty-fourth meeting, the HRC discussed draft Article 1 of the UDHR. Hansa objected to the use of gendered words such as 'all men' and 'brothers' because 'she felt they might be interpreted to exclude women and were out of date'.[57] Chairperson Roosevelt disagreed saying 'all men' was used in the general sense and implied human beings. The draft Article was put to vote and 'all men' was accepted. In the subsequent sessions, the matter was brought up and brushed away. Some members felt it was irrelevant as 'all men' automatically included women. The French representative highlighted the translation issues that were to happen if 'all men' was substituted with 'all men and women'. The United Kingdom and India joined hands and moved another resolution. It was only in the last session of the commission that Hansa's suggestions for gender-neutral terminology were accepted.[58]

Closer to home, starting with getting the CSW to adopt AIWC's words to successfully push the Indian draft for discussion during deliberations on UDHR, Hansa had done a stellar job in promoting liberal ideas based on justice and equality.

During this time, Hansa was also a member of a Constituent Assembly sub-committee on fundamental rights, alongside Rajkumari Amrit Kaur. The sub-committee brought to head several key issues Hansa had advocated for during her activism days.

In its report, the sub-committee suggested an expansive right to religion. Clause 16 of the report read: 'All persons are equally entitled to freedom of conscience and the right freely to profess and practise religion subject to public order, morality or health and to the other provisions of this chapter.' Hansa and Kaur disagreed with the broad scope of the right to religion. They were concerned that this might come in the way of social reforms.

They wrote to B.N. Rau, the Assembly's Constitutional Advisor: '... As we are all aware there are several customs practised in the name of religion e.g., purdah, child marriage, polygamy, unequal laws of inheritance, prevention of inter-caste marriages, dedication of girls to temples. We are naturally anxious that no clause in fundamental rights shall make impossible future legislation for the purpose of wiping out these evils. As worded, Clause 16 may even contradict or conflict with the provision abolishing the practice of untouchability... Indeed we have a further fear that validity of existing laws such as the Sarda Act, and the Widow Remarriage Act may even be questioned.'[59] Eventually, their opposition paved the way for a watered-down right to religion and empowered governments to restrict the right when enacting laws for social welfare (Article 25).

In their letter to Rau, Hansa and Kaur also suggested making the directive principles of state policy enforceable.[60] They were particularly interested in ensuring a UCC. A UCC would subsume all personal laws regarding marriage, divorce, guardianship, and other civil relations and replace them with one secular law. At the sub-committee meeting, they supported a proposal moved by Minoo Masani to incorporate UCC as a fundamental right. The proposal was rejected. Hansa and Kaur also supported removing barriers to inter-religious marriages, they pointed out how inter-religious couples had to renounce religion to solemnize a marriage under the Special Marriage Act 1872.[61] This Act was replaced in 1954 with a legislation that allowed marriages without the parties giving up their religion.

Hansa brought up the issue of a UCC during the Constituent Assembly debates. She highlighted that there were 'too many personal laws' that were dividing the country. Hansa continued to actively denounce the practice of purdah and was against providing any special privileges to minorities, other than those guaranteed under the fundamental rights. She blamed the British for promoting religious divide and wondered 'What do the minorities want? What can be their claims?' when the Constitution guaranteed equality in all spheres. She claimed, 'If they (minorities) want privileges, that is not in the spirit of democracy. They cannot ask for privileges.'[62] Like the issue of reservations, Hansa approached the debate without acknowledging the anxieties of the minorities.

Hansa carried forward the demands of the AIWC through her role in the Constituent Assembly. She kept underlining the abysmal status of women in the country, 'The average woman in this country has suffered now for centuries from inequalities heaped upon her by laws, customs and practices of people who have fallen from the heights of that civilization of which we are all so proud'. She also emphasized on the need for equality if India were to truly progress, 'This ancient land cannot attain its rightful place, its honoured place in this world without the cooperation of women. I therefore welcome this Resolution for the great promise which it holds, and I hope that the objectives embodied in the Resolution will not remain on paper but will be translated into reality.' Her efforts aimed at recognizing the individual status of women where their rights were not dependent upon a husband or a family.[63]

While she did welcome the Hindu Code Bill, she felt that it didn't adequately address issues of equality. 'This Bill to codify the Hindu Law is a revolutionary Bill and though we are not quite satisfied with it, it will be a great landmark in the social history of the Hindus.' When the Bill was referred to the Select Committee, she urged them to be futuristic in their vision, 'We have looked too much to the past. We must now look to the future. It is for the future generation that we are making this law.' She added 'We have to see that the future generation is not fettered by our own prejudices with regard to marriage or divorce or with regard to any other ideas that we may have today.'[64]

Hansa's unwavering dedication to women's welfare didn't always win her friends and admirers. The constitutional committee's push to define and enshrine the rights of women had irked a few male members. At the time, Rohini Kumar Chaudhuri from Assam called for 'protection against women'.[65] Having stressed the need for a progressive civil code, Hansa silenced Chaudhuri by saying, 'The world would have thought very little of the men if they had asked for protection against women in this Constitution; I am very happy to see that the Constitution does not include that provision. Otherwise men would have had to hide their faces before the world.'[66]

Post-Independence, Hansa continued to stay busy with women's rights and education reforms.[67] In 1949, Hansa was appointed the vice chancellor of Maharaja Sayajirao University of Baroda, which she attended many years ago and where her father taught.[68] Under her leadership, the university gained a great reputation in both sciences and humanities.[69] As the AIWC president, Hansa had spoken about the need for more home science seats in institutions around the country. She also reached out to Dr Flemmie Kittrell, the first African-American to earn a PhD in nutrition, requesting her help in building a home economics programme at the university in Baroda.[70]

Between 1958 and 1960, Hansa served on the executive board of the United Nations Educational, Scientific and Cultural

Organization (UNESCO).[71] She headed a committee on women's education that recommended adopting a co-educational policy at the primary school level. She also suggested doing away with the prevalent norm of separate curriculum for boys and girls. Her recommendations were accepted by the Indian Education Commission (popularly known as Kothari Commission) and subsequently formed part of the official policy.[72] She also went on to author multiple children's books such as *Prince of Ayodhya* and *The Adventures of King Vikrama*. In 1959, she was awarded Padma Bhushan for social work.

Hansa died in 1995, having left an indelible mark on Indian polity and society. The first half of Hansa's life was spent striving to mainstream the ideas of equality and the promotion of education. The second half accorded her an opportunity to implement these ideas. As India's representative, she deftly handled international politics and played her part in shaping a global order that was founded on equality and justice.

KAMALA CHAUDHRI

'What I believe is that marriage is just a compromise for the lifetime... If under any circumstances the separation be deemed essential then I think the legal right must lie with the woman.'

– In support of divorce in the Hindu Code Bill on 13 December 1949[1]

A true rebel and patriot, Kamala Chaudhri defied her family who were loyal to the British. Besides being a politician, Kamala used the might of the pen to advocate for gender equality through her short stories. She also wrote and spoke about the importance of sound mental health – almost eighty years ago – which was not only taboo but also unheard of in the mid-twentieth century. Her debates in the Constituent Assembly were grounded on the keen observations on patriarchy indicated in her writings.

***

Kamala was born on 22 February 1908 in Lucknow.[2] Her father Rai Manmohan Dayal was a loyal deputy collector to the British government.[3] They were financially well-off and had a comfortable life.[4]

In May 1923, at the age of fifteen, Kamala was married to Dr J.M. Chaudhri, who was from Meerut. The couple had two sons and a daughter.[5] Over time as the freedom struggle progressed, the deputy collector's daughter formed her own views of the British, which she espoused. She even succeeded in transforming her husband into a 'resolute supporter' of the idea of Indian independence.[6]

Kamala was passionate about writing fictional stories about the world around her. She completed a master's degree in Hindi literature from Punjab University.[7] She wrote poems and short stories on patriarchy, feminism, and even mental health – a subject that became mainstream only in the recent decades. Some of her short story collections were – *Unmaad* (1934), *Picnic* (1936), and *Yatra* (1947).[8] One of Kamala's short story collections *Belpatra* was published in 2016 by her daughter, Dr Ira Saxena. The book also contains a letter written by renowned Hindi novelist Premchand in 1934, wherein he praised Kamala for her writing skills.[9]

In Kamala's notable short story, 'Ankhe Khuli' (Realization), she reflected upon the gender stereotypes prevalent in society and the discrimination that daughters face from their own parents. Two of her stories – 'Swapna' and 'Rup' – shed light on the societal problems faced by widows, while 'Sadhana ka Unmaad' was about the deteriorating mental health of a married woman who was lonely and dissatisfied with her marriage.[10]

In another short story, 'Kartavya' (Duty), the protagonist's husband leaves her to die after their boat capsizes.[11] In an existential monologue, the author questions the man's supposed love for his wife and the meaning of belonging: 'If Usha had died, would he have been heartbroken?... After a decent interval and after observing a few social niceties, he would have married again. That foolish woman would also believe that her husband loved her very much... Woman, Man, Father, Son – all this is an illusion, a mere web of attachment. Nobody actually belongs to anybody else.'[12]

In 1930, at the age of twenty-eight, Kamala joined politics. She was secretary of the Mahila Charkha Sangh that followed the Gandhian practice of weaving and spinning yarn.[13] As a staunch follower of Mahatma Gandhi, Kamala was devoted to the fight for independence.[14] She joined the Congress during the Civil Disobedience Movement between 1930–31.

As a result of her activism, Kamala went to jail several times.[15] She also rose in the ranks of the Congress – being elected to the City Congress Committee, then District Congress Committee, and the Provincial Congress Committee. She rose from the grassroots to the national level of the party by becoming the senior vice-chairperson at the fifty-fourth All India Congress Committee session held in November 1946.[16]

Kamala was elected to the Constituent Assembly from the United Provinces (now Uttar Pradesh). On 9 December 1946, she signed the registry as a member of the Constituent Assembly.[17]

During the Constituent Assembly debates, Kamala was vocal in her support for the Hindu Code Bill and countered passionately those opposed to various parts of the Bill.[18] Praising the Bill and championing women's rights, she said, 'My personal feeling is that this Bill will prove as sort of a panacea for our women community and the progress of our Indian society, and this will go a long way to benefit our womenfolk who are even today being degraded to the lowest ebb.'[19]

In support of the provision to end polygamy in the Bill, Kamala emphasized the mental trauma faced by women whose husbands took more than one wife. She opined, 'It is a great injustice done to woman that the husband is allowed to enter into matrimony once, twice, thrice or even four times in the very life time of the legally wedded wife. For a woman this custom is horribly painful and demands utmost sympathy… For a woman, no other suffering is more tormenting than the distress of having a co-wife.'[20]

The provision for the right to divorce in the Bill was criticized by various members of the assembly calling it a Western influence that would lead to the breakdown of our society. Kamala's stance on divorce was clear and she addressed their concerns in the following words: 'The people here have come to believe that the right to divorce provided in the Bill would result in the destruction of the structure of our society and our culture would go to dogs. I do not understand how people give rise to such apprehensions and how they resort to such talks.' Well-versed with the Bill, Kamala added, 'But as far as I have studied this Bill I have not come across anything concerning the dissolution of marriages that can be called an innovation, or anything that has not been allowed and permitted by our sacred texts and holy scriptures.' She backed up her argument by adding, 'All the conditions that have been laid down for the dissolution of marriages, or in what manner the marriages can be dissolved, or for what reasons divorce can be granted. I think all these conditions do exist in our *Shastras*.'[21]

Kamala didn't agree with the anti-Hinduism colour that the Bill was painted in by some members of the assembly, 'Those who oppose this Bill have expressed the opinion that this will prove harmful to our religion as well as culture. This thing does not appeal to me at all. This is another thing that the brain and heart of our countrymen have been framed in such a way that anything said in the name of religion highly appeals to the sentiments of the people. On the altar of this very religion – in what manner did we accentuate our communal feelings?' She added, 'In the name of this very religion, we have seen the murder of Mahatma Gandhi – the father of the Nation.'[22]

She was speaking about the death of Gandhi, who was murdered on 30 January 1948, by radicals who blamed him for the partition of India and Pakistan.

The Hindu Code Bill faced severe opposition on another count – equal inheritance rights for daughters. The provision was dubbed as 'foreign culture'. According to her, this was not true. Kamala based her arguments on Indian literature – specifically folk songs performed at weddings since time immemorial. She said, 'This sentiment finds ample expression in our folksongs which have existed for the last hundreds of years. This sentiment did not get into our folksongs at the time of our mothers and sisters but has been there since the times of our grand and great-grandmothers when there was not even a trace of foreign culture anywhere and when it had not set any kind of seal on our culture.'[23]

She expressly stated that it was an injustice to deny daughters a share of their father's property. Kamala argued further, 'I think that the provision relating to the daughter having a share in her father's property is very much in consonance with the times and compatible with our faith and culture and I hope it will be considered in a very generous spirit. Nature has made a boy and a girl equal in the eyes of their parents. Then why is it that a boy should have a share in his father's property but a girl should have none?'[24] Despite the strong arguments put forth by various members including Kamala, the Hindu Code Bill was shelved, and it took many years for it to see the light of the day yet again. The work she and many other women leaders put into the Bill would benefit Indian women many years later.

Kamala continued to serve as a member of the Provisional Parliament till 1952.[25] After that, she worked for the education of girls in rural areas. She contested the 1962 Lok Sabha elections from Hapur in Uttar Pradesh on a Congress ticket. She secured 81,999 votes and defeated her nearest opponent with a 28,000-vote margin.[26]

In her political career, she focused on making girls and women independent through education and skilling like sewing, weaving, pottery, etc. She also helped women get trainings through village industries so that they could have a source of income.

As seen from her speeches on the Hindu Code Bill, Kamala was a rationalist who had a deep understanding of how patriarchy functions in the society. In an era when any discussion on mental health was unheard of, she used her pen to draw attention to the subject through fictional stories of women who were oppressed and gaslit in marriages. Not just that, Kamala used the floor of the highest law-making body of the country to highlight the mental health trauma and angst of women whose husbands took many wives. Her knowledge about Indian literature also enriched the law-making process and brought in an interesting perspective to her arguments. Even though her achievements and contributions were remarkable, there isn't much public record available about her body of work.

Kamala died in 1970, leaving behind a great legacy as a champion of women's rights. In memory of her mother, her daughter Ira wrote the following heartwarming words to commemorate Kamala, her work and life: 'My heart swells with pride as I remember my mother, Kamala Chaudhri, a freedom fighter, poet, and writer who was elected to the Constituent Assembly and later joined the Lok Sabha... She followed the dictates of Gandhi, practising Satyagraha devotedly and restoring peace before partition. Through the stories shared by her about the freedom movement, I developed a keen insight into the tumultuous period enabling me to feel the determination of people to endure and suffer for the sake of freedom.'[27]

LEELA ROY

> 'We have to admit that most of the girls remain illiterate because they do not get proper opportunity. Girls are eager to learn but they are denied the opportunity. Therefore, the system of education should be such that everybody should be able to acquire it easily irrespective of being rich or poor'
>
> – On access to education at the Annual Function of Nari Siksha Mandir in 1926[1]

Leela Roy was a member of the Shree Sangha, made up of a group of revolutionaries who were disillusioned by Gandhian principles. The only woman member, Leela faced opposition from most male members – who believed it was no place for a woman. Leela, of course, boldly chartered her own path in the revolutionary cause, as well as for all other women who followed.

★★★

In 1905, the British government cleaved Bengal into two parts – West and East – with some regions transferred to Assam. The colonial rulers cited difficulty in administering a population of 78 million spread over 189,000 square miles as the reason behind the partition.[2] However, the real hidden agenda was the infamous divide-and-rule policy that was synonymous with the British. The division of Bengal sought to widen the chasm between the Hindus and Muslims by offering advantages and powers to the latter in the form of East Bengal and Assam, and weaken the awakening nationalist movement by splitting the Hindus into two different provinces.[3]

The Bengali Hindu population, however, greeted the decision with stiff resistance.[4] Instead of slowing down or losing steam, the movement against the colonizers gathered momentum and spawned various militant revolutionary groups comprising young men.[5] The writings of Swami Vivekananda and Bankim Chandra Chattopadhyay inspired and instilled in them 'a kind of military courage and selfless service' for the motherland.[6] Though independence was the main target – their immediate goal was to defy and terrorize the British administration through political robberies and even assassinations of senior public officials, based on the Irish model of revolution. Radical newspapers such as *Jugantar*, *Swadhin Bharat*, and *Sandhya* propagated the idea of armed revolution.[7] As a result, several attacks, including bomb blasts, were carried out over the years.

When Mahatma Gandhi launched the Non-Cooperation Movement based on ahimsa, the armed groups of Bengal decided to give this new strategy a try and planned no major activity between 1920–22.[8] In fact, it was the violent Chauri Chaura incident in another part of the country that ended the movement. On 5 February 1922, a gathering of 2,000 burned down a police station in Chauri Chaura, Gorakhpur, United Provinces (now Uttar Pradesh) after a violent altercation with the police. The incident led to the death of several policemen and officials.[9] Doubtful about the efficacy of the Gandhian approach, the Bengali groups reverted to armed conflict, and more revolutionary organizations sprung up in Bengal in the summer of 1923.[10]

One of these bodies was the Social Welfare League, popularly known as Shree Sangha, led by Anil Roy, a Bengali revolutionary. It functioned on the principle that a successful revolution necessitates the education and awareness of marginalized communities. The organization provided facilities such as night schools, group study circles, and wrestling centres for the physical and mental growth of young men from low-income Hindu and Muslim families.[11]

In 1926, Leela Nag, who was in her twenties, became the first woman to join the all-male Shree Sangha. Most members opposed her entry because the revolutionary movement precluded women from membership. While some members recognized that these prejudices were a result of a male-dominated society and rued the fact that even 'revolutionary' movements were affected by them, others opposed the entry of women to the movement because they simply believed that women tied men down with emotions and made them weak.[12]

Unhappy with the blatant sexism she encountered,[13] Leela decided to work hard and prove herself, and pave the path for more women to get involved with the revolutionary movement. However, her rapid rise in the hierarchy caused rifts within the organization.[14] The conservative faction left no stone unturned in their vendetta against Leela. Disregarding her efforts and hard work, they attributed Leela's success to her closeness with the founder. Violent clashes often broke out between the factions that supported Leela and the conservatives. It ultimately led to a split in the organization, with the conservatives breaking away to form another group.[15] Unfazed, Leela recruited women into the movement. Some of these women later laid down their lives for the cause.[16] After the arrest of Anil in 1930, Leela took charge of Shree Sangha – a woman now led the organization that once didn't allow women in its fold.[17]

***

The story of Leela or Leelabati Nag began on 2 October 1900.[18] Her father, Rai Bahadur Girish Chandra Nag, was a civil servant and her mother Kunjalata was a homemaker.[19] Originally from Sylhet (a district in present-day Bangladesh), the Nags were in Assam at the time of Leela's birth, due to Girish's posting as the sub-divisional officer of Goalpara.[20] It wasn't just her father who was in government service, Leela's maternal grandfather Prakash Chandra Deb Choudhury was the first Indian superintendent in the secretariat of Assam in 1891.[21] Leela grew up in an upper-middle class family, and had six brothers and a sister – of which only three of her siblings survived their childhood.[22]

Despite being in the civil services, Girish took an active part in the freedom movement and opposed the partition of Bengal. He along with others formed the Sylhet-Bengal Reunion League with the object to undo the partition.[23] Upon his retirement as deputy magistrate of Dacca (now Dhaka) district, Girish was elected to the Central Legislative Assembly from Assam in 1920.[24] Almost a decade later he resigned from his post in protest against the controversial salt tax.[25] Leela became aware of the prevailing socio-political situation early in life. She keenly observed her father's political involvements and her grandfather's patriotism.

Growing up, Leela was brilliant in academics. She attended Calcutta's Brahmo Girls School, which was considered to be the province's best school for girls at the time.[26] She then transferred to Eden High School in Dacca from where she passed matriculation in 1917.[27] After high school, she won a scholarship to pursue a bachelor's degree in English at Bethune College, Calcutta, the leading higher education institution for women in Bengal.[28]

Leela had the desire to be more than herself – to be of service to others. In a letter to her father on her seventeenth birthday, she wrote, 'I will consider myself to be very fortunate, if I am able to help even a single person in any capacity. Believe me, this is no vain lecture, this is my heart-felt desire and ideal.'[29]

Leela's inner calling to activism came to the fore during her college days where she emerged as a student leader.[30] Leela was the first woman student union representative of her college.[31] She showed immense leadership skills.

Leela refused to accept the status quo and stood up against what she felt was wrong. In one such instance, there was a rule for the college students to kneel before the Viceroy Lord Chelmsford's wife and Leela felt that the wife didn't merit such a stature just by virtue of her husband holding the official position. She organized a protest against this rule. In another instance, she demanded the college be closed to mark the death of Bal Gangadhar Tilak.[32] Apart from activism, Leela showed immense talent in sports, painting, and music.[33] She especially loved tennis.[34]

Leela was in college when Gandhi announced the Non-Cooperation Movement. His clarion call urging Indians to join the movement resonated with the youth. In response to Gandhi, many college and school students left their education to join the freedom movement. The prospect of being a part of this historic movement also intrigued Leela and her close friends. However, after much debate and discussion, they decided to complete their studies first, in the hope to attain political maturity and nuanced understanding before joining the freedom movement.[35] In 1921, Leela completed her graduation with flying colours – a gold medal and a cash prize of ₹100 for being the topper.[36]

Leela returned to her family in Dacca after college, with a deep desire to pursue higher studies. Coincidentally, the University of Dhaka was established in July 1921.[37] However, it was only open to male students. Determined to secure admission, Leela made a plea before the university authorities. Her request put the administration in a dilemma – mainly logistical concerns about how a lone woman would adjust in a campus of 800-odd men.[38] Her request was denied, which then stirred the spirit of activism within her.

With great intent, she reached out to vice-chancellor P.J. Hartog and demanded an environment for co-education. Seeing Leela's sincerity, he set up evening classes for Leela and three other young women who also placed similar requests. Having broken this gender barrier, Leela became the university's first female student to earn a masters' degree.[39] Leela soon became a figure of respect among her fellow students as well as teachers. This was also where she became close friends with Anil Roy, a student at the university.[40]

While at the university, Leela became actively involved in the women's suffrage movement. Earlier in 1919, despite the demand for women's right to vote by women's groups to the British government, the Montagu-Chelmsford reforms made it into a provincial issue.[41] Provincial legislatures were to pass their own laws. Now the women's suffrage movement focused on the provinces with women's bodies organizing campaigns. The groups in Bengal worked towards garnering the support of the elected members of the Bengal Legislative Council.[42] Leela became assistant secretary in one such group known as the Nikhil Banga Nari Votadhikar Samiti (All Bengal Women's Franchise Association) established by journalist and editor Kumudini Basu in Dacca.[43] They carried out public meetings to mould opinion in favour of equal voting rights. When the pro-suffrage Bill came up for discussion in the Bengal Legislative Council in 1921, its supporters were sure it would pass easily. But it got unfortunately defeated, with 60 per cent of the members voting against it. This, however, would be reversed in 1925.[44]

Due to her social work and activism, Leela became a well-known face. In 1922, she worked in the Flood Relief Committee of North Bengal, an initiative of Subhas Chandra Bose.[45] She formed the Dacca Mahila Committee to raise donations and relief goods for flood survivors. While working on the ground, she realized the massive lack of social and political awareness amongst rural women.[46]

This was in stark contradiction to the elite Brahmo community that Leela grew up in. She felt that she could play a role in shaping the consciousness of the women. But she also understood the direct link between financial independence and women's overall independence to pursue their interests. It was evident to her that education was the only medium through which women could secure complete financial security and awareness. She also knew that increased political awareness would ensure women a bigger role in shaping society. With this ultimate goal, Leela and twelve of her friends established a women's association called Deepali Sangha in December 1923.[47] As a first step, they focused on education. They built twelve free primary schools, adult education centres, and handicraft and technical training centres.[48] Amongst these, the most popular was the Nari Siksha Mandir. It admitted women from all walks of life – young girls, married women, widows, as well as older women. Other than education till the matriculation level, the institution also skilled women in sewing, handicrafts, forms of arts and culture, self-defence, history, and geography.[49] It also had a residency wing, which provided lodging to women who visited Dacca and had nowhere to stay. With branches all over the city, Deepali Sangha was a beacon of hope for the women of Dacca.[50]

Throughout her activism, Leela noted the clear demarcation of masculine and feminine roles even in the freedom movement. She did not believe in restricting women to picketing foreign shops or weaving khadi. Leela wanted Indian women to participate in the freedom movement, shoulder to shoulder as leaders capable of making their own decisions and going beyond the traditional posturing of women as just mothers or sisters. She wanted to equip and train women to be all-encompassing in their intellect, physical fitness, public speaking, and organizational skills.[51]

Educational institutions run by Deepali Sangha provided capacity-building in political awareness and skills, acting as an incubation centre for the women of the era. The association also gave women an avenue to gain education, greater public awareness, and rigorous physical training. It invited personalities such as Mahatma Gandhi, Rabindranath Tagore, Acharya Prafulla Chandra Roy, and Kshitimohan Sen to address the members.[52]

Leela was profoundly influenced by the teachings of Rabindranath Tagore. She first met him in 1925, when Deepali Sangha requested to felicitate him. The turnout of the gathering was phenomenal. Thousands gathered to see the polymath who said that he had never seen such a large congregation of women in the continent. Impressed with Leela's skills, Tagore invited her to take charge of the women's wing in Santiniketan in Bengal (now West Bengal). Though it was a huge honour for Leela, she declined her idol's offer.[53] Tagore respected her passion to serve the public and fight for women's rights and gave her his blessings to do what she wanted.

As she dived deeper into the women's movement, the need for drastic change became clear to her. She felt the need to jolt the system to an awakening, and that meant getting rid of the colonizers first.[54] She rationalized that once freedom was achieved, one could focus on the emancipation of women altogether. Deeply moved by her work with Deepali Sangha, her former classmate Anil urged her to join Shree Sangha. The members of Shree Sangha had often helped out with her organization's social activities in the past.

At this juncture, Leela was in a dilemma. She was unsure what would bear better results – a violent or a non-violent revolution. Ultimately, Leela chose the former. She joined Shree Sangha in 1926.[55] She already felt a close affinity with the members. After joining, she took on administrative roles.

In 1928, Anil proposed that she lead Shree Sangha along with him.[56] This didn't go down well with most of the men in the organization. Constant fights broke out between the factions for and against her, which ultimately led to the split of Shree Sangha. Her own brother Prabhat Chandra broke away from the body to join the newly formed Bengal Volunteers.[57] Leela, on the other hand, focused on recruiting more women in the fight against the British.

Deepali Sangha became the sister organization of Shree Sangha, but each woman was tested strictly before consideration for membership for the latter.[58] They were given tasks such as bombmaking, pick and drop of arms and ammunitions, and writing and distributing seditious pamphlets. Only those with exceptional performance were given the chance to join Shree Sangha. Those who didn't make it were streamlined into contributing towards the social activities of Deepali Sangha.[59]

Throughout this period, the revolutionary movement in Bengal was rising. When Gandhi announced the Civil Disobedience Movement in 1930, the revolutionaries of Bengal were ready to advance their goals. With the arrest of thousands of people across the country during the Dandi March in 1930, the revolutionaries got a chance to strike. It was time to take matters into their own hands. On 18 April 1930, more than 60 revolutionaries executed a well-planned raid in the city of Chittagong. In an attempt to loot, they attacked two government armouries and destroyed communication and transportation facilities. In the aftermath, the British were harsh in dealing with revolutionary activities by imprisoning suspects or even killing them. The next four years saw widespread arrests of revolutionaries across Bengal, with 2,167 people placed under detention.[60] Anil was arrested in 1930, and the responsibility of running both Shree Sangha and Deepali Sangha fell upon Leela's shoulders.

A year later, in 1931, *Jayashree Patrika* was launched as the mouthpiece of Deepali Sangha, with Leela as its founding editor. Its objective was 'to inspire the spirit of patriotism and a fearless desire to serve the country among the women of Bengal'. The magazine was deliberately founded after the Chittagong Armoury Raid, 'when the British came down heavily on all revolutionaries with ever new repressive measures to curtail individual rights'. The aim of *Jayashree* was 'to help' and 'stay focused ideologically and generate empathy and camaraderie' for the cause.[61] Incidentally, the name, *Jayashree* means victorious and was given by Tagore when Leela sought his blessings for her publication.[62] Through *Jayashree*, Leela brought together a group of feisty women who wanted to change the course of history by commissioning articles from other extraordinary women, on topics ranging from academics to socio-political work.

Jayashree was no typical women's magazine. Shakuntala Chowdhury, assistant editor of *Jayashree*, best described its content as 'Women's magazines meant household tips, cooking, sewing, knitting and so on. We wanted to stay away from all that. Ours was an endeavour for Indian independence – a journal through which women could express their own views and spread political awareness.'[63]

Nationalist sentiments were high after the Dandi March and Chittagong Armoury Raid, and the coverage of *Jayashree* was well received. But soon things were about to change for Leela. In December 1931, following the assassination of the Dacca district magistrate by two teenage girls affiliated to Deepali Sangha, Leela and her co-editor Renuka Sen were arrested.[64] Following this, both Shree Sangha and Deepali Sangha were banned.

While Leela was in prison, *Jayashree* was edited by Deepali Sangha members like Chowdhury and others. But various government restrictions and financial impositions made operations exorbitantly difficult for them. Ultimately, the magazine shut down in 1936, only to be revived by Leela after her release in 1938.[65]

From 1931 to 1937, Leela stayed in several jails. After her initial stay at Dacca prison, Leela was transferred to Rajshahi, Suri, Midnapore, and then Hijli for striking against the jail authorities for poor treatment of prisoners.[66] Many women revolutionaries of Bengal were also in jail around this time. Another revolutionary Helena Dutta who was with her in Hijli Jail said, 'Pre-eminent revolutionary leader Leela Nag came forward to help us in our imprisonment. She guided us through those days with love and affection in such a way that the days became lively, sprightly and sweet.' According to Dutta's recollection, Leela was regarded as an older sister, someone who the women in prison would look up to. She added, 'She was firm yet soft, she taught us to be disciplined and well organized. The way she protected us in every possible way, is unique and unthinkable... Didi was our teacher in every way.'[67]

Leela was known for her dual nature as a revolutionary and a sensitive person. Her contemporary Bina Das commented, 'The firm personality of Leela was evident in various incidents while we were in jail. Similarly we were impressed by her poetic, artistic and loving nature. Often I found her in a small cell, sitting alone with her sitar in front of her, lost in thought'.[68]

After their release from prison in 1938, both Anil and Leela were attracted to the growing socialist faction in the Congress and decided to merge Shree Sangha with it. Party president Subhas Chandra Bose nominated Leela to the Women's Sub-Committee of the National Planning Committee.[69] Leela presided over the committee in West Bengal's Bankura district.[70] She also proposed the formation of Congress Mahila Sangha, a forum for women of every political affiliation in Bengal. Bose endorsed it and the forum organized political dialogue and networking opportunities for women who aspired to join the freedom struggle.

However, shortly the ideological rift between the left and right wing within the Congress led to Bose's departure from the party in April 1939. Leela was in agreement with his principles of centralized economy and strong national governance and soon followed him to his new party, Forward Bloc, with Anil.[71]

Bose trusted Leela and relied on her for the operations of the organization and mobilizing of youth and women. According to Leela, the Forward Bloc believed that 'inactivity is nothing short of national betrayal… it worships at the temple of youthful dynamism.' In complete agreement with the new party's agenda of giving India its freedom, she added, 'The vision of a free India taking her proud place in the Comity of Nations has stirred its soul… This is the cause it has sought to serve, a cause which is dearest to all patriotic hearts'.[72]

Though both Leela and Anil were completely caught up with nationalist work, they tied the knot in May 1939.[73] She was now known as Leela Roy. In terms of their commitment to their work, nothing changed after marriage. Around this time, the now revived *Jayashree* started publishing articles that were written by men, transitioning from the mouthpiece of Bengali women to become a magazine of universal interest.[74] Anil was a regular contributor to the magazine. In a world of many ideologies, the magazine clarified its ideology in its July 1939 edition:

'Communism, socialism, fascism and Gandhism, these four ideologies are in circulation in today's world. *Jayashree* represents a special position among these conflicting ideologies.'

Jayashree supported a socialist economy, opposed atheism, and politically believed that 'a mass movement for independence is the only path to follow' and it urged for 'a united anti-imperialist front.'[75]

Anil and Leela were committed to their anti-imperial stand, and did not favour supporting the British forces. When few leaders had the courage to critique Gandhi, both of them did so openly. Anil criticized the leader's call to support Britain during World War II.[76] Leela, in an article called 'A Grave Tragedy', accused the Congress of giving dictatorial powers to Gandhi to negotiate with the British. She wrote, 'Mahatma has his sainthood against any normal charge of dishonor. So in the last desperate resort, the Working Committee has put him up as their spokesman, even at the conscious sacrifice of their convictions'.[77]

In another instance, Leela boldly called out Gandhi's sexism in 1940 when he wrote in *Harijan*, an English newspaper that it was 'degrading that woman should forsake the hearth and shoulder the rifle. It is a reversion to barbarity and the beginning of the end.' Leela's years of work with the Deepali Sangha was to bridge the gap in opportunities available to women and to do away with the societal gender stereotypes that Gandhi exhibited in his article. Criticizing his patriarchal notion, Leela wrote a rebuttal in *Jayashree,* 'Such artificially constructed divide between the home and the world is absolutely unnecessary – all workplaces outside the house or inside should be equally accessible to both men and women and they should have equal rights in exercising their choice according to their disposition and needs. If, due to lack of practice, the initial outcome of entering a new field of work happens to be undesirable, that is transitory and applies equally for both men and women'.[78]

After Bose's house arrest and subsequent disappearance from Calcutta in January 1941, Leela and Anil shouldered major responsibilities as his most trusted compatriots.[79] As Bose travelled across the world to galvanize support, Leela was made the editor of the party's mouthpiece, also called *Forward Bloc*.[80] However, in 1942, *Jayashree* was forced to shut down again for its articles against the government.[81] Following this, both Leela and Anil were rearrested.[82]

This time Leela's stay in jail was gruelling. She fell seriously ill in Dinajpore Jail, but the authorities refused to provide treatment. To make sure that she was heard, her supporters protested against the government on the streets as well as at the Bengal Legislative Assembly.[83] It was after this that she was then admitted to Calcutta Medical College for treatment and recovery. Leela was finally transferred to Alipore Jail.

While in Alipore Jail, she received a secret message from Bose wherein he praised her and said, 'The day is not far off when you will be free to shine and lead Indian women once again'.[84]

Such words of encouragement spurred Leela to sharpen her mind instead of sitting idle in jail. She took up reading, like most political prisoners of the time. In a letter to her husband lodged in another jail, she complained about the lack of good reading materials, 'One may eat whatever one gets, but I would rather starve than stuff my mind with something I dislike.'[85]

Leela was still in jail when Subhas Chandra Bose died in a plane crash in 1945. She was released in 1946 after four years in prison.[86] She never was able to reconcile with the news of Bose's death and, like many others, carried on believing that he was still alive. In her later years, she was in regular touch with a Gumnami Baba who was speculated to be Bose living in disguise. She also once wrote to him: 'I am like the rock for the greatest patriot and one of the greatest men of the age, not because I think it to be my duty but because I cannot do otherwise.'[87]

After getting out of prison, Leela resumed the publication of *Jayashree* and *Forward Bloc*, eager to carry forward the legacy of Bose, her idol and inspiration.[88] On what would have been his fiftieth birth anniversary in 1947, she wrote, 'Today Netaji means much more than a human being. The name has come to stand for an idea lived and an ideal achieved.... The Forward Bloc had endeavoured to live and propagate that idea. India must be made safe for freedom, democracy and socialism.'[89]

In the run-up to India's independence, she was nominated to the Constituent Assembly in 1946. She was deeply anguished by the idea that India would have to undergo partition.

In August 1946, Calcutta saw widespread communal riots, known as the 'Great Calcutta Killings'. More than 50,000 people were injured while around 15,000 died. Leela risked her own life by being on the ground and tried hard to save as many people as possible. According to a survivor's account, 'She [Leela] saved innumerable innocent Muslims at the cost of her own life. It ought to be cited as a unique precedent in the annals of history... I still shudder at the thought of how she rescued me in a car, from the disturbed area of Park Circus.'[90]

Strongly opposed to the partition, her hometown of Dacca eventually fell in East Pakistan. This must have shaken her up. In a meeting with Jawaharlal Nehru, after learning that there would be no alternative to the partition, she promptly resigned from the Constituent Assembly.[91] Around this time, communal riots reached Noakhali, Bengal, which was to be a part of East Pakistan. Reports of thousands of women being raped and abducted were emerging. So, Leela headed there straight, and dedicated her energy into rescue and rehabilitation of the women. Gandhi also camped there for months to help, and the two became closely associated.

Leela still hadn't accepted the partition and knocked on all doors in search of a glimmer of hope. In June 1947, she and her husband went to meet Gandhi in Patna, Bihar to plead against the partition. Gandhi said, 'My lips are sealed, go and meet Jawaharlal and Sardar Patel. If you are able to organize a movement against partition, I will lead you.'[92]

All their attempts to prevent the division failed and Dacca became a part of Pakistan, where Leela and Anil continued to live. A few months after independence, the Pakistan government issued an arrest warrant for both of them for their activism.[93] With no option left but to protect themselves, the couple abandoned their birthplace and sought refuge in West Bengal in India.[94]

At first, Leela and Anil chose to live amongst the Muslim community of West Bengal in order to safeguard them from the riots that continued well after the creation of Pakistan. They worked for the welfare of the refugees under the aegis of the East Bengal Minority Welfare Central Committee. The body helped refugees procure documentation, including citizenship and voting rights.[95]

In 1949, Leela assumed the secretaryship of the committee and made high-level representations to the chief minister of West Bengal, and various central ministers including the prime minister regarding the seriousness of the refugee crisis. She fought for permanent settlement of the refugees, with land of their own and to provide a source of income so as not to depend on doles from the government.[96]

Both Leela and Anil wanted to contest the first general elections of independent India held in 1951–52 to carry forward the ideals of Bose.[97] However, before the idea could concretize, Anil was sadly diagnosed with cancer. He died on 7 January 1952.[98]

Leela was crestfallen at the demise of her life partner and compatriot. She for some time withdrew herself from public life to grieve. But in April 1952 when news of a shortage of food in the Basirhat jurisdiction of West Bengal was reported, Leela sprung to action. She went to survey the area and raise her concerns to the government which resulted in relief efforts.[99] It was as though public service was in her blood, and she couldn't give up. Around this time, she also started an education centre for girls at her house in Calcutta – it was like life coming full circle.[100]

She jumped back into politics soon after. The Socialist Party led by Jayaprakash Narayan, and the Kisan Mazdoor Praja Party led by J.B. Kriplani merged in 1952 to form the Praja Socialist Party (PSP). During this time, the Forward Bloc had been going through intense divisions. Members were essentially divided between pro-Marxist groups and non-Marxists, including Leela. The non-Marxist group was later called 'Subhasist Forward Bloc'.

Leela saw the formation of the PSP as an opportunity to take forward Bose's beliefs. In September 1953, she arranged for a merger of the Subhasist Forward Bloc with the PSP. Jayaprakash Narayan said, 'By this merger, the leadership of Netaji Subhas Chandra Bose has been brought into the very heart of the Socialist movement in India'.[101] Though Leela was made a national-level member, she preferred to work with the cadres at the grassroots, for serving the public was in her blood.[102]

Unfortunately, after the death of her husband, Leela's physical and mental health were not the same. After she suffered two heart attacks, one in 1955 and another in 1957, her health took a drastic turn.[103]

The first attack was a rude awakening for her, and she finally understood that she needed to focus on her health. She often took off to the beaches of Puri (in now Odisha) with her nephew and niece. She also seemed to be facing an existential crisis at this point in her life, which was reflected in her writing: 'The ocean brings new messages for me each and every moment. Whenever I come here, I am tormented by the questions – who am I? From where have I come, and where will I be going? This makes me very sad.'[104]

Despite her failing health, the call of duty reigned supreme in her life. In 1960, Leela accepted the request of the leaders of the PSP to become the president of the West Bengal unit.[105] She campaigned across the state for the elections of 1962 and tried her best to steer the party to victory. But the failure to do so made her quit active politics in mid-1962.[106]

As time passed, her health was getting worse. In 1963, Leela was diagnosed with retinal haemorrhage, and she became extremely weak. She then suffered a stroke in 1967 but continued to edit *Jayashree* against the wishes of friends and family. It was as though she knew she was running out of time and pushed herself to utilize every minute she had left in an attempt to improve the world. In a letter dated 22 May 1967, she wrote, 'It is undoubtedly very clear that I have come to the end of my life. Mother Kali is our protector, and she destroys us when we complete our assigned work in this world. I have realized that my duties are over.'[107]

On 4 February 1968, a cerebral stroke sent her into a coma that lasted for nineteen months.[108] Leela breathed her last on 11 June 1970.[109] Her death was mourned across the political spectrum, with everyone appreciating her life in public service.

In 2008, Prime Minister Dr Manmohan Singh unveiled a portrait of Leela, along with other social and political activists, at the Central Hall of Parliament.[110] However, in spite of her dedicated service, only a few in the country today are aware of this firebrand revolutionary and her unwavering commitment to women's agency and upliftment. Her life was best summarized by the following condolence message of Prime Minister Indira Gandhi in the Lok Sabha in 1970: 'Srimati Leela Roy was widely respected for the courage and devotion with which she worked for the national cause braving many dangers. She encouraged and stood by a large number of revolutionaries. Her work for women's franchise in Bengal and her intrepid services to organize relief at the time of the Noakhali riots will be long remembered.'[111]

MALATI CHOUDHURY

'When the eminent jurists like Shri Gopalswamy Ayangar, Shri Ambedkar, Munshiji, Durgaben Deshmukh, sitting in the first row, were found busy in writing the Constitution of our country collecting materials from the constitutions of different countries, I, sitting in the last row, was feeling like a helpless school student. The thought crossed my mind that I did not have a place in the Constituent Assembly.'[1]

– On her experience in the Constituent Assembly in a diary entry from 1971

Malati Choudhury was nicknamed 'Toofani' by Mahatma Gandhi for her swift and efficient rehabilitation work on the field. She never hesitated to help riot-affected people in the most violent of areas and jumped at the opportunity to lend a hand. She would go on to earn many similar nicknames, which epitomized her spirit of being of service to those who needed help. In spite of being put behind bars on several occasions, she would come out stronger and do even more for the oppressed. She continued being true to her nature of service even after Independence and raised her voice countless numbers of time when it mattered the most.

★★★

As India inched closer to independence from British rule, the Congress and the Muslim League, the country's two main political parties, were unable to reach an agreement on the road ahead. While the Muslim League did not budge from its demand for Pakistan, the Congress was against a partition on religious lines. As a result, the political impasse showed no signs of ending.

In the summer of 1946, the restless Muslim League refused to become a part of the interim government.[2] Furthermore, Muhammad Ali Jinnah asked Muslims to observe 16 August 1946, as Direct Action Day. Prior to the agitation, he declared, 'The Muslims of India won't rest contended with anything less than the immediate establishment of the independent and fully sovereign state of Pakistan... Now the time has come for the Muslim Nation to resort to Direct Action... Never before in the whole life history of the Muslim League did we do anything except by Constitutional methods.'[3]

Building on Jinnah's clarion call, the leaders of the Muslim League made rousing speeches. One of them remarked, 'Direct Action means resort to non-constitutional methods, and that can take any form which may suit the conditions under which we live.'[4]

Such inflammatory words stirred the masses. On Direct Action Day, the Muslim League–ruled province of Bengal saw unprecedented communal violence between Hindus and Muslims. The 'Great Calcutta Killing', a carnage that lasted five days, witnessed the deaths of 15,000 people with more than 50,000 injured.[5] It took intensive military operations to restore peace and only a semblance of normalcy was achieved by 20 August 1946.[6] This episode further deepened the chasm between Hindus and Muslims in the region leading to a tense atmosphere across the country.

Exactly seven weeks after the Calcutta massacre, on 10 October 1946, communal riots broke out in the Muslim-dominated district of Noakhali in Bengal and the princely state of Tipperah (present-day Tripura). These acts of violence carried on for weeks without any intervention from the government.[7]

As news of the riots spread across British India, Mahatma Gandhi and various other leaders including Leela Roy reached Noakhali in Bengal, which would later be a part of East Pakistan, in the first week of November.[8] He tried to restore peace by camping there, and through dialogues with community leaders. On hearing of Gandhi's presence at Noakhali, Malati Choudhury wrote to him expressing her wish to be of service there. She had years of experience working at the grassroots with the marginalized communities of Orissa (present day Odisha). Gandhi declined her offer saying, 'It will not be right for you or anyone else to come here at present. There is darkness all around which will not be dispelled but only deepen with the arrival of outsiders. The best thing is to remain where you are and do your duty.'[9]

Heeding Gandhi's advice, Malati went to Delhi instead, as a representative of Orissa in the Constituent Assembly.[10] The Assembly began its first session on 9 December 1946 and in the following days, it debated and discussed the framework of independent India. Malati felt dwarfed as she sat amidst legal luminaries such as Dr B.R. Ambedkar, Durgabai Deshmukh, K.M. Munshi, and Gopalaswami Ayyangar. Additionally, she was unhappy with the attempt at writing the Constitution by borrowing from other countries.[11] She felt she was dozing away in the backbenches while the country was aflame. Perhaps she sensed that she would be of more help to the people on the ground than sitting inside the Parliament.

Eventually, she resigned from the Assembly. She immediately headed off to the riot-affected areas of Noakhali. Gandhi who didn't want her to come to the riot-affected area was deeply impressed by the pace and efficiency of her rehabilitation work and gave her the name 'Toofani'.[12] Malati would go on to amass even more nicknames.

***

Born on 26 July 1904, in an aristocratic family in Calcutta (now Kolkata), Malati Devi was the youngest of barrister Kumud Nath Sen and Snehalata Sen's four children. Unfortunately, tragedy struck her family when Kumud Nath died. Malati was just three.[13]

Her educated and independent mother Snehalata was the daughter of Behari Lal Gupta, who, in 1869, became one of the first Indians to be selected as an elite Indian Civil Service (ICS) officer.[14] In 1872, a maverick of his times, he faced social backlash from his community for marrying outside his religion.[15]

In 1882, during his tenure as the presidency magistrate of Calcutta, Behari Lal initiated the controversial Ilbert Bill, which led to the trying of European criminals in Indian courts.[16] The discourse surrounding the Bill was significant in galvanizing nationalist sentiments amongst Indians. He also served as a justice of the Calcutta High Court before his subsequent move to Baroda in 1909. In later years, he served as the Dewan of Baroda (1911–13).[17] Behari Lal ensured that Snehalata completed her undergraduate studies at Bethune College, Calcutta.[18] She had a flair for words and authored various stories and books.[19] She also took up teaching at Darjeeling's Victoria Girls' High School to raise her children.[20] As fate would have it, she later became a teacher at her alma mater, Bethune College.[21] Snehalata also translated some writings of poet and social reformer Rabindranath Tagore, her father's close friend, from Bengali to English.[22]

With a strong educational background, Snehalata created an environment that encouraged learning in her household. Her sons Prodyot and Kula Prasad both went on to become prominent civil servants. Being the youngest, Malati Devi – or Minu – was the pampered child with a rebellious streak. In fact, when Gandhi launched the Non-Cooperation Movement in 1920, Malati was about to appear for her matriculation examinations. The passionate sixteen-year-old who was eager to join the uprising, ran off to a relative's place in Rangpur (in present-day Bangladesh).[23] Snehalata travelled there to persuade Malati to change her mind. After hearing her mother out, Malati relented and went back to take the examination. She also secured a first-class.[24] Malati always had the calling for the cause, she just had a few years more left before she would be a prominent voice of the movement.

Malati did the unexpected when it came to choosing an institution for higher education. Instead of Bethune College, her mother's alma mater and Calcutta's most popular college for women, she chose Visva Bharati, Tagore's university in Santiniketan. At the time, however, the university didn't have provisions for female students.[25] That of course did not deter the spirited teenager who preferred Santiniketan's ashram-like experiential learning environment over government colleges.

Being close family friends with Tagore, Malati directly wrote to him requesting for admission to the institute. With no accommodation for female students, the request made Tagore think of a solution. He decided to offer Malati's mother, Snehalata, a job to become the superintendent of the new girls' hostel to accommodate female students at the university. Her mother accepted the offer and both of them moved to Santiniketan.[26]

Malati's desire to learn at Santiniketan led to the entry of the first girls' batch of 1921–22.[27] This multicultural and multilingual university focused on the all-round development of students.[28] Classes here were held in the open so that students could experience life outside the confines of a room. A lifestyle without luxuries was followed in an attempt to harbour self-discipline and self-reliance among students.[29] Tagore insisted on promoting Indian languages to enable freedom of thought and creation unhindered by the limitations of expression in a foreign language. Studies of folk literature, fine arts, music, and various cultures – Vedic, Puranic, Sikhism, Jainism, Buddhism, Islam, Zoroastrianism, and so on – were also carried out.[30]

Malati became her own person at the university. She took up music and learned to play various instruments, including the veena and the flute.[31] She also trained in Rabindra sangeet, or Tagore songs, earning praise from Tagore himself for her singing.[32] Malati also immersed herself in the world of art and drama. According to Snehalata, her daughter benefitted greatly from her experience at the university. She even attributed

Tagore's teachings, patriotism, and idealism to influencing her daughter's life.[33]

In 1925, her fifth year in Santiniketan, Malati met a young man, Nabakrushna Choudhury, from Sabarmati Ashram in Ahmedabad.[34] After learning to weave and spin at Sabarmati, Nabakrushna came to Tagore's university at Gandhi's behest. During his ten-month stay at the university, Nabakrushna fell in love with the vibrant and strong-willed Malati.[35]

Born in a Kayastha family of Jagatsinghpur in modern-day Odisha,[36] Nabakrushna was the youngest son of Gokulananda Choudhury and Padmavati Devi. His father was a zamindar and an eminent lawyer in Cuttack.[37] His brother Gopabandhu was a revolutionary who quit the ICS to join the Congress.[38] Gokulananda was known for his progressive values and even arranged his son Gopabandhu's marriage to Rama Devi, the daughter of a Christian friend, against the wishes of his orthodox wife.[39] However, when Nabakrushna expressed his desire to marry Malati, Gokulananda was no longer alive. His mother Padmavati had serious reservations against this love marriage. But with the support of his brother Gopabandhu, Malati and Nabakrushna got married in Calcutta in July 1927.[40] At the wedding reception, held four days later in Cuttack, Malati Choudhury made her debut as an Odia bride, her head bowed, face veiled, and ankles adorned in silver jewellery.[41]

Malati's efforts at fitting into the Choudhury household met with only partial success.[42] Within a few months of marriage, the young couple moved to a village called Tarikund near Cuttack. Malati's lifestyle underwent a sea change here. From soft gossamer-thin saris, she switched to wearing coarse khadi outfits. Inspired by Gandhi's teachings, the duo even took to farming and planted hybrid seeds of potato, sugarcane, and groundnut.[43] They spun and sold khadi, besides running night schools for adults and young boys who were cowherds. They also became parents to a baby girl named Uttara.

During their stay in Tarikund, they came in contact with Gurucharan Mohanty, a Marxist who had returned to India from England. Discussions on Marxism with Gurucharan left a deep impression on the minds of Malati and Nabakrushna.[44]

In December 1929, the historic Lahore session of the Congress passed the 'Purna Swaraj' resolution. The party directed its provincial and district units to prepare volunteers for the launch of civil disobedience. Gopabandhu, Nabakrushna's brother, was appointed secretary of the Utkal Provincial Congress Committee, the provincial unit of the Congress. The Swaraj flag, saffron, white, green with the spinning wheel in the middle, was hoisted in Cuttack on 26 January 1930, despite the government's bid to stop the event.[45] Malati was among those in attendance. Her presence motivated women to join the movement. In fact when Malati donated gold bangles to the Satyagrahi fund, she inspired women to pledge money and their jewellery to the movement.[46]

When Gandhi launched the Dandi March against the salt tax on 12 March 1930, volunteers of the Utkal Congress gathered at Inchudi, a coastal village in Balasore district on a similar exercise. On April 20, Malati and her sister-in-law Rama led hundreds of women in making their own salt.[47] They replicated this act of resistance at Srijang, Kujang, Ganjam, and other parts of Orissa. The successful salt satyagraha at Inchudi was considered second only to Gandhi's Dandi March.[48]

The crackdown on the movement saw the arrests of countless Congress leaders and volunteers. Since a lot of leaders were incarcerated, Malati stepped up by organizing protest meetings in Cuttack, Balasore, Puri, and Berhampur.[49] At one of these meetings, she set fire to a heap of mill-made clothing items.[50]

In June 1930, Malati was appointed secretary of Cuttack district Congress. She led volunteers in the picketing of shops selling liquor as well as foreign clothes. Malati was eventually arrested for picketing during the Legislative Council elections in September 1930 and sentenced to six months' imprisonment.[51]

At this time Nabakrushna and Gopabandhu were already in jail.[52] Rama was also arrested in November 1930 and with that, the whole Choudhury family was in jail. With no immediate family to live with, Malati's two-year-old daughter Uttara joined her mother in Bhagalpur Jail.[53]

The Civil Disobedience Movement and the arrest of nearly 60,000 people including Gandhi garnered worldwide attention in the press. Gandhi was released from jail in January 1931 for negotiations with Lord Irwin, the then viceroy of British India. In March, the Gandhi-Irwin Pact led to the end of the movement and the release of the political prisoners.[54]

As a result, Malati and her family too were released from prison in March 1931.[55] Out of jail, Malati jumped back into the cause and continued to strengthen the freedom movement. She recruited children as part of Vanarsena, a group formed by Indira Gandhi, who was a teenager at the time, out of a desire to contribute to the freedom movement. Malati even organized picketing at places in Cuttack. On 26 January 1932, Malati was arrested again and this time sent to Hazaribagh Jail.[56] By this time, she had given birth again to a son named Binayak who went to jail with her and Uttara.[57]

The year 1932 was significant for marginalized communities in India. The British decided to introduce separate electorates for religious minorities and depressed classes. While Dr Ambedkar welcomed the move, Gandhi opposed it. Gandhi believed it would create divisions among Hindus.[58] On 18 August Gandhi wrote to British PM Ramsay MacDonald, 'I have to resist your decision with my life.'[59] Eventually, the British asked the Indian leaders to come to a solution or agreement by themselves. When Dr Ambedkar refused to 'sacrifice a rightful demand', Gandhi went on a fast unto death.[60] This forced Dr Ambedkar to compromise, and resulted in the Poona Pact, which doubled the number of reserved seats in the legislatures in lieu of separate electorates.[61]

Gandhi's agenda was to achieve social reforms by engaging and changing the mindset of upper-caste Hindus. He entreated

Dr Ambedkar 'not to deprive Hinduism of a last chance to make a voluntary expiation for its sinful past'.[62] Gandhi founded the All India Harijan Sevak Sangha and changed the name of his periodical from *Young India* to *Harijan*. Gandhi also went on a Harijan Yatra covering more than 20,000 kms across the country in an attempt to raise awareness and change the minds of the upper-caste by inter-mingling with lower-caste Hindus.[63]

Malati joined the Orissa leg of the Harijan Yatra. One day, tired from his travels Gandhi cancelled his visit to a Harijan village on account of fatigue. The news came as a blow to the morale of the villagers who were anxiously awaiting the first-ever visit by an upper-caste Hindu. Malati upset with his decision immediately rushed to Gandhi. She told him that he was wrong in dropping his plan so he apologized.[64]

To Malati and Nabakrushna, socialism and independence were two sides of the same coin. Their dedication to depressed and financially weaker sections of society led them to found the Utkal Congress Samyabadi Karmi Sangha in 1933. It became the socialist unit of the Congress party in Orissa. Nabakrushna edited a weekly magazine called *Sarathi* as a mouthpiece of the organization,[65] which bore the slogan, 'Let the Workers Unite' on its cover.[66]

They practised what they preached and even donated their farm in Tarikund to the organization. Malati even sold her wedding jewellery in order to cover the expenses of the publication.[67]

Around this time, more and more peasant uprisings were taking place across India. The socialists within the Congress fold organized camps in Cuttack and Puri to understand the oppression of peasants by landowners, moneylenders, and even the police. The party workers used the pages of *Sarathi* to describe the plight of farmers.[68] This was a concrete step in the direction of forming the Utkal Kisan Sangha in 1935, of which Congress leader Hare Krushna Mahtab was the president and Malati, the secretary.[69]

Malati's resolve to see the end of the zamindari system drove her to build a strong relationship with the people at the bottom of the agricultural pecking order. In order to establish this she walked 20–30 km on a regular basis to farmers' villages. To get a deeper understanding of their day-to-day problems, she often stayed with them. Wherever she went, she made it a point to sing songs of rebellion and she even played the flute.[70]

In 1936, their province was split into two separate provinces – Bihar and Orissa. Nabakrushna was elected to the Orissa Legislative Assembly in 1937. The provincial government enacted a few laws, including one that ended bonded labour, heralding reforms for farmers' rights.[71] Malati with her on-ground experience played a decisive role in the upliftment of peasants.

Meanwhile, in the neighbouring region of Dhenkanal, a princely state, a people's movement for a responsible government was gaining momentum. In essence, the people desired a system of governance with checks and balances and accountability. They wanted the integration of the princely states – known as Garjat states – with Orissa.[72] In 1937, in a setback to the pro-farmer reforms, the rulers were given absolute power under a new law aggravating the oppression of the peasants.[73] The resistance and protests to this new law claimed many lives.

Wherever there was oppression, Malati was at the forefront, fighting against injustice. As part of the resistance movement, the only woman leader of the Garjat movement, Malata organized a gathering of 55,000 people on 2 September 1938.[74] However, the outbreak of World War II brought the Garjat resistance to a grinding halt.[75]

Almost four years later, the August 1942 session of the Congress passed the historic Quit India resolution in protest of India's involvement in World War II. Out of the five Congress representatives of Orissa at the session, Malati was the only woman.[76] Soon after the session, most of the leaders were put behind bars. Because of the danger of being incarcerated, Malati and the other Congress leaders met in secret and decided to steer the movement from underground.[77] At the same time, the leaders were also driven to take action to meet their political goals by whatever means necessary. Given Malati's popular image, her colleagues wanted her to be arrested in public view to gain the sympathy of the masses.

Malati decided to play her part to perfection. Instead of heading directly to Cuttack, she along with another leader, took a detour and travelled to Bhubaneswar via Madras to buy time and court arrest according to their plan.[78] On the morning after her arrival in Cuttack, Malati was arrested while on her way to address a meeting. As planned, her arrest evoked strong emotions among the people.[79]

Malati spent nearly three years in prison before her release on 1 April 1945.[80] After her release she became the president of the Utkal Pradesh Congress Committee.[81] During her time in Cuttack Jail, Malati often thought about the Garjat movement and the children who lost their parents to it and wished to open a school for them. She decided to set it up in a town named Angul, on a piece of land that she owned.[82]

After being released from jail, Malati made her plans for the school public and received overwhelming support from the Garjat leaders as well as the common people. In fact, donations for the school poured in from well-wishers across the world because of the goodwill attached to her name.[83]

Malati named the school Bajirout Chhatravas, in memory of a twelve-year-old ferry boy who was shot dead when he refused to ferry the British across a river.[84] The school was formally inaugurated on 11 May 1946 and was open to both girls and boys.[85] One of the first teachers at the school was Uttara, Malati's daughter. Malati would remain the school's president for over four decades, until the Orissa government took charge of it in 1991.[86]

In 1946, Malati became the only woman from Orissa to be nominated to the Constituent Assembly. She, however, felt out of place and resigned soon after. Her calling was somewhere else. Malati was in fact driven by her life mission of working for the underprivileged, and instead, wanted to help the women and girls affected by the Noakhali and Tipperah riots on the ground.[87]

While Malati pressed ahead with relief and rehabilitation work, Nabakrushna remained busy with his duties as the revenue minister in the provincial Orissa government.[88] In 1948, the duo faced a personal tragedy – Binayak, their only son, died by suicide.[89] A traumatized Nabakrushna gave up his ministerial position[90] for a quiet life with Malati.[91]

But Prime Minister Jawaharlal Nehru wanted Nabakrushna to return to politics. One afternoon, two Assembly members from Cuttack visited Nabakrushna at Bajirout Chhatravas in Angul to convince him to take on the chief ministership of Orissa as the incumbent chief minister, Harekrushna Mahtab, was about to join Nehru's cabinet and they needed a replacement.[92] Not one to run away from the call of duty, the distraught Nabakrushna returned to head the government in 1950 as chief minister. Malati, on the other hand, chose to stay away from the limelight and continued her work in rural areas.[93]

Independence did not change the fate of millions of Indians. Their lives were still caught in a web of social inequalities from caste bias to lack of basic resources. With the British gone, it was time for the believers of socialism to invest in an apparatus for social change. The Utkal Nava Jeevan Mandal (UNJM), for example, was set up for the cause of tribal welfare, with Malati as the treasurer.[94] Among the UNJM's aims and objectives were the setting up of maternity and child welfare centres, dispensaries, libraries, gymnasiums, co-operative societies, and much more.[95]

In 1951, when Malati was made the UNJM secretary and president,[96] she worked in the remotest areas of Koraput, Ganjam, Sundergarh, Dhenkanal, Sambalpur, and Phulbani districts.[97] She was anguished at the plight of the tribal people. In 1952, in *Gramasevak*, an Odia magazine, Malati openly criticized the corruption of the government her husband headed. In the article, she commented about the prevalence of unpaid labour and unfair taxation of tribal people.[98] 'The revenue department… is yet to settle these lands in favour of the cultivating tenants. Instead after the abolition of Zamindari, the government is snatching away these lands from the possession of the cultivating people.'[99]

The UNJM was successful in eradicating immoral practices such as *goti* (bonded labour and debt enslavement), *bethi* (forced unpaid labour), and *magana* (forced contribution) in these tribal areas.[100] Her work made Malati a loved leader among the tribespeople. They called her 'Numa' – yet another nickname, meaning the one with whom they shared their sorrows and joys.

Though Malati's work was mostly focused at the grassroots, she occasionally helped Nabakrushna in governance, sometimes in rather unconventional ways.

Once in the town of Angul, a twelve-year-old cowherd called 'Nepali Baba' claimed to cure diseases with the help of the bark of a tree.[101] On hearing this, thousands of curious followers from across Orissa and neighbouring states thronged Angul in the hope of seeing the self-proclaimed spiritual leader. The town lacked clean drinking water and had poor sanitation, which led to an outbreak of cholera. Soon, the number of casualties as a result of the disease increased as steadily as the influx of followers.[102] Angul became the epicentre of cholera.

Due to a fear of backlash from religious quarters, the government hesitated to intervene. Malati stepped in and requested the local member of the Legislative Assembly and a teacher from Bajirout Chhatravas to accompany her to a meeting with the cowherd.[103] There she bluntly asked the boy to showcase his supernatural powers. Upon his failure to do so, she slapped him and reprimanded him strongly. He was later arrested by the police.[104] In order to avoid people gathering and spreading the disease further, the government immediately imposed a ban on the entry of visitors to the area. This was followed by setting up medical facilities to treat the patients and evacuating the devotees by bus and train.[105]

Despite a fairly good run as chief minister, Nabakrushna could not deal with the politics of power by those who kept eyeing his chair. In 1956, he finally gave up both the chief ministership and the membership of Congress.[106] The very next day, Malati and her husband left for Bajirout Chhatravas in Angul for a life away from active politics yet again.[107]

Now retired from politics, Malati and Nabakrushna channelled their energy into the running of the school and the UNJM. In 1957 and 1958, the duo conducted *padayatras* across the state to promote the Bhoodan and Gramdan movement, which were land reform movements that aimed to convince the landed to 'gift' their land to the landless.[108]

In the Ganjam and Koraput areas, the police tortured tribespeople on the grounds of 'suspected' collusion with Naxalites. Malati and Nabakrushna camped for six months at a village on the Orissa–Andhra Pradesh border in order to help reduce police brutality against innocent villagers.[109] To protect their rights, the Orissa Civil Liberties Committee was set up in 1968 with Malati as the president. It was amongst the country's first voices against fake encounters.[110]

As Gandhians, Malati and Nabakrushna espoused communal harmony through their work. In 1964, they went to Assam on hearing of the bloodshed between the Assamese and Bengalis.[111] Similarly, when communal riots broke out between the Hindus and Muslims in Rourkela, a city in Orissa, they amicably engaged with community leaders and restored peace.[112] In addition, during the Bangladesh Liberation War of 1971, when lakhs of refugees flocked to the India–Bangladesh border, Malati joined the Bharat Shantisena, a group started by fellow Gandhians, for relief work.[113]

In 1975, a state of Emergency was declared by Prime Minister Indira Gandhi which restricted basic freedoms, imposed strict press censorship, and imprisoned several political opponents. Both Malati and Nabakrushna were vocal against the proclamation of Emergency and were subsequently imprisoned on the orders of the chief minister of Orissa, Nandini Satpathy.

While in prison, Nabakrushna suffered a stroke, which left him paralysed.[114] In a massive blow to their work, the government also cancelled all grants to organizations run by them.[115]

After the end of the twenty-one-month Emergency, the fight against social injustices brought the Choudhurys back to politics in 1977. But this time it was Malati who took the plunge.

On her release, to register her anger democratically, Malati contested against the incumbent chief minister as an independent candidate in 1977, but lost. Nandini Satpathy secured 31,829 votes whereas Malati polled just 4,063 votes. The result came as a shock to many leaders. A press statement issued by Malati reads: 'I chose to contest this election on the dictates of my conscience. I never had and never will have any desire to be a member of the Assembly anytime.'[116]

While voters rejected her, various institutions honoured Malati for her immense body of work. She was feted with the National Award for Child Welfare (1987), the Utkal Seva Sammaan (1994), and the Tagore Literacy Award (1995). In 1988, the Jamnalal Bajaj Award was conferred too for her work in the emancipation of women and children. But she refused to accept the award from the hands of Rajiv Gandhi, the then prime minister. It was later sent to her home in Bajirout Chhatravas.[117]

Unfortunately, a series of personal tragedies struck her in the 1980s, which broke her. She lost two grandsons in 1983, followed by the death of Nabakrushna in 1984. Her daughter Uttara too died in 1988.

Though the series of bereavements drained her strength, she continued to be one with strong principles and discipline. In fact, once in the summer of 1997, she declined a meeting with Biju Patnaik, the then chief minister of Orissa, because he was tardy by an hour.[118]

Following a brief illness, Malati breathed her last in March 1998, at the age of ninety-four.[119] Malati left giant imprints on the history of present day–Odisha. She lived a simple life without any desire for position or power but gave her absolute best for the welfare of the people. In the book *Fragments of a Vision* (1972), author Erica Linton captures Malati's unmatched bond with the people. She wrote: 'Malati is no longer young and uses up her energy at a rate that leaves others falling by the wayside. The demands made on her are never ending, and the love she feels for those whom she is trying to help is being amply reciprocated. I knew – for even in this one short day I had ample opportunity to watch people's reaction; to see a young girl weep on her shoulder; a young tribal woman who had married a Gramdan worker belonging to a different tribe and feeling herself a stranger amongst the people of Akili [a village in Gajapati district, Odisha]. She had known Malati since she was a child, and was clamouring to be comforted by her as she had been when a small girl.'[120]

PURNIMA BANERJI

'I personally feel that this Constitution has provided us with the means for changing the structure of society. It will all depend on us whether we are able to establish that sovereign democratic republic, not for the hollow benefit of registering one's vote and passing legislation, not a democracy which will simply maintain the status quo or which will take upon itself the policy of laissez faire, but a democracy which will combine with it the healthy principle that the government governs best which governs least, with the principle that it should encourage the active citizenship of the country.'

– In hope that the Constitution would usher true democracy in the Constituent Assembly on 24 November 1949

Purnima Banerji's life remains an enigma. As one of the most vocal members of the Constituent Assembly, she was at the centre of key debates that shaped independent India. She was the sister of Aruna Asaf Ali – an icon of the Quit India movement. The Nehru family doted on Purnima, particularly Indira Gandhi. Yet, the historical records have sparse mention of this fiery leader.

★★★

Purnima was born to Upendranath Ganguly and Ambalika Devi in 1911. She was the third of five children in the household, younger than Aruna by two years. Both Upendranath and Ambalika hailed from influential families with close ties to

Rabindranath Tagore, poet, writer, playwright, and social reformer. The families shared such a close bond that it was Tagore who gave Purnima her name.[1]

Her mother, Ambalika was the daughter of Troilokya Nath Sanyal, a leading Brahmo Samaj missionary in the mid-nineteenth century. Sanyal was a musician and a folk theatre actor credited with creating Brahmo Sangeet, a form of devotional music praising the god Brahma. Tagore adopted this music form and popularized it among the middle-class Bengali Hindu society that started calling these songs 'Rabindra sangeet'.[2] Upendranath was 'an adventurous, liberal Brahmo who had migrated from Barisal in modern Bangladesh'[3] to the United Provinces (now Uttar Pradesh). His younger brother, Dhirendranath, went on to become a noted film director. Another brother, Dr Nagendranath Ganguly, was married to Mira Devi,[4] Rabindranath Tagore's youngest daughter.

While the exact details of Purnima's schooling and college are hard to tell because of a lack of records, it can be assumed that she received some formal tutoring based on her sister's educational background, which is well-documented. Aruna, her sister, was a student of Lahore's Sacred Heart Cathedral and later the All Saints' College in Nainital. Purnima studied for her intermediate examinations (some records suggest it was BA exams) while she was lodged in Lucknow Jail. Sucheta Kripalani, who was also in the same jail, wrote about Purnima requesting authorities to transfer her to the cells meant for solitary confinement so that she could concentrate, as the barracks were too noisy. The officials were taken aback as solitary confinement was meant as a harsh punishment. They relented once Kripalani offered to accompany Purnima.[5]

Purnima's intervention in the Constituent Assembly makes it clear that she was well-informed and capable of holding her own in any debate. Her letters to Jawaharlal Nehru and Indira Gandhi show that they discussed books they had read or intended to get their hands on. Purnima was also an avid birdwatcher and wrote to Nehru about being a 'bit of an expert in bird watching' and Dehradun having 'some of the loveliest birds'.[6]

Purnima was a minor when she married Pranab Kumar Banerji, the son of a leading Allahabad-based lawyer, Pyarelal Banerji. In fact, she was married before Aruna tied the knot with Asaf Ali. A book on Purnima's brother-in-law, Asaf Ali, says that he first met Aruna at Pyarelal's house in Allahabad, around 1927–28. Purnima could not have been more than seventeen years of age at the time.[7] It was two years later that the government enacted the Child Marriage Restraint Act 1929, which fixed the marriageable age of women at 14. Pyarelal had a flourishing legal practice and was a contemporary of Motilal Nehru at the Allahabad High Court.[8] The Nehrus and the Banerjis were well acquainted with each other which may have brought Purnima close to Vijaya Lakshmi Pandit, Indira Gandhi, and the rest of the Nehru family. In fact, the Nehrus dotingly nicknamed her 'Nora'. Purnima was seen very often at Anand Bhawan, the residence of the Nehru family in Allahabad (now Prayagraj).[9]

Purnima was lively and charming. An office-bearer of the All India Women's Conference (AIWC), she was pivotal in organizing its activities in Allahabad. At its fourteenth session, AIWC president Begum Hamid Ali was impressed by her work ethic. Praising her effusively, Begum Hamid Ali noted how Purnima was 'moving about like a nymph, radiating joy like the full moon to everyone who may come in contact with her.'[10] Purnima was a pillar of support for the freedom fighters who needed help in Allahabad. When Lal Bahadur Shastri's wife, Lalitadevi, fell ill, he wrote to Purnima requesting her to look after Lalitadevi. Purnima took her under her care and helped Lalitadevi through the illness.[11]

The time spent at Allahabad, then the centre of Congress political activities and proximity with the Nehru clan brought her close to the freedom movement. It also shaped her ideology as she remained a firm socialist throughout her life.

Economic justice had been a key platform for the Congress since its former president Dadabhai Naoroji wrote his seminal *Poverty and Un-British Rule in India* in 1901. The demands for workers' rights were gaining momentum, especially after the Bolshevik Revolution of 1917 in Russia, which overthrew Tsarist autocracy. A decade later, at the 1928 Calcutta session, the Congress welcomed the Nehru Report – a draft Constitution – that proposed far-reaching constitutional demands. The report also mentioned the improvement of economic conditions and protection of labour. One of the articles read: 'Freedom of combination and association for the maintenance and improvement of labour and economic conditions is guaranteed to everyone and of all occupation.'[12]

Jawaharlal Nehru, one of the authors of the Nehru Report, was deeply impressed by the Russian experiment of organizing the economy on socialist lines.[13] His sentiments were shared by Jayaprakash Narayan and Dr Ram Manohar Lohia. In 1933, the Congress Socialist Party was formed with Acharya Narendra Dev as president and Narayan as secretary. Lohia, Achyut Patwardhan, Kamaladevi Chattopadhyay, Minoo Masani, Purushottamdas Trikamdas, and Sampurnanand were among the notable delegates who participated in the party's first session.[14] Socialism was the common thread between Purnima, Narayan, and Dr Lohia. Aruna, Purnima's sister, was also one of the leaders of the socialist movement.

Prior to that, Purnima's association with the Congress led her to take part in the Civil Disobedience Movement. It resulted in her first recorded jail term. On 26 January 1932, Purnima, along with Vijaya Lakshmi and several others, were arrested for organizing a public event where the independence pledge was being taken.[15] She soon rose to become secretary of the Allahabad Congress Committee. Purnima even organized 'trade unions and addressed kisan meetings in Allahabad'.[16] Among the things she felt deeply against was the practice of purdah. During a municipal election, Sitaram Nishad, a Congress worker from

Allahabad, introduced his wife Ramrani Nishad to Purnima. Ramrani's face was covered in a *chaddar*, a cotton shawl worn over a sari, that was 'a symbol of respectability and purdah'. The sight of the veiled woman irked Purnima, and she ordered Ramrani to take off the *chaddar*. That ended purdah for Ramrani.[17]

In 1940, Congress launched individual Satyagraha in response to Britian's unilateral decision to make India a party to World War II. As the war was raging, plans to organize a mass movement were replaced with an advocacy programme. Under the individual Satyagraha plan, Congress workers would go to the people and preach against the war. Kripalani and Purnima were among those designated to offer Satyagraha in the United Provinces. They were both arrested for the act.[18] Months later, Purnima was arrested once again for participating in the Quit India Movement. This time she shared jail barracks with Vijaya Lakshmi. They were later joined by Chandralekha, Vijaya Lakshmi's daughter, as well as Indira Gandhi.[19]

The letters between Nehru and Indira give us a peek into Purnima's, or Nora as they fondly called her, life from the early 1940s. The successive jail terms had left Purnima with frail health and in 1943, she fell severely ill. She had been diagnosed with tuberculosis before and the doctors were worried that the ailment had resurfaced.[20] Nehru was concerned and rued how Purnima neglected her health. Writing to Indira, his daughter, he observed, 'I am sorry to learn about Nora's health. She is quite extraordinarily careless and observes no rules or discipline.'[21]

The letters also throw light on Purnima's marital problems with Pranab Kumar. On 5 June 1945, Indira wrote, 'The Banerjis are a most peculiar family. Nora has been divorced for some years now but she continued living in the same house and referring to P.K.B. as "my husband". Now he has married a girl from Delhi. Nora, I hear, has started wearing what she thinks is the Hindu widow's garb but she is still going to live there all together.'[22]

Jail sentences, poor health, and domestic problems did not stand in Purnima's way of public service. When Jayaprakash

Narayan faced arrest, she promptly filed a habeas corpus petition. In Narayan's words, Purnima was courageous to take 'such a risk' 'in those dark days, in spite of delicate health'. The petition was, however, rejected.[23] Purnima's career in the legislature began with the provincial elections of 1946. She served on various committees of the United Provinces Legislative Assembly.[24] The same year, she was elected to the Constituent Assembly. At thirty-five, she was one of its youngest members, alongside Dakshayani who was thirty four.

Her first speech in the Assembly was delivered two weeks after India's independence. The members were discussing fundamental rights and religious instructions in schools. Purnima moved an amendment for the addition of a clause that read: 'All religious education given in educational institutions receiving state aid will be in the nature of the elementary philosophy of comparative religions calculated to broaden the pupils' mind rather than such as will foster sectarian exclusiveness'.[25] She reasoned that exposure to diverse religious thoughts is important for young minds. Her speech came against the backdrop of ghastly violence perpetuated by the partition of India. Purnima said, 'The State should be perfectly entitled to see that in the formative age of the child, when he is of the school-going age, the religious instruction is controlled and that the syllabus is of such a nature that the child will develop into a healthy citizen of India capable of appreciating each other's point of view.'[26]

Purnima's amendment gives us a picture of how the constitutional framers conceptualized secularism. They did not want to eschew religion from the public sphere but recognized how it was an essential part of people's psyche. Purnima was advocating for secularism where the state proactively worked to instil respect for diverse religious thought. On the other hand, her colleague Renuka Ray moved an amendment that called for disallowing religious instructions in government-aided schools. Eventually, Purnima's amendment was defeated while Ray withdrew her amendment.

The same day she moved another amendment. Purnima wanted to add the words 'state-aided' after 'state' in one of the clauses that read: 'No minority whether based on religion, community or language shall be discriminated against in regard to the admission into State educational institutions, nor shall any religious instruction be compulsorily imposed on them.' Her argument was that if an institution receives aid from the state, it must adhere to secular norms. The amendment was supported by Hussain Imam and Hriday Nath Kunzru. However, Vallabhbhai Patel disagreed with her reasoning. Patel spoke of how the clause was intended to provide a safeguard for minorities and bringing state-aided institutions within the purview should be left to the 'legislature to be adopted wherever conditions were suitable'.[27] Five decades later, the Hon'ble Supreme Court referred to her speech in the landmark T.M.A. Pai case. The Court was dealing with several issues in the case, including the extent of autonomy minority institutions have regarding admissions. The Court held that when minority institutions take aid, they must comply with certain government regulations. They cannot outright give preference to one community and must observe certain standards of merit.[28]

In another intervention, Purnima moved to reduce the age of qualification to the legislative councils in the states from 35 to 30. Her suggestion was accepted by the Assembly and is reflected in Article 173 of the Constitution.[29]

On the question of the relevance and composition of the Upper House, Purnima felt that it could serve a useful function and bring to the legislative process members who were not cut out for the 'rough and tumble of active politics'.[30] Three weeks later, the Assembly debated on the composition of the electoral college for the Upper House in state legislatures. Purnima was happy at the inclusion of teachers as a constituency in legislative councils. She also suggested expanding the scope of the term 'social service' under which the governor could nominate members to the council. Purnima insisted that women's organizations and their members eligible for 'nominations should not be left out'.[31] Purnima also advocated for greater devolution of powers to panchayats and local bodies. Agreeing with Ambedkar's amendment to empower local bodies to levy taxes on professions, Purnima expressed the hope that taxation powers of local bodies, alongside other rights, was going to help bring 'swaraj to the people'.[32]

Purnima's commitment to socialist ideals was evident in the debate on right to property. At the time, the draft constitution included right to property as a fundamental right. Article 24 (1) of the draft read: 'No person shall be deprived of his property save by authority of law'. Article 24 (2) provided payment of compensation should the right be abridged. Article 24 (3) provided the exceptions to the compensation clause.

Jawaharlal Nehru proposed significant amendments to Article 24 and moved for a more diluted right to property.[33] Purnima, however, felt that the proposed amendments did not go far enough. She wanted additional exceptions to the compensation clause. In her view, the state ought to have the power to abridge property rights without paying compensation should it be towards ensuring economic justice.

To this end, she said, 'We have already said that an adequate means of livelihood to men and women shall be provided and the economic resources of the country shall be so handled as to avoid concentration in the hands of a few and to avoid its working to the detriment of the common people. At that time when these clauses were under consideration we also felt, and some of us felt very strongly, that in the Fundamental Rights the right of livelihood, the right of earning honourable bread, should be guaranteed to all people.' Purnima argued that bringing about a 'new order of society' would 'take some time and therefore the right of livelihood' was included in Directive Principles of State Policy. She added, 'We consider these Principles to be absolutely essential and in fact our guiding star in the future. For that reason, if provisions are not made in this article dealing with

Property Rights and the economic policy of the future State is in any way fettered and made rigid, we feel that we shall not be able to succeed in these articles which we have already passed.'[34]

Purnima's views on property rights echoed the opinions of her Socialist Party colleagues. Socialist leaders were unhappy with Congress's reluctance to nationalize 'existing industries', accusing the latter 'of acting in the interests of the capitalist class'.[35] Eventually, the right to property as a fundamental right was extinguished in 1978 with the enactment of the 44th Amendment. It continues to be a legal right today.

The extent of the right to life and liberty was subject to intense debate in the drafting committee and the Constituent Assembly. Initially, the agreement was on curtailing the right only according to due process of law. It meant that if the government wanted to abridge the right, it had to adhere to established legal principles. Later, the words 'due process of law' were replaced by 'procedure established by law'. The latter allows the state a greater room for restricting freedoms. Some members felt that 'due process' was vague and undemocratic as it gave primacy to judges' opinions over the wish of the elected legislature.[36]

There was heavy criticism of the Assembly replacing the due process clause. Several leaders and the public had themselves faced unlawful detention and punishment. The Rowlatt Act of 1919 allowed detention without trial and had been vociferously opposed, eventually leading to the Jallianwala Bagh massacre. By allowing the legislature to curtail the right to life and liberty by 'procedure established by law', the Assembly was perceived to be giving a free pass to future governments to do as they please. Responding to the criticism, an article was drafted that provided protection against unlawful arrests and granted rights to detainees (present Article 22).[37]

Purnima moved four amendments to the draft article. Perhaps having been unlawfully jailed herself, she was passionate towards the cause even more. In her speech, she called for expediting the process to ensure that nobody suffered at the hands of law, limiting the duration to which a person could be detained without proper trial, and compensation to the families of the detained. She suggested that charges against a detainee must be framed within fifteen days and the accused released if trial doesn't start six months after the detention. She added, 'Continuous detention from month to month without a person getting a chance of appearing, or considering himself, sufficiently defended... is highly arbitrary'.[38]

She spoke about how important it was to be able to draw a salary and how even those imprisoned should be able to do so, especially if they are the only member earning in their family. With great conviction, she debated, 'I do earnestly plead that he should be given a maintenance allowance. It should not be left to the arbitrary will of any one to deprive anybody of his liberty and then later on to decide, by leaving it to their sweet will, as to how his dependents shall live and maintain themselves.'[39]

Her amendments on the matter were not accepted. The right of detainees continues to be a contentious issue even today. Governments have enacted legislations that allow detention without trial for long periods. The Supreme Court has held that the accused cannot be 'subjected to unending detention pending trial'. However, in the absence of a clear constitutional guarantee, several accused continue to be detained without trial.[40]

Originally, the Constituent Assembly had 15 women members. This number fell to 11 following the resignations of Leela Roy and Malati Choudhury, Vijaya Lakshmi's appointment as ambassador to the USSR, and Sarojini Naidu's demise in March 1949. When the Assembly sought to fill the vacant seats, Purnima suggested that only women should replace women.[41] Her suggestion, however, was not implemented.

Purnima's final speech in the Assembly was made on 24 November 1949, two days before the adoption of the Constitution. Despite some concerns, Purnima was jubilant about the Constitution. She expressed happiness at the fact that the Constitution gave citizens a chance to mould their lives for the better and establish an equitable society. It was important for Purnima that the Constitution should not be relegated to a document that gives sanctity to an elected government but instead, it should provide a framework to deepen democracy. She noted, 'If we want to establish a democracy which should answer the needs of the growing pattern of society, we should place the means at the disposal of the people by which Governments can be established, which in its turn can be done by the right of free association and free expression of opinion, with the exercise of which institutions can be changed.'[42] She added, 'I personally feel that this Constitution has provided us with the means for changing the structure of society'.[43]

She wanted a more rigorous socialist agenda, reminding Congress leaders of its 1931 Karachi resolution that called for state control of 'key industries and all the mineral resources of the country', adding that the policy 'should have found a specific place in the Directive Principles of State Policy'.[44]

Purnima appealed to the men in Parliament to treat women's rights with seriousness. She urged her fellow members to not take the matter up with 'lightness of spirit' as the women like 'the rest of India' were 'standing upon a new threshold of life'. She passionately added, 'As between the purdah-system and the new life which awaits the development of her personality, she is finding a new place in her home and her country and it is difficult enough.'[45]

Two months after her final Constituent Assembly speech, she led the chorus of the national anthem after its official adoption. Purnima died in 1951 following a bout of illness aged forty. Though her name is not well known today, Purnima Banerji's imprints are firmly etched on the Indian Constitution.

RAJKUMARI AMRIT KAUR

'The worst opponents of social reform are men who are steeped in ignorance, who have never felt where the shoe pinches and who glibly talk of religion and tradition being in jeopardy whenever any attempt is made to get rid of their domination over women.'

– In the pamphlet 'To Women', June 1945

Six kilometres from India's Parliament stands the country's premier medical institution – the All India Institute of Medical Sciences (AIIMS). Every year, over four million patients and their families pour into the outpatient departments at the hospital's Rajkumari Amrit Kaur Block. For a lifetime consultation charge of a mere ten rupees, these patients get access to some of India's finest doctors and healthcare facilities. Among the 'temples of modern India', AIIMS is one of the country's foremost success stories. AIIMS's establishment is owed to Jawaharlal Nehru's vision and the untiring efforts of India's first health minister, Rajkumari Amrit Kaur, a name that reverberates loudly across the hospital complex and inadequately in history books.

***

Born in a royal family, Rajkumari Amrit Kaur renounced a life of luxury and immersed with missionary zeal into the struggle for freedom as well as the upliftment of the oppressed. In the three decades of her public life, she championed the movement for women's rights, served as an aide to Mahatma Gandhi at the most crucial juncture of the freedom movement, and oversaw independent India's foundation of public health infrastructure.

Amrit Kaur was born on 2 February 1889,[1] to Raja Sir Harnam Singh of Kapurthala, a princely state in Punjab, and Priscilla Chatterjee, daughter of a Bengali missionary Golak Nath Chatterjee. Kapurthala state was founded in the eighteenth century by Sardar Jassa Singh Ahluwalia, a Sikh leader renowned for his bravery in the battles against raiding armies from Afghanistan. He was conferred with the title 'Sultan-ul-Qaum', or king of the Nation. Jassa Singh's descendants built upon his glorious legacy and despite some setbacks, Kapurthala prospered over time.[2]

In the 1845–46 Anglo-Sikh War, Kapurthala met with defeat against the British and suffered the loss of territory. Subsequently, it sided with the British in crushing the Revolt of 1857. In return, the colonizers rewarded the rulers with lands in the Awadh region.

At the time of the revolt, Harnam Singh, Amrit's father, was only six years old. Born in 1851, he studied at the American Presbyterian Mission School in Kapurthala. In 1872, he left for Jalandhar following a disagreement with his elder brother.[3] Among the many Christian missionaries settled in Jalandhar at the time was Golak Nath Chatterjee, a former Bengali Brahmin who was the first Indian 'to be ordained as a Presbyterian minister'.[4] In 1874, Harnam Singh, apparently under the influence of Golak Nath, converted to Christianity and married Golak Nath's daughter Priscilla a year later.[5]

Upon conversion, Harnam Singh renounced his right to the Kapurthala throne, and as one biographical sketch puts it, he 'literally gave up his earthly kingdom for the Heavenly'.[6] The British were sympathetic to his plight and appointed him manager of Awadh Estates, a remunerative posting.[7] The family then moved to Kapurthala Palace in Lucknow.

Amrit grew up in a large family with seven brothers and spent most of her childhood in Lucknow and Shimla. Unfortunately, two of her older sisters had died in their childhood, which made Amrit the only daughter. As the youngest, she was pampered by her brothers, who doted on her. She loved riding, trekking, and exploring the forests with them.[8]

Passionate about women's emancipation, Amrit's mother believed in the importance of formal education for them. Though Amrit was initially homeschooled, Priscilla's resolve helped her gain admission to Sherborne School for Girls in Dorsetshire, England. Amrit was only eight when, despite her father's reluctance, she was sent abroad.[9] Amrit's performance in academics and her many talents dazzled everyone at Sherborne. She was the head girl, a coveted position at school, and captained the hockey, tennis, and lacrosse teams. Amrit was particularly fond of tennis. She is said to have played at Wimbledon[10] and is regarded as one of 'the finest female tennis players in India'.[11] She had also been dubbed as a 'connoisseur of things, cultural and aesthetic', as she was fluent in Italian and French and could play the piano and the violin.[12]

After school, Amrit attended Oxford University. She wanted to pursue medicine, however, her parents did not allow her to do so. Determined, Amrit nevertheless sneaked into lectures and absorbed a great deal through just listening to the teachers. During her university days, she travelled extensively across Europe, soaking in the diverse cultures.[13] Around 1909–10, she returned to a country that was resonating with the demands of self-government.

While Amrit was in England, her father was knighted in 1898. Two years later, he became a member of the Legislative Council of Punjab. Then a few years later, in 1907, he was conferred with the title 'Raja', which enabled him to start a separate branch of the Ahluwalia dynasty.

Harnam Singh's close ties with the British notwithstanding, he was a supporter of the nationalist movement. As World War I raged across Europe, the demands for self-government for India grew stronger. A 'Post-War Reforms' memorandum submitted by Indian leaders sought dominion status for the country and greater representation for Indians in the different branches of administration and armed forces. Harnam Singh put his weight behind the demands, making an impassioned appeal in the memorandum for the self-government status. He said: 'If, after a century of that (British) rule, we were still considered unfit for full participation in the government of our country, surely it would be neither a creditable reflection on the British Government nor in keeping with the high traditions of an Empire which has always stood for freedom and the true rights of nations... India will not be satisfied unless she is henceforth treated equally with the Dominions.'[14]

Harnam Singh's nationalist fervour rubbed off on the young and impressionable Amrit. Stalwarts of the Congress would frequent their residence; in fact, Amrit described her house as 'the rendezvous of all the leading Congressmen of the day'.[15]

Amrit credited senior Congress leader Gopal Krishna Gokhale, who was among Harnam Singh's close friends, for fanning her 'passionate desire to see India free from foreign domination'. Gokhale gushed to Amrit about Gandhi, who had at the time recently returned from South Africa, calling him a man 'destined to do very great things for India'.[16]

Amrit finally met Gandhi when she attended her first Congress event, the 1915 Bombay Congress session. At the session, Gandhi spoke about the plight of Indians in South Africa. However, it was not his speech but his conduct that swayed the twenty-six-year-old Amrit, sowing the seeds of a lifelong friendship between them. Amrit believed that 'there was a quiet strength, an earnestness, and a deep humility about him'. That was something that touched her heart and made her feel that she 'owed allegiance to him and his way of life'.[17]

Amrit continued meeting Gandhi post the Bombay session. On a visit to their home in Jalandhar, he asked her to give up all her 'foreign finery' and take to wearing khadi clothes instead. Amrit, however, refused to burn her foreign clothes and found the transition to khadi difficult – she found the homespun fabric 'too coarse' for her 'fastidious tastes'. While she was keen on immersing herself in the growing freedom movement, the lifestyle changes were too daunting for her to adapt quickly. Instead, she sought to help by donating money[18] and, on Gandhi's suggestion, took to spinning. Even then, she could not bring herself to wear khadi.[19]

Amrit was captivated by Gandhi's idealism and requested him to let her join him at the Sabarmati Ashram in Ahmedabad. The prospect of a difficult life at the ashram did not intimidate her. For someone who found the transition to khadi challenging, she was ready to take a giant leap and renounce luxury. Gandhi asked her how her parents would feel about the shift to the frugal life of the ashram – this was at a time she had not been keeping well. When Amrit told him they would resent her for it, Gandhi said, 'You must not hurt them, and you can work for me in your own environment without necessarily joining my ashram.'[20] It was a decade later that she finally moved to the ashram.

Amrit's next years were devoted to pioneering India's rapidly expanding women's rights movement. In 1927, prominent Indian women came together to form the All India Women's Education and Social Conference (later renamed All India Women's Conference or AIWC) in Pune. AIWC's principal objective then was social and educational reforms. Amrit was a founding member of the conference and, in a short time, she rose to assume the leadership mantle – she was the chairwoman from 1931 to 1932. She took the nascent organization to unprecedented heights. Amrit was also actively involved with organizing the All-Asian Women's Conference (AAWC). Praising her efforts, Renuka Ray, her future Constituent Assembly colleague, shared, '...in some countries... more than one illustrious person had said that "Rajkumari was the AIWC and the AIWC was her"'.[21] Amrit was one of the most recognizable faces of the Indian feminist movement internationally.

In 1933, she was part of an AIWC delegation, alongside Ammu Swaminathan, another member of the Constituent Assembly, that made an official submission to the Council of the League of Nations, pointing to the 'lack of representation of Indian female opinion in the Council'.[22] This was the first time that representatives of the all-India women's movement were claiming an independent space for Indian women in an international setting.[23] The growing global outreach reflected 'desires for recognition of their worth on the international stage'.[24] AIWC's engagement with international institutions is credited with making space for 'non-Western women and their ideas' in these bodies.[25]

Back in India, women leaders had also been advocating expanding adult suffrage, which, at the time, was a privilege of only the educated and the landed. Very soon, the demand for suffrage brought with it the question of reservation for women.

In December 1931, the British formed the Indian Franchise Committee under the chairmanship of the Marquess of Lothian, popularly known as the 'Lothian Committee'. Its main objective was to propose revisions to 'frame a scheme for the franchise and the constituencies of the new legislatures, central and provincial, suitable for the system of responsible government'.[26] Along with her AIWC colleagues, Amrit placed before the Lothian Committee a memorandum that called for equal rights for all citizens, non-discrimination, adult suffrage and, most importantly, no reservation of seats for women.[27] The demand for no reservation was a contentious one and a corollary to the larger debate that had engulfed the political circles.

In 1928–29, the Congress had set up an All Parties Conference to prepare a draft Constitution under the chairmanship of Motilal Nehru; his son, Jawaharlal, was appointed secretary. This draft Constitution, popularly known as the 'Nehru Report', called for far-reaching reforms. It claimed dominion status for India, introduced fundamental rights for all citizens, and a 'parliamentary system along with universal adult suffrage'.[28]

The report had no provision for separate electorates, a demand championed by a section of the Muslim League. Under separate electorates, seats were reserved for a community and only members of the community could vote in the elections. Congress leaders had been opposing separate electorates on the premise that it would widen the communal gulf between Hindus and Muslims, the two major religious groups.

The Lothian Committee recommended expanding the franchise for Indians, removing several existing disqualifications. It specifically called for granting voting rights to a larger section of the women population, increasing the women's electorate twenty-one times, and the reservation for them in provincial councils from 2 to 5 per cent.[29]

However, the Committee did not make any recommendation on separate electorates, referred to as a 'communal decision' in the report, as it was beyond its scope. The Committee's enquiry was limited to compiling information on different groups vis-à-vis their enfranchisement and suggesting measures to ensure their adequate representation in legislatures. Lord Lothian addressed the question of separate electorates in an address given at Chatham House in London in June 1932, saying, 'provision will have to be made, unfortunately, for representation in a communal sense'.[30]

In August 1932, British Prime Minister Ramsay MacDonald announced the 'Communal Award'. The award ensured the continuance of separate electorates for Muslims, Sikhs, Europeans, Anglo-Indians, and Indian Christians. The British also announced the extension of separate electorates to the Depressed Classes, taking India by storm.

The Communal Award met with fierce opposition from Congress leaders. In September 1932, Gandhi went on a fast demanding its withdrawal. He feared that the Award was going to deepen divisions among the Hindus and weaken the national struggle. Dr B.R. Ambedkar had supported the Award but Gandhi's fast forced him to negotiate an alternate governance framework. Gandhi broke his fast with the signing of the Poona Pact, an agreement 'arrived at between leaders acting on behalf of the Depressed Classes and of the rest of the Community'. Under the Poona Pact, seats were reserved for Depressed Classes among general electorate seats.[31] Under reservation, all voters were eligible to vote but the candidates belonged to a particular group. However, in separate electorates, both voters and candidates belonged to the same group.

The storm raised by the Communal Award reached the AIWC. Amrit, who was a staunch supporter of Gandhi, strongly opposed the Award by moving the following resolution on 23 December 1932: 'This Conference stands united (i) in its protest against the Communal Award as stirring the womanhood of India, and (ii) in its demand for a system of joint electorate.'[32] Amrit said, 'There is no question as to the reality of unity amongst us women. We want to send our best women and our best men to the councils – therefore we do not want the canker of communalism amongst us. Once we are divided into sects and communities all will be lost.'[33]

Aruna Asaf Ali, a prominent Congress leader and sister of Purnima Banerji, seconded Amrit's resolution, proclaiming that the 'difference which separated men did not exist' among women. She went on to make a case against reservations for women in general. Ali said, 'We hate those things which separate people into compartments or parties. We want no unworthy or incapable woman to represent us, no matter what her rank in life may be. Her patriotism and individual merit are the only things to qualify her for public office. Each voter should have the right to vote for all candidates regardless of sect or race.'[34]

It has been argued that over time the AIWC had changed its position, to align itself with the nationalist movement. It had initially supported reservations but opposed them later 'due to the broader context of the nationalist movement'.[35] The Congress wanted to do away with separate electorates as it saw them as reinforcing communal and caste identities. While condemning reservations was easier for upper-caste leaders, it fuelled alienation among other minority members, especially the Muslim leaders in AIWC.

The AIWC resolution was met with opposition by some Muslim members who were concerned that without separate electorates, Muslim women were going to be at a disadvantage due to their 'comparative educational backwardness'. One member pointed out that 'desiring the good of one's community did not imply' wishing harm on others. But their objections were 'brushed aside as creating barriers' and 'artificial communal hedges'.[36] The resolution was passed with only four dissenting votes.[37] AIWC's position on the Communal Award drove a wedge between its members. Muslim women's approval of separate electorates was disregarded as 'numerically unimportant' and their dissent was repeatedly ignored.[38] The AIWC passed another resolution condemning the practice of untouchability and calling upon women to work towards its abolition.

In April 1933, Britain appointed a joint select committee of the House of Lords and the House of Commons 'to consider the future government of India'. The committee called on Indian representatives to join them. Amrit, Dr Muthulakshmi Reddi, and Begum Hamid Ali represented AIWC, the Women's Indian Association (WIA), and the National Council of Women in India (NCWI) at the committee meetings.

The meetings witnessed a brusque exchange between Amrit and Ambedkar when the latter posed questions on the issue of women's reservation. Amrit reiterated that AIWC had always opposed reservation. On being grilled on the same issue multiple times, Amrit impatiently replied, 'I have already answered this question, have I not?' When Ambedkar persisted with the question, Amrit chose different words, 'May I give you the answer again? We object to indirect election first of all, because naturally we want direct election.'[39]

Three days after being called as a witness, Amrit made a statement before the select committee. A large part of her statement focused on AIWC's demand for adult suffrage. She claimed that they (AIWC, WIA, and NCWI) represented the opinion 'of the womanhood of India as a whole'. On the issue of separate electorates, she said, 'We women, are, therefore, determined not to let this spirit of separation, so highly detrimental to our national interests, enter into our ranks. Surely it must be recognized by all fair-minded people that to force us – against our will into a room and tell us that the door is locked, is against all canons of justice.'[40]

At the meeting, Amrit contended that the Communal Award had ignored the demands of a major community – the community of women. She passionately argued, 'When the Secretary of State says that the Communal Award was forced on His Majesty's Government by all the communities in India, we would remind him, in all humility, that 47 per cent of the population of India were never a party to it and will never accept it. It is a matter of extreme regret to us that our earnest and united and repeated demands have not met with any success. We are forced to wonder if any attempt has ever been, or ever will be made, to meet us in a spirit of co-operation.'[41] Reddi and Hamid Ali concurred with the statement. Amrit's fashioning of her stand as a community leader was an attempt to present the women's movement as being united and as unaffected by the narrow confines of religious identities. In reality, the outright rejection of separate electorates had already divided opinion within AIWC.

The opposition to reservation continued through the next decade, reverberating in the Constituent Assembly debates. During one of the debates on representation in legislative assemblies, Renuka Ray mentioned the opposition to reservation for women. 'Our [AIWC] representatives, the three women who gave evidence before the Joint Parliamentary Committee, made it clear in unequivocal terms – [I may say that Rajkumari Amrit Kaur was one of the three women] – that we did not want reservation, but in spite of our protests, and in direct contravention to our desires, reservation of seats was brought into the 1935 Act. This Act has been so great a factor in bringing dissensions in our fold and has at last divided the country.'[42]

Amrit emerged as one of the foremost voices of the women's movement. In an article published in the *Modern Review* (April 1933), she elucidated the problems faced by the women in India – such as insufficient educational facilities, the customs holding up reforms – calling for a change in outlook on how women are treated. 'The proper status of women in modern societies must, therefore, be discussed and settled in the light not of history, but of ethics,' she wrote. She also talked about how a democratic society is one 'based on respect for the fundamental fact of human personality'.

In April 1934, the *Modern Review* carried another piece by Amrit, in which she wrote on 'The Responsibilities of Women as Citizens of India'. The article gave a window into her ideology. She tried to harmonize rights, religion, and spirituality, an interesting attempt, considering religious practices were in conflict with the larger social welfare agenda in several instances. 'The women of India must see to it that our State is a great moral agency. We must, at all costs, stand by principles for principles alone are constructive and ideals are never translated into facts without faith. Great things are never achieved except by "the rejection of individualism and a constant sacrifice of self to the common progress"'.

'If, therefore, we want to become citizens in the fullest sense of the term we have got to give the highest place to the moral and spiritual values of life without which all material *gain* or political freedom is mere dross.'

The increased bent towards spirituality could be attributed to her life at the Sabarmati Ashram. Amrit had previously requested Gandhi to let her join him at his ashram, which he declined, citing her parents' displeasure. After losing her father in 1930, Amrit settled her family affairs and took up active work with Gandhi. She initially worked to organize a spinner's association in Jalandhar. A few years later, in 1934, she joined him at Sevagram,

Maharashtra, where Gandhi had established his base after shifting from Sabarmati in Gujarat.

Life in the ashram was a challenge but this time Amrit was prepared. Gandhi was empathetic towards her, ensuring that she was not unduly burdened by the vagaries of an austere life. Amrit would go on to share, 'He [Gandhi] would not allow me at first to sleep on the ground. I was not made even to wash up my own plates.'[43]

Dr Sushila Nayar, Amrit's contemporary and successor as health minister, wrote of the remarkable change the princess went through in the 1930s. 'I used to see her there sitting near Bapu dressed in fine silks and wearing long earrings as also other beautiful jewellery. All this changed when she came to live in the Ashram. I never spoke to her in those early days. She was a princess, too high for an ordinary student.' She went on to describe Amrit's transformation: 'Under Gandhiji's influence Rajkumari Amrit Kaur took to khadi. She sat on the floor and ate at the Ashram.'[44] Aruna Asaf Ali attested to the change the princess underwent: 'Though Rajkumari was a princess belonging to the feudal aristocracy of those days, she became a disciple of Gandhiji and decided to live the austere life of his ashrams.'[45]

Amrit served as Gandhi's English language secretary, travelling with him often. He was quite a hard taskmaster. Once, when an important matter slipped Amrit's mind, Gandhi wrote to her that 'an ideal secretary keeps her chief straight where he is going astray. She hovers round him and watches all the movements about him, picks up his papers even torn – lest he might have torn important ones in mistake, collects all she had given him if it is to be found anywhere. Therefore she leaves after him and seeks what he has left behind and, if not owned by anybody else, collects it.'[46] But, despite the occasional admonition, it was clear that Gandhi relied on her. He sent her as his representative to negotiate with the Dewan of Travancore.[47] The Travancore State Congress (TSC) office bearers, including activist and politician

Annie Mascarene, had been demanding the removal of the Dewan. Gandhi was keen on avoiding any friction between TSC and the state government.

In 1938, Amrit undertook a tour in Gujarat's Kathiawar region, spreading the word against untouchability and impressing upon people the need to adopt khadi.[48]

Amrit was devoted to Gandhian ideals with religious ferocity. In an article on Gandhi, she alludes to what she considered his Christ-like habits: 'I am again and again reminded, in his dealings with human beings, of the great prophet of Nazareth, who came not to be ministered unto but to minister.'[49] Gandhi, on his part, was deeply affectionate towards her. Their letters revealed a close friendship. He jokingly called her 'rebel', 'my dear idiot', and often signed off as 'robber' or 'tyrant', and once 'Robber, Tyrant, and Co'.

Amrit was equally committed to the Congress, but she did not shy away from expressing disapproval over the party's decisions. Aruna Asaf Ali, writing for a book dedicated to Amrit, narrated an incident when Amrit criticized Jawaharlal Nehru over the absence of women in the Congress Working Committee (CWC), constituted in April 1936. Amrit was keen on taking up the matter officially. She was 'suggesting a communication to him (Jawaharlal) from the AIWC "deploring the fact that a woman has not been appointed a member of the Working Committee"'.[50] In December 1936, the old committee was renominated, with the addition of Sarojini Naidu as a member.[51]

Amrit was rightly incensed at the lack of women in the highest decision-making body of the party. The Congresswomen had been at the forefront of the freedom struggle, many of them had even faced imprisonment. Amrit herself faced jail time. She was first arrested in Bombay (now Mumbai) for taking part in the Salt Satyagraha in 1930.

Different profiles of her suggest that Amrit was even imprisoned and convicted for sedition in 1937 for advocating Congress's cause in Bannu, in erstwhile North-West Frontier

Province (NWFP).[52] Undeterred by the conviction on sedition charges, Amrit continued raising her voice against British atrocities in NWFP – for instance, the bombing of tribespeople by the Royal Air Force in Waziristan. In her presidential address at the AIWC in December 1937, Amrit remarked, 'With what voice can we raise a protest against the Italian conquest of Abyssinia or Japanese ruthless aggression in China if we cannot condemn the bombing of villages on the North West Frontier or speak out against imperialistic designs wheresoever they be?'[53]

A descendant of Sardar Jassa Singh Ahluwalia, the famed warrior who staved off Afghan aggression during his time decades ago, Amrit's open support of the tribespeople from the Frontiers is an interesting turning point in history. Somehow, the ruthless British rule and its secular oppression against South Asians played a significant role in building ties among formerly warring people.

Amrit was at the forefront of the Quit India Movement too, leading processions in Shimla. She even sustained injuries after the police lathi-charged the protestors in one procession. Amrit was later arrested and kept in solitary confinement for eight weeks. The hardship took a toll on her health and she was placed under house arrest at her residence. Her sufferings were not just physical. While captive, Amrit lost one of her brothers, and to make matters worse, the authorities refused her permission to write to her sister-in-law to offer condolences.[54]

The indefatigable women's rights champion chose to write something else instead. Amrit used her time under house arrest to pen a detailed pamphlet on women in India. Titled 'To Women', it called upon women living in towns to take to villages and devote their time to social welfare. A keen advocate for indigenous industries, she urged parents to involve their daughters as well as sons in handicrafts. The future health minister even touched upon the importance of medical aid and education in the pamphlet. She even talked about how men hampered social reform by citing tradition. Amrit penned:

'Our men need to be educated just as much if not more. The worst opponents of social reform are men who are steeped in ignorance, who have never felt where the shoe pinches and who glibly talk of religion and tradition being in jeopardy whenever any attempt is made to get rid of their domination over women.'

Amrit was also unsparing of men keen on aping British lifestyle. 'I should also like to express my sorrow at the lack of pride in our men in their national dress. I know Indian men resent strongly the adoption by us women of European dress even when this is mainly for sport. But why do they go in for it themselves?' She pointed out the blatant hypocrisy of the men, who were dressed in 'ill-fitting European clothes' and spoke 'broken English' and urged the women to try their best 'to influence them in the right direction.'[55]

In 1946, Britain announced the creation of an interim government of India to help India (and Pakistan) transition from British control to independence. Amrit's name was included in the proposed list of ministers but was turned down by the Viceroy, Lord Mountbatten. The Viceroy recommended replacing Amrit with a Hindu member.[56]

Her status was soon to change. In 1947, Nehru invited her to be part of independent India's first Cabinet, where she took charge as minister of health. Amrit was the only woman in the Cabinet. Gandhi wrote to her the day after she assumed charge. 'So you are a Minister. You have to be firm and true… You should insist on teamwork. Then most things will come under your notice.' Two weeks later, he cheekily wrote to her, 'Are you in charge of physical health only or moral also? The latter seems to be worse than the former.'[57]

Amrit was elected to the Constituent Assembly from the Central Provinces and Berar. In January 1947, she was nominated to the fifty-member Advisory Committee – Amrit and Hansa Mehta were the only women on the committee, later joined by Begum Qudsia Aizaz Rasul. Amrit was also nominated to the sub-committees on fundamental rights (alongside Mehta) and minorities.

Indian society was rife with caste, communal, and class barriers. The Indian freedom movement encompassed within its fold various social reforms agenda. The Constitution makers were aware that the task before them went beyond preparing a charter of government. In fact, they had to prepare a charter of government that would help in achieving the progressive goals of justice, liberty, and equality.

It was clear that the Constitution would guarantee equality between people as a fundamental right. The framers added another clause that expressly prohibited the State from discriminating against any citizen – the present Article 15. They went a step further and assured citizens of free access to public places such as shops, restaurants, hotels and the use of wells, tanks, as well as roads [Article 15(2)]. For the countless citizens who had been turned away from shops, denied access to water in public wells, and forced to walk on unpaved paths, a constitutional guarantee of non-discrimination was a small, but significant, step in the battle for dignity. Fundamental rights are usually guaranteed against state policies. In extending them to the private sphere, the framers were breaking new ground.

During a discussion on Article 15, Amrit joined other members to highlight the need for positive discrimination. The members suggested that 'what was required was a general statement of principle prohibiting discrimination and at the same time a clause to enable the provision of separate amenities exclusively for women and children'.[58] This took shape in Article 15(3), which reads 'Nothing in this article shall prevent the State from making any special provision for women and children'.

At the Sub-Committee on Fundamental Rights meetings, Amrit joined forces with Mehta, her long-time AIWC colleague, to espouse women's rights causes.

In its draft report, the sub-committee suggested an expansive right to religion. The draft clause read: 'All persons are equally entitled to freedom of conscience and the right freely to profess and practise religion subject to public order, morality or health and to the other provisions of this chapter.' Amrit and Mehta disagreed with the broad scope of the right to religion. They were concerned that this might come in the way of social reforms. They wrote to B.N. Rau, the Assembly's Constitutional Advisor: '... As we are all aware there are several customs practised in the name of religion e.g., purdah, child marriage, polygamy, unequal laws of inheritance, prevention of inter-caste marriages, dedication of girls to temples. We are naturally anxious that no clause in fundamental rights shall make impossible future legislation for the purpose of wiping out these evils. As worded, Clause 16 may even contradict or conflict with the provision abolishing the practice of untouchability... Indeed we have a further fear that validity of existing laws such as the Sarda Act, and the Widow Remarriage Act may even be questioned.'[59] Their opposition paved the way for a watered-down right to religion that emphasized 'public order, morality, and health' and empowered the government to enact laws for social welfare (Article 25).

In their letter, Amrit and Mehta also suggested making the directive principles of state policy 'justiciable'.[60] They were particularly interested in ensuring a Uniform Civil Code (UCC). A UCC would subsume all personal laws regarding marriage, divorce, guardianship, and other civil relations, and replace them with one secular law. At the sub-committee meeting, they supported a proposal moved by Minoo Masani, another member of the Constituent Assembly, to incorporate UCC as a fundamental right. Unfortunately, the proposal was rejected.

They also supported Masani's other proposal that read: 'no impediments to marriages between citizens shall be based merely upon difference of religion'. This proposal was also rejected. The minutes of their dissent read: 'one of the factors that has kept India back from advancing to nationhood has been the existence of personal laws based on religion which keep the nation divided into watertight compartments in many aspects of life. We are of the view that a uniform civil code should be guaranteed to the Indian people within a period of 5 or 10 years.' Determined to remove barriers to inter-religious marriages, they pointed out how inter-religious couples had to renounce religion to solemnize a marriage under the Special Marriage Act 1872.[61] This Act was finally replaced in 1954 with legislation that allowed marriages without the parties giving up their religion.

Article 23 of the Indian Constitution prohibits human trafficking and forced labour. It, however, contains an exception clause empowering the government to impose compulsory service for public purposes. Amrit and Mehta vehemently opposed the inclusion of compulsory service as going against democratic norms. They said, '(we) would point to the danger of giving to the State powers of compulsion in any sphere of life. We would instead suggest the creation of paid social service in both the Centre and the units for the spread of education and other nation-building activities.'[62]

At the minorities sub-committee meetings, Amrit argued against giving special privileges to minorities. In a memorandum to the committee, Amrit said, 'Privileges and safeguards really weaken those that demand them.' She complimented women for refusing to demand any special privileges, and once again made the case to view women as one community. 'Women may be said technically to be the largest single minority in India. Not only have custom and usage dealt harshly with us, but even the law has militated and still continues to militate against us.' Amrit urged the minorities to trust in the 'goodwill of the majority and its own inherent moral strength', arguing that there was 'no reason why the interests of any individual or community should not be safe in the hands of a good person or persons, irrespective of their personal religion.' She said it was up to the majority to inspire confidence in the minorities,[63] a view echoed by Qudsia in the Assembly debates.

The sub-committee decided against continuing with separate electorates. However, it favoured the reservation of seats for minorities. The Indian Christians accepted reservations proportionate to their population. Amrit, a Christian by faith, dissented. She called special privileges in the name of religion 'doubly wrong' and going against the ideals of creating a classless society.[64] Eventually, the Constituent Assembly decided against minority reservations and limited reservations to the scheduled castes and tribes.

While Amrit could not actively participate in the Constituent Assembly debates due to her schedule as health minister, she was a pillar of strength for other women in the body. Reminiscing on their time, Renuka Ray wrote, 'During those days, the fourteen *(sic)* women who were members of the Constituent Assembly met very often together and it was under her guidance that we were able to put up a united and concrete stand in regard to Women's rights. I remember how disappointed the women were, as also Dr Ambedkar, the chairman, when it was finally decided that the UCC for the citizens should be placed in the Directive Principles of State Policy under Part IV.'[65]

Amrit had taken charge of the health ministry at a time when the health infrastructure was in shambles. The challenge before her was to lay the foundation of a robust healthcare network to meet the needs of a burgeoning population. She piloted several remarkable programmes against 'malaria, leprosy, and other venereal diseases'.[66]

One of her lasting contributions was piloting the Bill to establish AIIMS. One key objective behind setting it up was to attain self-sufficiency in the field of medical education.[67] Introducing the Bill in the Rajya Sabha, Amrit spoke of what she hoped to achieve: '… right up to this time – we have had to depend on scholarships, whether governmental or from abroad such as the Rockefeller Foundation is good enough to give us, to send a few chosen representatives of the medical profession to outside countries to get their postgraduate studies in the various limbs of the medical profession. I have always felt that it would be ever so much better for us if we could give the same knowledge, as these young men and women acquire by going abroad, in our own country… As I have often said, it has been one of my cherished dreams that an institute of this nature should come into being and that through it we may be able to serve our own people better, especially the people who live in our villages.'[68]

Setting up a world-class institute, however, required more than legislation. To do so, Amrit leveraged her personal connections with global leaders to secure finances and technology. The effects started showing very early. Between 1950–51 and 1955–56, the number of medical institutions increased by 16 per cent and the number of medical colleges and annual admissions by 40 per cent.[69] India also witnessed a sharp fall in the death rate (by 14 per cent) and a rise in life expectancy (between 1950 and 1957).[70] People's lives were changing for the better because of improved services.

Amrit's achievements as health minister were chequered by her views on family planning. She and Dr Sushila Nayar were accused of waging 'a rear-guard action against birth control'.[71] Amrit was an admirer of Gandhi, who was against the use of 'mechanical' birth control methods. It seemed that the Gandhian influence was too much to shake off. In a speech in Lok Sabha, Amrit made convoluted arguments against birth control, claiming that the government could do little. 'I agree with the woman member who said that there are lots of women who are anxious to have a certain amount of control because they have borne too many children. Well, as I have said, the God-given means of birth control are within the reach of each one of us. Why don't we use them?'[72] Such aversion to encouraging scientific methods contributed to the population boom in the following years.

Amrit was respected across the world and represented India at many international forums. In 1945 and 1946, she was the deputy leader of the United Nations Educational, Scientific and Cultural Organization (UNESCO).[73] She also represented India at the World Health Assembly as well as the International Red Cross Assembly.[74]

Amrit's keen interest in sports did not fade away in her later years. She was the founder and president of the National Sports

Club of India, chairperson of the National Institute of Sports, and even founder member of the Rajkumari Sports Coaching Scheme. Her love for tennis saw her helming the All India Tennis Association.[75]

After ten years as health minister, Amrit was dropped from the Cabinet in 1957. She, however, continued to be in Parliament as a Rajya Sabha member till her death.

Amrit passed away on 6 February 1964. She was cremated as per Sikh customs even though she practised Christianity.[76] The princess was the epitome of sacrifice for higher ideals. She renounced luxury and devoted herself to first the freedom struggle and then nation-building. Amrit touched countless lives and left her country a far better place than she inherited.

Writing in 1941, Margaret Cousins, founder of the WIA and a mentor to several women leaders, summed up Amrit's life with the following: 'She always dresses in pure khadi, eats the simplest vegetarian fare, loves flowers, and at her homes in Jullunder and Simla cultivates the loveliest blooms. Yet she could leave all and go on long, hard tours with Gandhiji, for spiritual nourishment and universal unity are her deepest concern. She reminds one of old-time Spanish saints, the ones worn almost to a shadow, with her long narrow face and her large dark eyes full of feeling. She never spares herself in her work for others. She lives only to serve.'[77]

RENUKA RAY

'A Constitution is but a paper document. It is the way in which it is worked that will determine its success or its failure. We are the framers of this Constitution and in our humble way, as a compromise amongst so many, we have done the best that we could have perhaps, although we must consider that there are many flaws left.'

– On the future of the Constitution in the Constituent Assembly on 19 November 1949[1]

Renuka Ray was born to privilege and was able to access the best educational institutes in the world. As a child of an illustrious family in Bengal, she inherited a front-row seat to both the reformist and the resistance movements. Very early on in life, Renuka developed a desire to be of service to the public and fight against injustice. But to do so, she had to walk the tightrope of choosing between violence and non-violence at different junctures in her life.

★★★

Renuka was born on 4 January 1904 to Satish Chandra Mukerjee and Charulata Mukerjee in Pabna (in present-day Bangladesh).[2] She was the oldest of four children. Her family was highly educated, and committed to social reform. Her father had secured a high rank in the Indian Civil Services (ICS) examination.[3] Renuka's mother, Charulata, was one of the first two women students at Calcutta's Presidency College in 1897.[4] Charulata later ran various schools and *mahila samitis* to educate girls and women.[5] She was also good friends with poet and activist Sarojini Naidu. She was a lifetime member of the All India Women's Conference (AIWC).

Renuka's paternal grandparents joined the Brahmo Samaj, a Hindu reform movement. They then proceeded to settle in Bhagalpur in modern-day Bihar, far away from the disapproving gaze of their orthodox Brahmin family and relatives.[6]

Renuka's maternal grandfather, Dr P.K. Roy, had an impeccable academic career. He graduated in psychology from the University of Edinburgh and received a doctorate degree from the University of London.[7] He went on to teach logic and philosophy at Presidency College in Calcutta (now Kolkata) from 1876.[8] In 1902, he became the first Indian to be appointed principal of the institute.[9] His wife, Sarala Roy, was focused on working on girls' education and founded several schools before becoming the president of the AIWC in 1932.[10] The Roy household was a hub where all the generation's best minds gathered together. Rabindranath Tagore, one of the regulars at the buzzing Roy household, is known to have dedicated his dance drama, *Mayar Khela*, to Sarala.[11]

In 1911, Charulata's father was appointed the academic counsellor at the High Commission in London. Renuka's family moved to London for two years, where the six-year-old Renuka attended Kensington High School.[12]

Upon returning to Bengal, Renuka became a resident scholar at Calcutta's Loreto House school.[13] The family would often spend Durga Puja holidays with the Mukerjees in Bhagalpur and Christmas with the Roys in Calcutta.[14]

A meeting with Gandhi at her relative's house, when he was in Calcutta to declare the launch of the Non-Cooperation Movement in September 1920, changed the college-going Renuka's life. Inspired by Gandhi, she and a friend, Lalita, quit college to join the freedom struggle.[15] Gandhi asked them to go door-to-door and raise awareness and funds for the movement. He also urged the teenagers to spin the *charkha* and learn Hindi.[16]

Renuka found the house visits 'interesting and varied'. These visits helped her gain a deeper understanding of the subjugation of women. Renuka captured the experience in her writings: 'In those days the women of orthodox affluent families lived in the *andar mahal* (inner court) and we could reach them only after getting consent from the men who were their guardians.' Renuka added, 'Sometimes the women would come to us through the bylane and ask us to return at specific times when the men were absent. Most of the women were responsive and donated their jewellery if they did not have enough cash with them.'[17] Renuka also helped organize various meetings where Gandhi addressed these women. She witnessed the potential and power of such gatherings. To help her figure out her career plans, Renuka decided to stay in Sabarmati,[18] and accompanied Gandhi on his way back to the ashram from Bengal.

Renuka found life in Sabarmati 'interesting and absorbing'. She fit in quite well into the new atmosphere and 'did not mind in the least the chores'.[19] For a girl of privilege, living an austere life in the ashram would have been a different world altogether.

Later that year, she went to Calcutta on a short visit. The plan was to return with Gandhi who was supposed to pick her up from Calcutta after his tour of Bihar. However, unknown to her, her father and Gandhi had a secret meeting in December 1920 and decided to send her to London to pursue higher education. Renuka was furious and protested against it. Gandhi intervened and explained the importance of getting an education in a 'free atmosphere' to an infuriated Renuka, and hoped she would, 'without becoming an anglicized girl,... take full advantage of the education and come back well equipped to serve [her] country with courage and an independent outlook!'[20]

In August 1921, despite her reluctance, she sailed to London with her family and secured admission in the elite Girton College,

University of Cambridge. But the idea of entering an aristocratic institution didn't appeal to Renuka. So she instead enrolled into the London School of Economics and Political Science (LSE).[21]

While in the UK, Renuka met and fell in love with Satyendra Nath Ray, a student at King's College. Though only a year older than her, Satyen was, according to Renuka, 'more mature. He provided a balance to [her] impulsive actions.'[22]

One important instance of Satyen's positive influence on Renuka occurred while the two were still in London. Renuka was urged by a cousin, who was a member of an underground armed revolutionary group, to join the revolutionaries. He even lent her a revolver and invited her to join him at the shooting range for target practice. While Renuka was sure of her goal to fight against the British, she was conflicted on the path to adopt. Growing up in the post-partition Bengal of 1905, she admired the extremist approach seeing the rise of revolutionary groups. But her family believed in fighting 'through constitutional methods'.[23] While she mulled over the suggestion of her cousin, Satyen spotted the revolver in her purse and was thunderstruck.[24] This prompted Renuka to realize that this was not the path she wanted to adopt.

Coincidentally, she also received a letter from Gandhi the very evening the gun was discovered. She credited the letter for making her realize how far she 'had deviated from the purpose and objectives' that she had sworn allegiance to before she had left India. It was a wake-up call that shaped her future. She soon returned the weapon and refused her cousin's invitation. 'It was lucky that I did so,' she later wrote in her memoir, 'because I learned much later that had I joined and then wanted to leave the only answer of the terrorists would be to shoot the defector.'[25]

Meanwhile, her education at LSE sharpened her progressive and socialist ideas.[26] In college, she attended lectures of eminent thinkers such as Prof. Harold Laski, political theorist and economist, Graham Wallas, social psychologist and educationalist,

Clement Attlee, who later became prime minister of the United Kingdom, as well as Welsh politician Hugh Dalton.[27]

In her second year, Renuka was elected to the student union. She was the only woman and only Indian in the body. It was around this time that she made acquaintance with many Indians who would go on to carve a name for themselves in the Indian freedom movement, including Krishna Menon, Subhas Chandra Bose, and Biren Chattopadhyaya.

Between her classes and political activism, Renuka had little time for anything else. Satyen pushed her to keep up with her studies. When Satyen cleared the ICS examinations, Renuka became concerned about losing her freedom after marriage to a civil servant. Nevertheless the two got engaged, once Satyen had assured her that she would be able to 'carry out [her] interests and that when he joined the covenanted service, he would not allow it to hamper [her] activities'.[28]

Renuka returned to India in August 1925. Gandhi was in Calcutta at the time. Renuka was embarrassed to reach out to him because she had not informed him about her engagement to Satyen.[29] But on finding out about the two, Gandhi sent for the young couple to visit him. Satyen and Gandhi had an interesting conversation:

Gandhi: I suppose you are aware of what you are going in for by deciding to marry Renuka, whose first priority will remain service to the country.

Satyen: I have overcome her hesitancy by assuring her that my career will not be allowed to interfere with her activities. As for me, I believe firmly that women have as much right as men to work according to their inclination and aptitude. There will no doubt be difficulties at times but I feel sure that we both have the strength and the courage to overcome them.

The young man's confidence impressed Gandhi. Later on, Gandhi joked, 'I shall try to make it not too hard for both of you and depute Renuka for such work that it will be possible for you to remain together as much as possible.' With Gandhi's blessings, the couple tied the knot on 26 October 1925.[30]

Satyen and Renuka had two children – a son, Rathindra, and a daughter, Ranjana.[31] Satyen's posting at Bankura district in Bengal – an area with a high tribal population – gave Renuka an opportunity 'to have first-hand experience and understanding of the basic structure of rural life in India'.[32] Renuka started working for women's welfare in Burdwan and Hooghly. She set up a few *mahila samiti*s that focused on maternity and child welfare, children's education, as well as crèches for working mothers.[33] While advocating for women's rights, she often faced opposition – even from women themselves.

One such incident was from the Women's Social Conference in 1928. It was Renuka's first time attending a national forum on women's rights.[34] Renuka and a few others advocated for the enforcement of monogamy and the rights to divorce and inheritance for women. Though the resolutions were passed with a huge majority, they faced stiff opposition from some of the attendees. Renuka was surprised that one of them was her grandaunt Lady Abala Bose, the first president of Bengal Women's Education League,[35] who had been advocating for women's equality and suffrage for decades.[36] It was now clear to Renuka that the feminists were divided on some of their demands.

At the same forum, a woman from the Brahmo Samaj attacked Renuka for demanding the right to divorce. 'You have only been married two or three years and you are already wanting a divorce!' she charged at Renuka. Renuka retorted, 'As Brahmos marry under the Special Marriage Act, you and I are already entitled to divorce and we have other necessary rights. It is for the vast majority of women in India that we want these rights so that if they need the help of the law they too will have equal treatment with men.'[37] Such incidents helped Renuka understand the division between the moderate and radical schools of feminism. She realized that the battle was between conservative and liberal ideas.

Renuka was always looking for ways to challenge the status quo when it came to women's rights. She also had an astute political sense. One example of this was when noted activist Margaret Sanger came to India to advocate for birth control. Renuka took it as an opportunity to spread awareness about family planning in Calcutta. She and her friends organized various meetings, braving media criticism for talking about such subjects in public.[38]

In 1930, Renuka attended her first annual session of the AIWC. The women at the Conference inspired her and she became deeply involved in its activities.[39] In later years, Renuka would set up various district chapters of AIWC in Bengal.

At the time, the AIWC was disappointed with the Sarda Act, which fixed the marriageable age of girls at 14 instead of 16, which was the demand of women's organizations. In 1934, it asked the government to set up a commission to reform the laws. As the social secretary of the AIWC, Renuka published a report listing out the various ways women faced subjugation based on religious laws – both Hindu and Islamic laws – and urged the British government to intervene. She wrote: 'Law can no longer remain static in a dynamic society. It is the duty of the State to adjust and suit the laws of a country to the requirements of the times.'[40] Renuka highlighted the importance of a uniform civil code to remove the legal disabilities of women in terms of their property rights, rights of widows, divorce, guardianship, and child marriage.[41] The issue of gender inequalities in the various personal laws of the country and the question of a uniform civil code remain hotly debated to this day.

In 1935, the Ray family decided to take a break from work and travel around the world. Renuka, Satyen, and seven-year-old Rathi went to Japan, China, the USA, and Britain – places where Renuka managed to address AIWC conferences – as well as touring Singapore, Malaysia, and Hong Kong.[42] She also met eminent personalities such as Chinese politician Madame Sun Yat Sen in Shanghai, actor Clark Gable in Hollywood,[43] and Indian journalist Syud Hossain in California.

The following year, Gandhi asked Renuka to focus on developing village industries that would benefit the rural population.[44] She developed plans to teach spinning and other useful handicrafts, besides encouraging good hygiene practices, cleaning ditches, and repairing pathways. Renuka got down to the job in all earnest and sent fortnightly reports to Gandhi. She also accompanied him on some of his anti-caste *padayatras*.[45]

Tagore was another influential figure in her life.[46] Satyen, too, was close to Tagore since childhood. In 1939, Tagore nominated her to the Karma Samiti (Executive Council) of the Visva Bharti University. Renuka credited both Gandhi and Tagore in helping her understand the needs of rural India.[47]

Despite her other engagements, Renuka remained committed to the women's movement. The latter half of the 1930s saw an increased demand for a uniform civil code to remove the legal disabilities of women. Renuka had earlier written about the need to reform personal laws. The enactment of the Hindu Women's Right to Property Act – also known as the Deshmukh Act – in 1937 was a watershed moment in the women's movement. The Act, though reformist, had flaws. It granted widows the right to the husband's property but without absolute ownership.[48] The Act also ignored the rights of the daughter in her father's property. Many women's organizations led by the AIWC took to the streets to protest the government's tokenistic attitude towards their demands.[49]

Renuka and some of her women colleagues turned to Gandhi for advice. He told them that the law is only one element, and that '…while he was all in favour of equality for women and the law should be altered, what was needed was the transformation of social attitudes'.[40]

The women's organizations devised a two-fold plan: they would spread awareness and gather public support, and then get the legislature to pass a truly progressive bill. To facilitate this, meetings and processions were held across the country. In

Calcutta, Renuka and her team received a tremendous response from the public;[51] both men and women joined in large numbers to support the legal reforms. However, there were also many men and women who opposed the reforms.[52]

Finally, in 1941, the government formed the Hindu Law Committee to review existing laws and appointed Sir B.N. Rau, a civil servant and jurist, as chairman.[53] The AIWC requested and was granted the right to nominate a member to the Central Legislative Assembly to help in the codification of the new laws.[54]

Rau chose Renuka to represent the women's organizations in the Central Legislative Assembly.[55] Initially, Renuka was reluctant to take on the role – she did not want to work with a government that was imprisoning her friends and fellow Indians during the Quit India Movement. Renuka herself was under threat of arrest many times during the movement. However, Rau reminded her of the women's cause and how unfair it would be to the people who had worked hard to get women a seat at the table, and in February 1943 Renuka became a member of the Central Legislative Assembly.[56]

On 23 March 1943, the Hindu Law Bills on Marriage and Intestate Succession were introduced in the Central Legislative Assembly.[57] The visitors' gallery was packed with women from across the country.

To the surprise of the British officials who had nominated her to the legislature, Renuka used this momentous occasion to argue for Indian independence from British rule. She insisted that the Bills being considered were mere 'half measures' and that only a 'free national government… answerable to the people would be able to bring in radical changes by which complete equality could be secured'. Her empowering speech donned the newspaper headlines the next morning.[58]

The Bill was opposed heavily by some of the members and was then referred to a Select Committee. Renuka took her seat at the table very seriously but there was only one other woman in the entire Assembly, and Renuka was 'overcome by shyness and embarrassment [because] the legislature and its lobby was overwhelmingly masculine.'[59]

However, Renuka managed to make her own place in the House and under no circumstance did she lose her spine or voice. In one instance during the Assembly's 1944 Budget session the government was one vote short to get the Budget passed. Some members of the Assembly assumed it would be easier to convince Renuka to vote for them, as she was the wife of a civil servant. When they saw that she wasn't agreeing, seniors and colleagues of her husband threatened her husband's career if she didn't comply. Renuka, however, was undaunted. She called up her husband and told him she was prepared to resign if she was putting him in an inconvenient position, but she 'could not vote with the government'. Satyen was unperturbed, humorously suggesting Renuka ask them whether she was 'nominated as [her] husband's representative, or as the representative of the AIWC'.[60] The government's machinations failed and they lost the vote.

When Renuka's term was over in 1946, she wasn't nominated again.

Other than political activities, Renuka was deeply involved in humanitarian causes. Renuka was the first member of the Central Legislative Assembly to rush to Bengal during the famine in 1943 and arranged 'a large amount of voluntary donations of food'.[61] Renuka was involved in the relief and rehabilitations committee of the Congress after the communal riots in the aftermath of Direct Action Day.[62] Both communities were devastatingly affected, she revealed: 'In certain parts of north Calcutta we used to rescue Muslims from the Hindu areas and vice versa and reach them to safety in hospital vans and ambulances meant for the wounded.'[63] She also accompanied Gandhi for relief work in the riot-affected areas of Noakhali (in present-day Bangladesh).[64]

Around the same time, in 1946, Renuka was elected to the Constituent Assembly on Gandhi's insistence that marginalized groups including women should be represented.

Yet again, she did justice to her seat at the table by participating in numerous debates, ranging from religious education, the Hindu Code Bill, the Devadasi system, and right to property. She also spoke against reservation for women in Assemblies and Parliament. Ironically, both her nomination to the Central Legislative Assembly as well as to the Constituent Assembly was on the basis of gender.

Renuka's opposition to women's reservation was because she considered reservation to be 'an impediment to our growth and an insult to our very intelligence and capacity'.[65] Her belief was grounded in the notion that reservation would limit women's representation to only reserved seats, and they would lose out on being considered for non-reserved seats. She also said, 'When there is reservation of seats for women, the question of their consideration for general seats, however competent they may be, does not usually arise. We feel that women will get more chances in the future to come forward and work in the free India, if the consideration is of ability alone.'[66]

Renuka was also against reservation for minorities, and believed it was 'not self-respecting for them'.[67]

Renuka was vocal against the inclusion of the right to property in the fundamental rights, and felt that 'this was not in line with the progressive ideas and the needs of [the] time'. Further, she felt that this would give the courts the power to determine the compensation of the estates acquired by the State.[68] She moved an amendment but it failed to get enough votes.[69] Eventually, in 1978, through the 44th Constitutional Amendment, the right to property was removed from the fundamental rights and turned into Article 300-A, a legal right.[70]

Another crucial amendment that Renuka moved was against the bicameral nature of the legislature. She found the concept of two legislative bodies in the state to be 'retrograde'.[71] Countering the popular rationale of the second chamber acting as a body of checks and balances, Renuka declared in the Constituent Assembly, 'when there is a Governor, in the Province and a President at the Centre, who is empowered to send back to the legislature any Bills which may have been enacted carelessly, for revision, I do not think that this excuse obtains.'[72]

However, the Constituent Assembly went ahead with the bicameral structure.[73] Not happy with the result, Renuka brought in an amendment to empower the state assemblies to abolish the second chamber.[74] It was successful.

Given her decades of work to uplift women, Renuka was extremely disappointed by the delays in passing of the Hindu Code Bill. As the term of the Provisional Parliament neared, Renuka and her colleague Durgabai Deshmukh went to Nehru to complain about the machinations to delay the Bill by the orthodox members of the body. Nehru assured them that it would 'be part and parcel of our election manifesto in the first elections in India', and once elected, 'we will not allow impediments to the passage of this vital legislation.'[75]

When Nehru returned as the elected prime minister of India, he pushed for the Hindu laws to be passed. Again, it met with stiff opposition. But between 1952 and 1956, it was broken down into separate Bills, in an attempt to get the Bills passed quickly. Even though Renuka was serving as a minister in West Bengal at the time, she helped the law minister H.V. Pataskar in garnering support for the Bills. She was finally victorious in the seeing the Hindu Code Bill being passed – this was something that would change the lives of women all across independent India for the better.

Even while Renuka served in the Constituent Assembly, she devoted her time to solving the post-Partition refugee crisis. She was the regional advisor for the eastern zone.[76] She worked in close proximity with Dr B.C. Roy, chief minister of West Bengal. She also was a member of India's delegation to the United Nations in 1949.

Renuka contested and lost the 1952 parliamentary elections from Hooghly.[77] Post-election when she and her friend Durgabai Deshmukh went to New Delhi, they were offered seats in the Upper House, or Rajya Sabha. Apparently, Nehru even offered to make an exception to the rule to not to induct anyone 'who lost their Lok Sabha seats' to the Rajya Sabha. However, both the women declined the offer.[78]

Renuka was still working as the regional advisor on the refugee problem when chief minister Roy asked her to join his Cabinet as the minister for rehabilitation. Renuka declined, saying she was neither a member of the assembly nor would she accept a seat in the Legislative Council. Roy then tried to convince her that she could be a minister if she found a seat in the Assembly within six months.[79] Renuka realized that he was serious and asked him if he had consulted anyone else about her appointment. 'His reply was that he had asked the only person it was necessary to consult and that was my husband. I still refused and left the place. When I rang him up the next day and asked him what he had decided about the refugee issue that I had placed before him, he told me, "It appears that women like to be advisers but not to take on any responsibility."'[80]

When Renuka shared this with her husband, who was then chief secretary of West Bengal, he suggested that she should accept the offer. 'When I asked him whether he had been consulted by Dr. Roy, he told me that the Chief Minister had merely asked him, "Have you any objection to stand up when your wife comes into the room?"' Satyen replied that he always stood up when any woman entered a room.[81]

Renuka accepted the Cabinet position. Within six months, she got elected from Ratua Assembly constituency in Malda.[82] In her memoir, she shared an anecdote from a banquet at the governor's residence in Calcutta. She was seated next to Clement Attlee, her teacher at LSE and former prime minister of the United Kingdom. Attlee turned to her and said, '"I used to know a young lady called Miss Mukerjee who was at the London School of Economics a long time back." My rejoinder was, "Perhaps, if you look at me more closely and make allowances for the years ... you will find her."'[83] Attlee was elated that his former pupil had become a minister.

Renuka's time as a minister from 1952–57 impressed upon her the need for Centre-State cooperation.[84] While she did some outstanding work to rehabilitate the refugees from East Pakistan, she felt that she could do better with more support from the Centre. As a result, she decided to enter the Lok Sabha to be in a position where she could influence the Parliament to give due attention to the refugee problem in West Bengal. Chief minister Roy was highly reluctant to let go of Renuka, but she was determined.[85]

Renuka won the 1957 Lok Sabha elections by securing 97,217 votes from Malda.[86] However, she was disappointed by the difference in the functioning of the Constituent Assembly and the Lok Sabha, as she discovered that 'group interests had become paramount and who should go to what committee and delegations at home and abroad seemed more important than how developmental work proceeded or how refugees could be absorbed into the economy of India'.[87]

In Parliament, she headed the Study Team on Social Welfare and Welfare of Backward Classes which later came to be known as the Renuka Ray Committee.[88] It toured the rural areas in the country and recommended pragmatic solutions to improve the lives of tribals. It also recognized intersectionality and suggested that those who are economically less fortunate should get greater benefits.[89]

Renuka was re-elected from Malda in 1962. After the deaths of B.C. Roy and Nehru, Renuka found it hard to survive the internal party politics of West Bengal.[90] Eventually, the Congress did not nominate her for the 1967 polls.[91] Prime Minister Indira Gandhi was unhappy with this and tried to intervene but the party parliamentary board didn't budge in its decision. Alternatively, Indira Gandhi asked her to come to the Rajya Sabha. Renuka declined and mentioned that she refused it during her father's prime ministership too.[92]

Thus, Renuka went back to Calcutta and focused on social work, an area that she had been dedicated towards since her teenage years. Even while she was occupied with ministerial or parliamentary duties, she had not detached from the women's movement. In 1953–54, Renuka served as the president of the AIWC.[93] After Satyen's death in 1969, she kept herself busy with work, which became her primary outlet.[94] She concentrated her energy on the Women's Coordinating Council, which was a body of various women's organizations.[95]

In 1988, Renuka was conferred the Padma Bhushan, the country's third-highest civilian award, for her contribution to public service.[96] She died on 11 April 1997 in Calcutta.[97]

She had a life extraordinaire. She was not swayed by power or positions. Renuka never abandoned her principles, and did not accept nominations for Rajya Sabha or the Legislative Council because she had spoken against the creation of such Houses. Every step that she undertook was rooted in high morals and values. Her lasting conflict between the use of violence and non-violence was settled in the later stages of her life. Though her sympathies for the armed movement didn't cease, she always believed in Gandhian non-violence. In the 1970s, when the Naxalite movement gained momentum, she wrote, 'If I were young today, without the guidance of someone like Gandhiji, I too would have rebelled against society and perhaps joined this group of Naxalites'.[98]

SAROJINI NAIDU

O YOUNG through all thy immemorial years!
Rise, Mother, rise, regenerate from thy gloom,
And, like a bride high-mated with the spheres,
Beget new glories from thine ageless womb!

The nations that in fettered darkness weep
Crave thee to lead them where great mornings break...
Mother, O Mother, wherefore dost thou sleep?
Arise and answer for thy children's sake!

Thy Future calls thee with a manifold sound
To crescent honours, splendours, victories vast;
Waken, O slumbering Mother and be crowned,
Who once wert empress of the sovereign Past.

– In her poetry collection *The Golden Threshold* (1905)

In 1835, T.B. Macaulay, a British politician, circulated 'Minutes on Education' that proposed the adoption of English as the official language in India. In this extremely racist treatise, Macaulay denigrated Sanskrit and Persian (the official language of the Mughal Empire) claiming that 'a single shelf of a good European library was worth the whole native literature of India and Arabia'. The objective behind the introduction of English was 'to form a class who may be interpreters between' the rulers and the governed.[1] Over the next decades, there did emerge a class of Indians that enthusiastically took to English. Sarojini Naidu was one of the few who mastered the language but was not content with merely being an 'interpreter' for the British rulers.

Contrary to their objective, Sarojini deployed her mastery over the colonial language to fight against the British Empire. At twenty-six, she was a literary sensation, an unofficial cultural ambassador of India. She led the Congress and emerged as one of the foremost national leaders. Besides fighting for independence, Sarojini indefatigably nurtured the feminist movement, mentoring leaders who took over the mantle in later years. Sarojini was one of the founding mothers of modern India in its true essence.

Sarojini Naidu was born on 13 February 1879 to Dr Aghorenath Chattopadhyaya and Varada Sundari Devi. Her parents were highly accomplished and renowned personalities of their time. Aghorenath was a scholar and social reformer who pursued eclectic interests. He belonged to a family of Sanskrit scholars well versed in the Vedas and Indian literature. His family 'were devoted lovers of nature and spent long sessions in forests meditating and philosophising'. He once came across a gang of dacoits who took a liking to him after he impressed them with his storytelling skills. These dacoits would later play a part in Aghorenath's marriage. One day, while taking a boat ride, Aghorenath caught a glimpse of Varada Sundari, who was only nine at the time, and fell in love with her. His dacoit friends helped him tie the knot with Varada at a very young age.[2]

The child marriage was in stark contrast to Aghorenath's reformist ideals. At fourteen, he was said 'to have broken his sacred thread and flung it into the Ganges' in protest. He also led a group of young men who took it upon themselves to rescue girls who had been married off by their families 'to very old and sometimes even moribund men in order to preserve the Kulin caste'.[3] These young men started the Banga Mahila Vidyalaya, one of the country's first institutes to impart matriculation studies to women, for educating these rescued girls.

After his schooling, Aghorenath moved from his village Brahamangar to Calcutta, where he came in contact with noted

Brahmo Samaj leader Keshav Chandra Sen. Aghorenath and his friends, who had been ostracized by their community, found refuge under Sen. Sen also came to Aghorenath's rescue when the latter had to go abroad for higher education after receiving the Gilchrist Scholarship. Sarojini's mother, Varada, who stayed back in India, received 'her early education together with lessons in housekeeping' at Sen's ashram.[4]

Aghorenath excelled at his studies and emerged as a leading chemistry researcher in a short time. In 1877, he received his doctorate in science from the University of Edinburgh.[5] Thereafter, he continued his studies in Germany.

Following his return from Germany, Aghorenath and Varada moved to Hyderabad where he took up a teacher's job in an English-medium school. Both husband and wife were devoted to the cause of women's education.[6] In 1887, Aghorenath helped establish the Hyderabad College (now known as Nizam College),[7] and Varada and Aghorenath then worked together to establish a women's college. His social reform agenda went beyond education. He was a votary of economic independence for women, abolishing child marriage, and establishing widow remarriage.[8] He also advocated for the introduction of the Special Marriage Act 1872 in Hyderabad state. Aghorenath also dabbled in politics. One of the first people to join the Congress in Hyderabad, he helped in propagating the Swadeshi movement.[9]

Aghorenath and Varada's home was a sanctuary for arts, literature, and a range of other interests and pursuits. Varada was a renowned singer, lyricist, and dancer. Curiously enough, Varada was also 'known to be [a] psychic'.[10] Aghorenath was a polyglot who wrote poems in both Urdu and Bengali. Though he had given up his career in chemistry, he hoped to strike gold by practising alchemy.

The Chattopadhyaya household was one of dreamers and doers. Sarojini wrote of her father, 'My ancestors for thousands of years have been lovers of the forest and mountain caves, great dreamers, great scholars, great ascetics. My father is a dreamer himself, a great dreamer, a great man whose life has been a magnificent failure… He has wasted all his money on two great objects: to help others, and on alchemy.'[11]

The eldest of eight siblings, Sarojini was born in 1879 and described as an 'overbearing' sister who took upon herself 'the right to rule the younger members of the family and the responsibility for things that were, in her opinion, the function of her father and mother'.[12] Sarojini was followed by Virendranath (1880), Bhupendranath (1882), Mrinalini (1883), Sunalini (1890), Ranendranath (1895), Harindranath (1898), and Suhasani (1901).

Her brother Virendranath was a revolutionary who lived in exile because of his involvement in anti-imperialistic activities. A leading figure of the Indian Independence Committee (formed in Berlin in 1914), Virendranath was a close friend of Vinayak Savarkar. Virendranath's revolutionary actions brought undue attention to the Chattopadhyaya clan. His infamy was such that Sarojini was advised to disown her brother and save her parents the trouble from government authorities. She 'impulsively wrote a letter' 'dissociating herself from her father and brother'. This earned her a rebuke from Aghorenath, who in turn 'exiled' Sarojini from his home. Aghorenath disagreed with Virendranath's revolutionary methods but was not going to outcast him from his family. Unfortunately, Virendranath spent his last days in Russia where he was executed during Joseph Stalin's Great Purge.[13]

Aghorenath and Varada ensured that their children received the best education. They had employed a governess to teach them English and French. Sarojini was a prodigal talent; she was an excellent student despite her lack of interest in formal tutoring. Aghorenath wanted her to master English, much to her annoyance. Sarojini wrote, 'I was stubborn and refused to speak it (English). So one day when I was nine years old my father punished me the only time I was ever punished by shutting me in a room alone for a whole day. I came out of it a full-blown linguist. I have never spoken any other language to him.'[14] The claim of leaving the room a 'full-blown linguist' is most probably an exaggeration propelled by poetic license.

Aghorenath was also keen on inculcating in Sarojini a scientific temper and steered her towards a career in mathematics or science. But the poetic instinct she inherited from her parents, proved far stronger. 'One day, when I was eleven, I was sighing over a sum in algebra: it wouldn't come right; but instead a whole poem came to me suddenly. I wrote it down. From that day my "poetic career" began.' When she was thirteen, she wrote 'Lady of the Lake', a 1,300-line poem, in six days as well as a drama. She did this 'just to spite' her doctor while she was ill, as he told her to 'not touch a book'.[15]

Sarojini was sent to Madras (now Chennai) to appear for her matriculation examination. She topped the Madras Presidency, earning her fame throughout the country. For three years after this brilliant performance, Sarojini was confined to her parents' home in Hyderabad as she was unwell. During this time, she interacted with a number of visitors from all walks of life who frequented the Chattopadhyaya residence. It is likely at one of the gatherings in her home that she met her future husband – Dr Govindarajulu Naidu, a young doctor who had just returned from England after studying medicine at the University of Edinburgh. Sarojini was smitten.

Sarojini and Naidu's love met with resistance from both their families, as the couple belonged to different castes.[16] There was also the concern that Sarojini was too young during their courtship as she was only sixteen in 1895.[17] The same year, Sarojini wrote a Persian play, a copy of which was sent to the Nizam of Hyderabad Asaf Jah VI. The Nizam was greatly impressed by her talents and granted Sarojini a generous scholarship to pursue higher studies in England. She was sent abroad against her wishes,[18] probably in the hope of breaking up the couple.

Sarojini sailed to England in 1895. She attended classes at King's College in London and later joined Girton College, University of Cambridge. Despite studying in world-class institutions, she would return to India without a degree because she didn't appear for any exams in England. But the exposure and the education turned her into a mature poet.

In England, she met Arthur Symons and Edmund Gosse, British poets and critics, both of whom read her poetry. Gosse offered her blunt but valuable feedback. He told her that her work was 'without individuality' and suggested she 'start again with the genuine vision of her own land'.[19] Symons saw promise in her work and encouraged her to publish a collection of poems. Sarojini took the well-meaning advice and changed her style to incorporate her Indian background in the poems. In 1905, she published her first collection of poems, *The Golden Threshold*. She dedicated it to Gosse, while Symons wrote the introduction.

While in England, she was engrossed in writing poetry. Unfortunately, her health deteriorated in the damp British climate and she may have even suffered a nervous breakdown. To recuperate, she left for Switzerland and then Italy.[20]

In 1898, Sarojini returned to India and married Naidu in December. Neither distance nor time had blunted their love. They registered their marriage under the Special Marriage Act, 1872, the same legislation that Aghorenath had helped implement in Hyderabad. Theirs in fact was one of the earliest recorded cases of inter-caste and inter-regional marriages in the country.[21]

The couple settled happily in Hyderabad and had four children, Jaya Surya, Padmaja, Ranadhira, and Leilamani. Sarojini's struggle with her health continued but she was 'steeped in romance and indulged in flights of fancy'. The poet had taken wings and she 'was at this time almost a mystic'.[22] Sadly, her bad health made Sarojini 'think a great deal about death and she often spoke as though she had been on the brink of it'.[23]

Sarojini, however, did not always dwell on death as a dark entity. She realized its inevitable nature and valued living in the moment. She adopted 'Eat, drink and be merry, for tomorrow we die!' as her motto and wondered if it was 'worthwhile to be anything but radiantly glad'.[24]

Sarojini scrupulously practised her philosophy of being 'radiantly glad'. She was the life of parties and always dressed in bright colours. Renuka Ray, describing a party in honour of Jawaharlal Nehru, wrote, 'Sarojini Naidu was there and with her wit and charm she kept everybody in roars of laughter and was the presiding deity on the occasion.'[25] Independence activist and lawyer Asaf Ali commented: 'Sarojini falsified my mental picture of her in every single detail. She was a full-figured, picturesquely dressed, heavily bejewelled person, radiant and restless, full of sparkling life and laughter.'[26] He added, 'She was becoming a great centre of attraction, and held her *durbar* almost daily at the Lyceum.'[27]

Sarojini had become an international literary sensation after the publication of *The Golden Threshold*. The collection was a bestseller and received rave reviews from newspapers and journals alike.[28] The *Review of Reviews* wrote, 'This little volume should silence forever the scoffer who declares that women cannot write poetry.' The *Times* read in her poetry a successful marriage of East and West. The *Academy* said, 'Full of beauty.... What is as delightful as surprising is its individuality: a perfection of its own that owes but little to any one.' Lilian Waring wrote in The *Englishman*, 'The Golden Threshold has that indescribable charm which acts like magic on the English mind.'[29] The praise, quite often, was tinged with a patronizing tone. Nonetheless, Sarojini emerged as one of the foremost Indian voices. Over the next decade, she published two more poetry collections – *The Bird of Time* and *The Broken Wing*.

At the turn of the century, Sarojini took to social service. She initially worked in Hyderabad, coordinating social and relief work, but craved more. She was invited to speak on different discussion forums across the country. Her speeches touched upon a wide range of issues. Sarojini also campaigned for women's emancipation and warned against the narrow nationalism she saw brewing. In 1902, she addressed large crowds in Calcutta and

Bombay, exhorting women 'to come out of seclusion, to work and to take up careers'.[30]

In 1903, at a lecture organized by the Historical Society, Pachaiyappa's College, Madras, Sarojini urged young students to foster a spirit of brotherhood and think beyond the narrow binaries of region, religion, and nationalities. 'I beg of you, my brothers, not to limit your love only to India, because it is better to aim at the sky, it is better that your ideals of patriotisms should extend to the welfare of the world and not be limited to the prosperity of India and so to achieve that prosperity for your country; because, if the ideals be only for the prosperity of your country, it would end where it began, by being a profit to your own community and very probably to your own self.' At the lecture, Sarojini recalled her father's advice, 'Be not limited even to the Indians, but let it be your pride that you are a citizen of the world.'[31] This lecture was one of the earliest warnings against narrow nationalistic ideals.

A few years later, Rabindranath Tagore, in his novel *Home and the World*, directly addressed the question of fervent patriotism through the words of one of his characters: 'I have nothing against your worship (of country) as such, but how is it you propose to conduct your worship of God by hating other countries in which He is equally manifest?' Sarojini and Tagore had access to similar social circles (they would later become friends) and may have even contributed to each other's views on nationalism.

At the Indian Social Conference, held in Calcutta in December 1906, Sarojini was indignant that people were still passing resolutions in favour of female education. Sarojini raised pertinent questions and called out Indian men: 'Does one man dare to deprive another of his birth right to God's pure air which nourishes his body? How, then, shall a man dare to deprive a human soul of its immemorial inheritance of liberty and life? And yet, my friends, man has so dared in the case of Indian women… Therefore, I charge you, restore to your women their ancient rights, for, as I have said, it is we, and not you, who are the real nation-builders, and without our active cooperation at all points of progress, all your Congresses and Conferences are in vain.'[32]

Sarojini was unsparing in her assessment of Indian men. In another speech, she said, 'Do men of our days deserve sati? What sort of men do we find now? They are not men at all. They can be called the degenerate descendants of ancient heroes.'[33]

Her speech at the Indian Social Conference in 1906 earned her the appreciation and eventual friendship of Gopal Krishna Gokhale, a senior Congress leader. Their comradeship was based on their mutual love for the motherland and the desire for Hindu-Muslim unity. Once, Gokhale asked her, 'What is your outlook for India?' Sarojini replied, 'One of hope.' He then asked, 'What is your vision of our immediate future?' She answered, 'Hindu-Muslim unity in less than five years.' Gokhale responded, 'Child, you are a poet, but you hope too much. It will not come in your lifetime or in mine. But keep your faith and work if you can.'[34]

Gokhale and Sarojini had great hopes for Muhammad Ali Jinnah in their quest for religious amity. Sarojini shared a deep bond with Jinnah and helped 'build a circle of admirers'[35] around him in England. She hailed him as an ambassador of Hindu-Muslim unity. She was in fact relying on Gokhale's assessment of the man. Jinnah reciprocated the adulation and confided in Sarojini his ambition to become the 'Muslim Gokhale'.[36] She saw in Jinnah 'the Mazzini of the Indian Liberation' – Mazzini was an Italian nationalist who fought for Italy's unification. Unfortunately, in later years, Jinnah dropped his secular ideals and campaigned for India's partition.

When Gokhale introduced Sarojini to Mahatma Gandhi, another lifelong comradeship was born. In July 1914, Gandhi had arrived in London from South Africa. Europe was in the throes of World War I and Gandhi suggested that Indians should help the British with the war effort. And so, the Indian Voluntary Corps was formed in August 1914 and Sarojini joined as a volunteer.[37]

When Sarojini went to meet Gandhi at his dwellings in London, she was amused by the austerity of the surroundings and the sight of a 'little man with shaven head' who was a household name by then. She let out an inadvertent laugh, and Gandhi remarked, 'Ah, you must be Mrs Naidu! Who else dare be so irreverent? Come in and share my meal.' Sarojini declined with a cheeky reply, 'No thanks. What an abominable mess it is.' In her own words, this unusual exchange was the genesis of a friendship, 'which flowered into real comradeship, and bore fruit in a loving, loyal discipleship, which never wavered for a single hour through more than thirty years of common service in the cause of India's freedom'.[38]

Sarojini and Gandhi worked together till the end. They were a formidable team. She succeeded him as Congress president in 1925. She was a key member of his inner circle, participating in the Dandi March and facing several arrests. Gandhi called her the 'Nightingale of India' and she called him 'Mickey Mouse'. She followed him as a leader but playfully mocked his austere methods, once famously saying that it cost a lot of money to keep Gandhi in poverty. Of his food choices, she said, 'Good heavens, all that grass and goat milk? Never, never, never!'[39] She even joked about his views on chastity. Gandhi enjoyed the camaraderie and her 'merciless teasing'.[40] When Gandhi was assassinated, Sarojini was 'stoic in her grief' and asked a loud mourner to 'stop snivelling'. She asked, 'Would you rather that he had died old and decrepit in his bed? This was the only death great enough for him.'[41]

Like her mentor Gokhale, a magnetic personality who attracted a slew of talented people to the fight for independence, Sarojini inspired women to reach for the sky. She also influenced the other women in the Constituent Assembly. Sarojini was the northern star for those who wished to serve their country. Vijaya Lakshmi Pandit said, 'Women like Annie Besant and Sarojini Naidu filled me with the ambition to be like them. To be an orator, to be able to sway people with my words, this was my great ambition.'[42] Renuka Ray, whose mother was friends with

Sarojini, shared, '[Sarojini] was a leader who could arouse the young to great heights of enthusiasm... Her skill of combining poetic language and style was new to us.'[43] Hansa Mehta said, 'In this close companionship with Sarojini Devi I learned much about people and things. In fact, she brought me out of my shell so to speak and made me do things I otherwise would not have dreamt of doing.'[44]

Irish-Indian suffragette and feminist Margaret Cousins called Sarojini 'the brightest star amongst the galaxy of Indian women publicists'.[45] She further said, 'Sarojini Devi became more and more popular as a soul-stirring orator, a poetess, a politician, an unofficial ambassadress of India to foreign lands, an acknowledged leader of the united Indian people, a position she still retains. In her person she ensures that womanhood will be found in every move of every game on the political chessboard.[46]

Cousins's praise of Sarojini's work and growing influence in the fight for women's rights was not exaggerated. Sarojini was the face of the suffragist movement in India. In 1917, she led a delegation of fourteen women to present a memorandum on governance to Edwin Montagu and Lord Chelmsford. At the 1916 and 1917 sessions of the Congress, Sarojini made rousing speeches in support of resolutions calling for self-rule.[47] As expected, her vision of a free and modern India was powered by equal rights for and empowerment of women. This was reflected in the aforesaid memorandum that demanded better education, health, and maternity services for women along with voting rights.[48]

In 1918, in a resolution at its Bijapur session, Sarojini asked the Bombay Provincial Conference to place its support for women's franchise in India on record. In her speech, Sarojini referred to the nomenclature and demanded that 'the word "man" should include, politically speaking, "woman" in discussing the rights of citizenship.' Sarojini was clear that enfranchisement was not a largesse but a matter of justice: '... the women of India should not appeal to the chivalry of the men of India but to their sense of justice.'[49]

In September 1918, at a special session of Bombay Congress, Sarojini moved another resolution that read: 'Woman possessing the same qualifications as are laid down for man in any part of the scheme shall not be disqualified on account of sex'.[50] The resolution was enthusiastically passed and paved the way for the adoption of similar resolutions in other provinces.

In 1919, a deputation of women submitted a memorandum to the Joint Committee of the Lords and Commons to consider the Government of India Bill. Sarojini made an eloquent appeal for voting rights: 'I have spoken to the youths in their academies, to the women in their walled gardens, to the merchants in the marketplace, to the peasants in the shade of their fig and banyan trees, but how shall my prophecy be realized and how shall my country take her pre-destined place worthily in the noble World Federation of liberated peoples, until the women of India are themselves free and enfranchised, and stand as the guardians of her national honour and the symbols of her national righteousness?'[51]

The deputation earned a substantial victory. Britain enacted the Government of India Act 1919 (based on a report by Montagu and Chelmsford), which, while having no provision for voting rights for women in the Central legislature, allowed provincial legislatures to enfranchise them. It was now for the Indian men to step up and stay true to their democratic ideals.

In March 1919, another Act would be passed greatly affecting the basic freedoms of the Indian people, as Britain enacted the Anarchical and Revolutionary Crimes Act of 1919, popularly known as the Rowlatt Act. The Rowlatt Act conferred on the police far-reaching powers. Provisions of the Act violated principles of natural justice, allowing arrest without warrants, juryless trials, and the accused's right to know of the evidence against them. Sedition was considered an offence that would attract the provisions of Rowlatt Act. Gandhi decided to launch a Satyagraha against the Act.

On 17 March, Sarojini addressed a public meeting in Madras where she made a forceful case for repeal of the Act and lent unstinted support to Gandhi's Satyagraha. His methods had caused consternation amongst some people. At the time, Satyagraha was criticized for promoting irreverence for law and authority, and for setting a dangerous precedent that was going to create a tradition of lawlessness. Sarojini, however, defended Gandhi, 'There are times in the history of nations, as of individuals, when the customary law of caution, of order, of reverence to constituted authority must fail before the inspiration and the impulse and the intuition of the moment's demand.' She added, '... the great law of Satyagraha is the very instinctive law of self-defence against aggression and against tyranny that we Indians have followed, because Satyagraha is that form of historic resistance to outside devastating and disintegrating influences which has kept the life and spirit of Indian people today'.[52]

Three weeks later, General O'Dwyer ordered indiscriminate firing on a peaceful crowd that had gathered in Amritsar's Jallianwala Bagh. Hundreds of innocent women, men, and children died at the site. The Jallianwala Bagh massacre left the country in a state of shock and anger. It laid bare the oppression and cruelty of the colonial regime that had till then fashioned itself as a benefactor of the Indian people. Tagore renounced his knighthood in protest. Gandhi and Sarojini too joined Tagore in returning state honours. She gave back the Kaiser-i-Hind, which was awarded to her for her relief work during the Hyderabad floods of 1908.

The following year, Sarojini addressed the House of Commons in England on the massacre. Unsparing in her criticism, she admonished the British for their inhuman treatment of Indian men and women. 'Not only were the men mown down as if they were grass that is born to wither; but they tore asunder the cherished purdah, that innermost privacy of the chaste womanhood of India. Therefore, Englishmen and Englishwomen, my sisters were stripped naked, they were flogged, they were outraged.' She thundered, 'You deserve no Empire. You today have lost your soul; you today have the stain of blood-guiltiness upon you; no nation that rules by tyranny is free; it is the slave of its own despotism.'[53] Montagu accused her of spreading falsehood, requesting her to withdraw her statements. Letters were exchanged between the two. Sarojini in her reply cited several statements made by women who faced atrocities at the hands of the authorities.[54]

In 1920, Gandhi launched the Non-Cooperation Movement. It coincided with the visit of Edward, Prince of Wales. A welcome procession in Bombay in his honour ran into Congress volunteers who pelted stones at the motorcade.[55] Soon riots broke out and it was left to the Congress leaders to quell the violence. Sarojini was among those who ventured out to broker peace. According to one account, 'Time after time she would go out amongst the rioters in the different areas of disturbance.'[56] At the Congress session held in December in Ahmedabad, she stood in support of Gandhi's resolution calling for civil disobedience.[57]

The movement was withdrawn in 1922 following violence in the Chauri Chaura town of the United Provinces, where a mob burned down a police station, killing twenty-two official personnel. A month later, Gandhi was charged with sedition for inciting disaffection against the government by writing three articles.[58] He was sentenced to six years in prison but was released early on health grounds. In March 1922, Britain repealed the Rowlatt Act.

As the fight against the Rowlatt Act was going on, strides were being made when it came to voting rights for women. In 1921, Madras became the first province to grant women the right to vote, followed by Bombay and the United Provinces.[59] Earning voting rights around the same time as their American and some European counterparts – members of 'mature' democracies – is a testament to the perseverance and brilliance of Indian women leaders.

The women leaders did not let up after the initial success. The right to vote, while monumental, was conditional upon ownership of property, income, and other statuses, which excluded a substantial number of women. In fact, in Bombay, Bengal, and the United Provinces, less than 1 per cent of women could exercise franchise.[60] Further, women still did not have the right to sit in legislative bodies. Indians had been demanding a universal franchise right. The Nehru Report, a draft Constitution, prepared by an All Parties Conference in 1929, committed itself to equality. It called for equal civic rights for all citizens. Britain was not keen on expanding the right and women's organizations had to consistently struggle for years. It was only with the adoption of the Constitution in 1950 that all women acquired the right to vote.

To make their voices stronger, in 1927, several women-led organizations joined hands to form the All India Women's Conference (AIWC).[61] Sarojini was a key member of the AIWC and helped it grow and sustain. In 1930, she presided over its fourth session. Here she made a famous speech, refusing to be identified as a 'feminist'. According to Sarojini, 'To be a feminist is to acknowledge that one's life has been repressed. The demand for granting preferential treatment to woman is an admission on her part of her inferiority and there has been no need for such a thing in India as the women have always been by the side of men both in councils and in the fields of battle. We women recognize our responsibilities. Therefore, it is that our rights are taken for granted. The consciousness of what we ought to do for our people is deep in the hearts of our men. Still sometimes we have to struggle against the chivalry of men who want to have protective legislation for us. We have to educate the manhood that the spiritual reform of the world is woman's great work.'[62]

In her passionate defence against the label of 'feminism', she put women on a fictitious pedestal. The romanticism ignored the prevailing reality and came from a position of privilege. Without 'protective legislation' in the form of reservations and nominations to the assemblies, it was obvious that women would be at a disadvantage. In later years, it became AIWC's official policy to oppose reservations and separate electorates for women, finding its way to the Constituent Assembly debates. Renuka Ray had in fact called reservation for women 'an impediment' and 'an insult to [women's] intelligence and capacity'.[63]

AIWC's work had its share of hurdles but that did not hassle Sarojini. Once a group of young men heckled Sarojini as she took the dais at an AIWC event. They raised slogans of 'Down with the women's social rights'.

Appalled at such atrocious behaviour, Sarojini made a forceful intervention, forcing the men to retreat. She said, 'I am shocked and ashamed to find that my own brothers can be so uncultured and un-Indian in their ways as to not only come in and forcibly occupy the front seats at a meeting convened by women but behave in this ungentlemanly and outrageous fashion. We have no objection to your attending our meeting as women always like to encourage their brothers. If you want to say anything, you must ask me as president to give you an opportunity and to come up one by one to the dais. We are not afraid of you. We know we will convert you to our ideas but only please behave as Indians and cultured gentlemen.' The front seats that had been occupied by the hecklers soon emptied, to be filled by genuine supporters who had been waiting outside the hall.[64]

Sarojini's tireless advocacy for women's rights was concurrent with her contribution to the freedom struggle. This meant long periods of absence from home. In Naidu, she had a partner who stood behind her like a rock. Margaret Cousins described the couple's equation with the following words: 'There was the protecting strength and upholding of her clever, quiet husband with his sense of power'.[65] When people passed judgments on Sarojini for not spending time at home, she retorted with, 'My home, my husband and my children are now as much my care as ever. They know that my public work does not interfere with my care for them. They and I are thankful to you for your interest in us.'[66]

In 1925, at the Kanpur session of the Congress, Gandhi proposed Sarojini's name as president. She became the second woman, and the first Indian woman, to head the Congress party. She took to the rostrum 'amidst scenes of intense enthusiasm and prolonged and loud cries of "Bande Mataram", Allah-o-Akbar", and "Sarojini Naidu ki jai"'. Her presidential address was extempore. She spoke in English and started with, 'Friends, I have asked the permission of this great gathering to address you in a language that is not ours because today I have been made the mouthpiece of a nation in struggle, the consolation of a nation in sorrow, the heart-beat of a nation in agony and the promise of a nation determined to win freedom at the uttermost sacrifice.'[67]

In her speech, she addressed Indian men and their misogyny, telling them that in elevating a woman to the post of president, they had somewhat redeemed themselves. A large part of her speech was focused on admonishing Indians in the choicest words for their failure to mount a defence in honour of their country. She declared, 'Today you are a mere imitation – cheap imitation – the fifth rate imitation of second rate models of the West. You have forgotten your own art. You have forgotten your own language. You do not know how to evolve your own music. You have betrayed your own inheritance because you have run after false gods and your intellect has bowed down in worship to the gods that slave you and your imagination burns incense at the shrine of those that devour the honour of your race.'

Sarojini also addressed the divide within Congress. The suspension of the Non-Cooperation Movement had created fissures within the party. And Sarojini called for unity under Gandhi's leadership: 'Today is it not the duty of the Liberals, the Conventionalists or Independents – no matter what particular label they attach to their names – no matter what be their shibboleths to return to the Congress?' She concluded, 'I am not afraid of the ultimate sacrifice. I am only a woman. I am only a woman but I am the standard bearer of your honour and I will see to it – the women of India will see to it – that you men shall no more betray the heritage of our nation.'

The speech garnered favourable comments from the international press. The *New York Times* went to the extent of calling Sarojini the 'Joan of Arc' who had risen to inspire India. Unlike the speech, her term as president was unremarkable. Congress was struggling with the divisions within its rank and anti-government activity was missing. Sarojini devoted her energies to organizational work.[68] Unfortunately, her presidentship saw the differences between the various party factions widen further. At a Congress Committee meeting in Ahmedabad, a group of leaders abstained and 'virtually broke away' from the party. The internal squabbles took a toll on her mental health.[69]

Her experience as president shaped her into an adroit politician adept at party machinations. In 1932, she became Congress's acting president by virtue of being the only Congress Working Committee, the foremost decision-making body within the party, member outside prison. Sarojini never again headed the party but played a key role in political affairs.

In the 1939 Congress elections, Subhas Chandra Bose was elected president. Gandhi was not pleased with the outcome and declared that 'the defeat of Subhas's rival was his own defeat'. However, Bose was a minority in the Executive Committee of the party. Gandhi's followers wanted the president-elect to nominate 'the Working Committee in accordance with the wishes of Gandhiji'. It was in effect a vote of no-confidence in Bose's leadership and he offered to resign. The leaders met in April to chalk out a peaceful resolution to the conflict. Sarojini chaired the meeting after Bose's refusal to preside in light of his resignation offer. She said she wanted Bose to continue and called the leaders to cooperate with him. At the same time, she wanted Bose to cooperate with them as well. The differences could not be reconciled and Bose refused to withdraw his resignation. Sarojini insisted on the immediate election of a new president. Some leaders protested, pointing out that only the delegates were empowered to elect the president. She brushed aside their concerns, later saying, 'Yes,

I have got to act unconstitutionally.' Dr Rajendra Prasad was then elected president.[70]

Her commitment to Gandhi's leadership remained absolute. Gandhi relied on her implicitly, often defending her transgressions. When someone criticized her for not wearing pure khadi, he retorted, 'Whatever Sarojini wears is purer than what you wear'.[71]

In 1928, Gandhi sent her to the USA to counter 'anti-India' propaganda. She was also there as an AIWC delegate to attend the Pan-Pacific Women's Conference.

During her visit, Sarojini addressed multiple meetings across the USA. At the World Alliance for Peace banquet, she noticed that the hall was decorated with flags of all 'free nations'. She questioned the futility of the talks when India remained subjugated: 'The only guarantee of abiding world peace [was a free India] and till they could hang India's banner dyed in the red of hope, the green of her courage, and the white of her faith among other world symbols of liberty, there could and would be no more peace in the world.'[72]

The symbolism of having a flag was dear to Sarojini. One of her two speeches at the Constituent Assembly was on the national flag. She narrated her despair at India not possessing a flag. 'I was asked to speak at a peace celebration in New York soon after the peace had been signed. Forty-four nations and their flags fluttering in the great hall in which the Assembly met. I looked at the Flags of all the Nations and when I spoke I cried that though I did not see in that great Assembly of Free Nations the Flag of Free India, it would become the most historic Flag of the world in the not distant future.' Sarojini also described a 'moment of anguish' for her when, at a women's International Conference in Berlin, India did not have a flag. She added, 'But at my suggestion some of the women Indian delegates tore strips from their saris sitting up till the small hours of the morning to make the Tricolour Flag, so that our country should not be humiliated for the lack of a National Banner.'[73]

Eventually, when the Indian flag was adopted in 1947, she was jubilant. Saluting the flag of a free nation was a heart-warming moment for those who had toiled for years. Their struggles came at great sacrifice. Active participation in Congress was a ticket to prison. Sarojini along with several of her Congress colleagues faced several jail terms and bouts of poor health but continued fighting for independence.

In March 1930, Gandhi launched the Salt Satyagraha. The production and distribution of salt was a profitable monopoly of the British, and a number of laws prevented Indians from selling or even producing salt on their own. To make matters worse, Indians had to pay heavy taxes to purchase salt. To challenge these laws, Gandhi decided to march from Sabarmati to Dandi town on the coast of Gujarat. No woman was part of the cohort that marched with Gandhi. Sarojini joined him at Dandi and stood beside him when he broke the law. Later, when Gandhi was arrested, she assumed the leadership role. Sarojini led a peaceful procession of volunteers for which she was arrested.

She called the prison 'The Garden of Seclusion' in her letters to her children. When asked about her jail experience, she wittily responded, 'I had a splendid time; did not want to come out. I had planted some beautiful anthuriums, and just as they were coming into flower, we were all put out again.'[74]

In 1931, she travelled to England with Gandhi and other leaders to attend the Second Round Table Conference. The Congress had historically boycotted the First Round Table Conference. Sarojini's reputation preceded her and she was welcomed with great warmth. When someone asked her what India was going to do with all the Victoria statues across the country, she replied, 'Cut off their heads and put mine in their place.'[75]

She was again arrested in 1932. This time, she was classified as an 'A-class prisoner', entitled to services superior to what most other inmates got. From there she was transferred to Yerawada prison where Gandhi had been incarcerated. She was beside him when the negotiations for the Poona Pact were underway. In

1940, Congress launched individual satyagraha. Sarojini went to prison once again, and also during the Quit India Movement. The prolonged jail terms worsened her health and she left prison on a stretcher.[76]

Following her release, she threw herself back to work. As Partition became inevitable, she was despondent. Hindu-Muslim unity had been a very important focus area for her, and she was anguished to see her motherland partitioned along religious lines.

In 1946, she was elected to the Constituent Assembly from Bihar. In her first speech at the Assembly, made on 11 December 1946, she said she hoped that the Partition would be stalled. 'I see gaps in this House and my heart is sore because of the absence of those Muslim brothers to whose coming I am looking forward under the leadership of my old friend Mr Muhammad Ali Jinnah.'

Her speech was one of hope and optimism for the Constituent Assembly. 'I hope those that call themselves the original masters of this land, the tribal people will realise that there is no distinction of caste, creed, ancient or modern, status in this Constituent Assembly. I hope the smallest minority in this country will, whether represented politically, or I do not know by what other means they may be represented – I hope also that the Princes of India, many of whom I count among my personal friends, who are so hurried, so anxious, so uncertain or so afraid today, will realise that the Constitution for India is a constitution for the freedom and emancipation of every human being in India, whether Prince or peasant.'[77]

Sarojini made only one more speech thereafter, on the resolution regarding the national flag. She was appointed governor of the United Provinces, the first woman to occupy the position. She was initially reluctant and is said to have remarked, 'You are putting a wild bird in a cage.'

On 15 August 1947, she made an emotional speech in Lucknow. 'Oh world of free nations, on this day of our freedom, we pray for your freedom in the future. Ours has been an epic struggle, covering many years, and costing many lives. It has been a struggle, a dramatic struggle. It has been a struggle of heroes chiefly anonymous in their millions. It has been a struggle of women transformed into strength they worship. It has been a struggle of youth suddenly transformed into power… it has been a struggle of young men and old men, of rich and poor, the literate and the illiterate, the stricken, the outcast, the leper and the saint.'[78]

The same year, India hosted the first Asian Relations Conference. It was a platform for Asian nations, many of whom had recently gained independence, to come together and review post-War conditions. Sarojini presided over the gathering. A true internationalist, she was suited for a role that required non-partisanship. She proclaimed, 'We do not cry for the moon. We pluck it from the skies and wear it upon the diadem of Asia's freedom.'[79] The Conference set the tone for India emerging as a pivot in international affairs, eventually culminating in the creation of the Non-Aligned Movement.

On 30 January 1948, when Nathuram Godse assassinated Gandhi, all hell broke loose. Stoic in the face of grief, Sarojini made a radio broadcast in Gandhi's memory two days after his death. She recalled his selfless service. She was defiant in grief, urging the listeners to walk his path. 'I say the time is over for private sorrow. The time is over for beating of breasts and tearing of hair. The time is here and now when we stand up and say, "We take up the challenge" to those who defied Mahatma Gandhi. We are his living symbols. We are his soldiers. We are the carriers of his banner before an embattled world. Our banner is truth. Our shield is non-violence. Our sword is a sword of the spirit that conquers without blood. Let the peoples of India rise up and wipe their tears, rise up and still their sobs, rise up and be full of hope and full of cheer.'[80]

In Gandhi's passing, she lost a leader and dear friend. For three decades, they had formed a rock-solid partnership, her faith in him never wavering. Shortly after he breathed his last, she put aside her grief and went about preaching his gospel. That needed inner strength and Sarojini commanded an unending reservoir.

Sarojini passed away on 2 March 1949 from cardiac arrest. Sarojini rose to every challenge and inspired countless others. She left a lasting impact on every sphere she touched. Sarojini built modern India and has given the world a life story to emulate.

Nehru, then prime minister, paid her a moving tribute in Parliament, 'Just as the Father of the Nation had infused moral grandeur and greatness to the struggle, Mrs Sarojini Naidu gave it artistry and poetry and that zest for life and indomitable spirit which not only faced disaster and catastrophe, but faced them with a light heart and with a song on her lips and a smile on her face… She knew how to sacrifice herself for great causes. She knew also to do that so gracefully and so graciously that it appeared an easy thing to do and not anything containing travail of spirit… She lifted our struggle into a higher plane and gave it a certain touch which I cannot think anybody else can give or is likely to give in future.'[81]

SUCHETA KRIPALANI

'We are seeking to have a society where men and women should be equal, where people of all castes will be equal. We are trying to bring about a perfect democracy of which we have dreamed all these years. We are pledged to give women equal status in society.'

– On the importance of equity in society in the Constituent Assembly (Legislative) on 24 February 1949

In the 1952 general elections, 24 women were elected to the Lok Sabha, which accounted for 5 per cent of the total members. In Uttar Pradesh, India's most populous state, eleven women were elected to the legislative assembly, which was only 2.2 per cent women representation. A decade later, in 1962, there was a marginal improvement in the representation of women, with their percentage in the Lok Sabha and Vidhan Sabha going up to 6.7 and 4.6 respectively. Uttar Pradesh was clearly lagging in ensuring political justice for women. There was some redemption when Sucheta Kripalani became chief minister in 1963, India's first woman to head a government. A staunch nationalist, Sucheta was a Gandhian who became known for her underground activities during the Quit India Movement and thereafter, running relief camps in Noakhali and Delhi. A teacher of constitutional history, she was a member of the Congress when she was elected to the Constituent Assembly. She later resigned from the party and stood in opposition when she felt it was losing its ideological moorings. Throughout her life, she displayed exemplary courage in standing up to those in power.

Sucheta was born to Surendra Nath Mazumdar and Prembala in Ambala (then in Punjab) in June 1908. Surendra Nath hailed from an illustrious Brahmo family. His father, Dinanath, was one of the twelve disciples of the noted Brahmo leader Keshav Chandra Sen. Dinanath was employed in the railways but left his job to become a full-time preacher[1] after coming under Sen's influence. The spirit of renunciation for a higher cause ran in the family.[2] Dinanath was given charge of undertaking missionary activities in Bihar and later sent to Punjab and Sindh. Surendra Nath was born in Patna. He would go on to complete his training in medicine at the Lahore Medical College. Sucheta's mother, Prembala, was the daughter of Manmatha Nath Dutt, a distinguished scholar who is credited with translating several Hindu epics and texts from Sanskrit to English.[3] Prembala's maternal family, too, was deeply involved in the activities of the Brahmo Samaj and were followers of Sen.

The religious and intellectual proclivities of the Mazumdars and Dutts found their way into Surendra Nath and Prembala's household. After his studies, Surendra Nath joined the Punjab Medical Service[4] and the duo set up a home in the state. Theirs was a 'happy and boisterous family' with nine children. Since the couple was related to leading Brahmos, their home became a centre of social and cultural functions. The father was indulgent towards the children, while the mother was a disciplinarian. All of their children received formal education in the leading institutions of the time.[5]

Sucheta and her sister Sulekha studied at Loreto Convent in Shimla, after which they were sent to a boarding school in Allahabad. Subsequently, they attended Queen Mary's School in Delhi. A reticent Sucheta described herself as 'dark, dull, and agonisingly shy'. She initially struggled with her studies but turned around to become a high-scoring student.[6]

Sucheta was fourteen when she had her first brush with nationalistic activity. In 1921–22, Edward VIII, the Prince of Wales, was on a royal tour of India.[7] The students of Queen Mary's School were scheduled to welcome the prince in Delhi. However, the royal tour had come only months after the Jallianwala Bagh massacre, which shocked the Indian public. Sucheta and Sulekha were outraged at the thought of standing in honour of the Crown in whose name the killings were carried out. At the same time, they couldn't refuse to join the welcome party and decided to be absent during the event. The abstention left them ashamed for lacking 'sufficient courage to refuse' to honour the prince.[8]

Following the Jallianwala Bagh massacre, the Non-Cooperation Movement was launched by Gandhi in 1920, which renewed the patriotic fervour in the people. Indians responded positively to Gandhi's call for Satyagraha. One among them was Jivatram Bhagwandas Kripalani who was known by many names –JB, Professor, Acharya-ji, and Kripalani. Sucheta's cousin, Dhiren Mazumdar, was then a student at Banaras Hindu University (BHU), an area of Kripalani's influence. Dhiren idolized Kripalani and narrated stories of his time with his leader. Fuelled by the spirit of Satyagraha, Dhiren was a conduit for bringing Gandhi's philosophy into the Mazumdar home. Inspired, Sucheta took to khadi. She was joyous when she got her hands on her first khadi sari. Dhiren also arranged for her first 'Gandhi darshan' in 1924 in Delhi. For a young woman like Sucheta, seeing Gandhi was an exhilarating moment. She shared, 'We waited, all elation and excitement, in a crowded room, having a look at the great man! Little did I then imagine how close to him I would get one day!'[9]

Despite having a window into the world of freedom fighters, Sucheta was focused on her education. She topped the intermediate examinations, winning a gold medal and a scholarship. She wanted to pursue medicine, but it was ruled out by her father.

By then, the family had moved to Lahore, and Sucheta and Sulekha were enrolled in Kinnaird College for Women. Tragedy struck the Mazumdars when Sulekha, who was diagnosed with rheumatic fever and heart ailments, passed away. Her untimely death marked the beginning of a rough patch for the family. Surendra Nath couldn't bear the loss of his daughter and his health subsequently suffered.[10] He became seriously ill in 1927 and passed away two years later. The family's savings had been all but exhausted on Surendra Nath's treatment, and after their father's death, they had to drastically cut their expenses.

Shortly after, Prembala moved the family to Delhi, where they rented a small flat. The young Sucheta had trouble adjusting to the new environment. Despite the tough times, Prembala ensured the children received a good education.[11]

Sucheta, who had graduated from the Government College for Women in Lahore, enrolled at St. Stephen's College for her master's in history. The only woman in the class, she was picked on by her male classmates. The titters died down when she outscored them in all but one paper. She described her feelings, 'I heaved a sigh of relief. I had no longer to bother about the sniggering of the boys. My reputation in St. Stephen's was established.'[12] Continuing with her stellar academic record, she graduated at the top of her class and earned another gold medal.

Sucheta's completion of studies coincided with key national events. In 1927, the British announced the appointment of the Simon Commission to review the working of the Government of India Act 1919 and propose further reforms. The Congress decided to boycott it because it had no Indian representative. In 1928–29, the Congress had set up an All Parties' Conference to prepare a draft Constitution under the chairmanship of Motilal Nehru; his son, Jawaharlal, was appointed secretary. This draft Constitution, popularly known as the 'Nehru Report', called for far-reaching reforms. It claimed dominion status for India, introduced fundamental rights for all citizens, and a 'parliamentary system along with universal adult suffrage'.[13] In December 1929, the Congress passed the Purna Swaraj resolution that called for complete independence. The political activity gained pace with Gandhi launching the Civil Disobedience Movement through the Dandi March. While the Congress followed Gandhi's non-violent methods, there was a clamour for the revolutionary overthrow of the British government. A section of leaders, disillusioned by Gandhi's methods, concluded that taking up arms against the British was the only way to expel them from India. In 1931, the British hanged three prominent young revolutionaries, Bhagat Singh, Sukhdev Thapar, and Shivaram Rajguru, to death at the Lahore Central Jail. They had been convicted for the murder of a British police officer, which was planned to avenge the death of Lala Lajpat Rai, a prolific leader who was killed when he sustained injuries while taking part in a peaceful protest against the Simon Commission in 1928.

Sucheta was working as a teacher in Lahore when the trio were sent to the gallows. The hangings led to an outpouring of emotions and a huge procession joined the families for the last rites. The anti-British atmosphere was rising and the people of Lahore 'acted as if shaken by a storm'. Sucheta was itching to join the freedom movement but was held back by familial obligations.[14] Yet again, she had to stop herself from joining the cause she was so passionate about.

From Lahore, Sucheta moved to Banaras Hindu University (BHU) as a lecturer in history at the Women's College. The position provided Sucheta with financial stability and a year later, her family moved in with her. At BHU, she met Kripalani and Dr Verrier Elwin, British-born Indian anthropologist and tribal activist, who were on a tour to popularize khadi. She was greatly impressed by their intellect and formed a close friendship with the former. Kripalani would often call on her whenever he visited Banaras.[15]

After the January 1934 India–Nepal earthquake, the region of Bihar suffered several casualties and devastation. Congress leaders, including Kripalani, converged in the state to assist with relief operations. He encouraged Sucheta to join them. She took leave from university and followed Kripalani to Bihar. The relief work was her first experience working in a rural setting. Sucheta was shocked by the extent of poverty and inhumane conditions. The relief work brought her in close contact with Gandhi as well as Jamnalal Bajaj, an industrialist (founder of the Bajaj Group) who was overseeing the work. Bajaj was impressed with her and asked her to leave BHU and join the Mahila Ashram in Wardha, in modern-day Maharashtra. Sucheta made a trip to Wardha but declined the offer. She was put off by the rigidity and puritanical beliefs of Vinoba Bhave, a prominent Gandhian activist, who was on a fast because two young ashram residents had sinned by falling in love.[16] The rigid beliefs at the ashram were endorsed by Gandhi and almost cost Sucheta her blossoming relationship with Kripalani.

Over time, the couple's bond grew stronger. They enjoyed each other's company and regularly exchanged letters. They were both united in their desire to see a free and prosperous India. Kripalani suggested that the two should marry as he felt that their friendship would invite taunts and criticism from orthodox society. Kripalani shared he 'would have been satisfied with [their] friendship. But, in those days, that would have led to loose talk, in which the woman suffers more than the man'.[17] So they decided to tie the knot.

Unfortunately, the union faced multiple roadblocks. For instance, Sucheta's mother wanted 'the life of a normal housewife' for her daughter. Kripalani, twenty years Sucheta's senior and committed to an austere life, was not the most attractive prospect in her mother's eyes. Kripalani's sister, too, opposed the match as she felt it was going to impair his reputation. However, the most fervent resistance came from Gandhi.

Gandhi feared the marriage would distract Kripalani from the freedom cause. He attempted to dissuade Sucheta, saying, 'If you marry him, you will break my right arm.' Sucheta tried reasoning, telling him he was not going to lose a worker but gain one; but Gandhi was not one to budge easily. Gandhi's persistence paid off and a heartbroken Sucheta agreed to call off the wedding. Gandhi won but was not content. He then asked her to give up Kripalani completely. 'You have to give him up in thought, word and deed, have no contact, no letter even,' he demanded. Sucheta relented once again. Gandhi had won again, and this may have prompted him to push a little further. Gandhi continued to push her and told her, 'If you remain unhappy, it will oppress Kripalani; so, you must marry someone else'.[18] By then, Sucheta had had enough. She refused to accede to any unjust demand and decided to follow her heart.

The couple got married according to Brahmo rites in Banaras. A small reception was held at Anand Bhawan, Allahabad, organized by Vijaya Lakshmi Pandit. The marriage was registered at Anand Bhawan with Jawaharlal Nehru as a witness. Kripalani and Nehru were close friends and the former even waited for Nehru to be released from jail to formalize the marriage.[19]

Unsurprisingly, Gandhi refused to bless the union, saying that 'he could only pray' for the couple. The marriage irked Gandhi and he told Padmaja Naidu – Sarojini Naidu's daughter and a close friend of the Nehrus – that he disapproved of it. Naidu curtly responded with, 'Where do you come in? It is their business. They are both majors.' Over time, Sucheta and Gandhi made peace with each other and formed a solid partnership.[20]

Sucheta and Kripalani adopted celibacy. In an interview, she said they had been 'living like two friends' out of love and regard for Gandhi's views. She felt Gandhi was obsessed with the idea and went overboard in advocating abstinence.[21]

After the wedding, Sucheta and Kripalani maintained a long-distance relationship for two years. She was based in Banaras, looking after her family, and he was in Allahabad. They visited each other on weekends and spent holidays together. In 1938, she took a year-long leave from work and joined him in Allahabad, followed by her resignation in 1939. Kripalani was working from Swaraj Bhawan and the couple would make it their home. Swaraj Bhawan was then the nucleus of Congress politics in the United Provinces.

Free from familial obligations, Sucheta was keen on starting political work, but Kripalani initially dissuaded her. According to him, 'Sucheta could have helped me in my work as the General Secretary of the Congress. But I did not want her to do that. It would not have been the full utilisation of her talents, which at the time only I knew. I wanted her to follow her own bent of life and to grow. She was quite capable of that.'[22]

Despite the differing views on Sucheta's role in politics, the couple shared a deep respect for each other's work. Their personal and professional lives were intertwined. At the time of their marriage, Kripalani was one of the leading Congresspersons. Sucheta became his trusted aide and helped execute his vision. After independence, when Kripalani quit the Congress to form the Kisan Mazdoor Praja Party (KMPP), Sucheta joined him. In 1956, Sucheta left KMPP and returned to Congress. Now, husband and wife were on opposing sides in Parliament. This invited derision from several people. Kripalani noticed the awkward situation as people were not accustomed to spouses having opposing political opinions. To his credit, Kripalani stood firmly behind Sucheta. When a minister taunted him saying that 'even his wife does not agree with him', Kripalani retorted with, 'I did not marry a highly educated wife to work in the kitchen and breed children'. Kripalani further explained, 'We talk of modernism but beneath our skin we think and behave in old ways! We were criticised both ways as was politically advantageous to our opponents. It was the old mentality that the wife was the appendage of the husband in spite of universal franchise.'[23] Theirs was truly a partnership of equals.

Sucheta's political journey started at the grassroots when she joined as a worker at the ward level in Allahabad. Later, she took charge of the foreign affairs department, ultimately handing it over to Dr Ram Manohar Lohia. One of her more lasting legacies was the formation of the women's wing of Congress, now known as All-India Mahila Congress.[24] Unlike other women leaders in the Constituent Assembly, there is little evidence of Sucheta's active involvement with the All India Women's Conference (AIWC). Her priority lay in establishing women's units for Congress across the country.

After the handover of the foreign affairs department to Lohia, the Congress asked Sucheta to organize the women's department in 1940. The department's goal was to raise the political consciousness of women and position Congress as the vehicle of social change.[25] Gandhi's active encouragement created more space for women in politics. However, organizing them under a political banner was a challenge. Sucheta left no stone unturned and travelled from state to state for the task. The lack of finances was a major concern. The provincial units were reluctant to set aside money for the new department. Unfortunately, 'without money women's work could not be organized, as many of them needed some assistance for coming to the office, touring'.[26] This mammoth project was put on hold after her arrests in 1940 and 1944. After her release from prison, she tried reviving the department in 1945 but met with resistance from the provincial committees.[27]

In 1940, the Congress launched individual Satyagraha in response to Britain's unilateral decision to make India a party to World War II. As the war was raging, plans to organize a mass movement were replaced with an advocacy programme. Under the individual Satyagraha plan, Congress workers would go to the people and preach against the war. Sucheta, who was selected to offer Satyagraha at Faizabad in United Provinces, was promptly arrested. She was sentenced to a year in prison.

Meanwhile, the Congress upped its ante by demanding absolute freedom from British rule. On 8 August 1942, its leaders passed the Quit India resolution in Bombay. Both Sucheta and Kripalani were in attendance. To quell the protest, the police started arresting Congress leaders. As Kripalani was being taken away, he told Sucheta to not go back to Allahabad and instead oversee the work in Bombay. Thinking on his feet, he specifically asked her to avoid the United Provinces.[28] Sucheta managed to escape arrest because the warrant had been issued in the United Provinces.[29]

The key task before the workers who had escaped arrest was to ensure party activities did not suffer due to the detention of the entire senior Congress leadership. Sucheta, Ram Manohar Lohia, and Achyut Patwardhan went underground and created a separate cell, known as the Central Directorate. The Central Directorate would send propaganda bulletins and other information to the All India Congress Committee (AICC), from where it was transmitted to workers. Another leader, Aruna Asaf Ali, later joined the directorate. Lohia, Aruna, and Achyut were all senior members of the Congress Socialist Party. The socialists, long on the sidelines of the main party, had now assumed control. A government report noted: 'The Congress Socialist party, from being a left-wing revolutionary group within Congress, subject to the limitations imposed by the right-wing leaders, became overnight the controlling group of the whole Congress organization… The tail began to wag the dog.'[30]

Offices were set up in different locations in Bombay. The underground group collected information, raised finances, and assisted workers who were in trouble with the authorities.[31] By September 1942, a few activists had even organized an underground radio station called the Congress Radio to counter government propaganda transmitted through the All-India Radio (AIR). The radio started with a nightly programme that was broadcast at 8.45 p.m. The bulletins comprised national news and talks by freedom fighters.[32] Congress workers would collect information and pass it on to Lohia and Sucheta who forwarded it to the radio team. The location of the underground station had to be constantly changed and the broadcast team worked closely with Sucheta.[33] The broadcasts were made by Usha Mehta, a student-activist with immense courage, with the help of other activists. Sucheta feared that the radio team was going to be discovered by the police and urged Lohia to stop the operation. She reminded him how Mehta's life was at risk; but Lohia overruled her.[34] The Congress Radio was active till November 1942 when it was unfortunately seized. Mehta was arrested along with the other organizers and was sentenced to four years' imprisonment.

Although Congress was committed to non-violent means, the pent-up anger amongst some workers and the public led to violence and sabotage of government property. The police came down heavily on these dissenters.

With a warrant out for her arrest, Sucheta had to steer clear of the authorities and take on guises to evade them while travelling around the country to coordinate Congress activities. Once, while travelling to Delhi for a demonstration on 26 January 1943, she stopped at Vrindavan in the United Provinces, in the garb of a religious Hindu woman. On her way back, she changed into a bright silk sari to escape surveillance.[35] Sucheta was finally arrested in Bihar. She was in the state for some work when her cousin, with whom her mother and brother were staying, invited her over. For someone who was extraordinarily cautious, she knew she was risking jail time when she decided to accept the invitation. But she continued regardless. After her arrest in Bihar, Sucheta was sent to Lucknow Jail and this time categorized as a 'dangerous prisoner'. She was released in 1945.

Sucheta commented on how 'utterly tired' she was and felt 'discouraged' over the controversy that had broken out vis-à-vis activists employing violent and non-violent means.[36] In fact, the debates over the use of violence turned the Quit India Movement into a cauldron of disagreements. Most of the senior Congress leadership was in prison and, despite the best efforts of others, there was no real central control over the movement. The socialists actively promoted violent means. Jayaprakash Narayan too was in favour of 'guerrilla attacks on British targets'.[37] In 1943, Sucheta met Gandhi in prison and apprised him of their activities. Gandhi, however, disapproved of the 'violent activities carried on in the name of Congress'.

Gandhi's admonition probably had an impact. Sucheta and her colleague Sadiq Ali broke from the pro-violent group of Lohia, Narayan, Aruna, and Patwardhan, and advocated discontinuing violent methods. Sometime later, Patwardhan complained to Narayan that Sucheta was 'turning a priest'.[38] In September, Sucheta resigned from the central directorate. Years later, Sucheta said that the whole question of violence and non-violence was a 'great moral dilemma' for her. 'In the spur of enthusiasm, young as I was, I hadn't cared for anything. I had thought: Let us just somehow or other push the British out the quickest we can. Therefore, whatever had been done by the people, we had not only condoned but we had connived at and helped.' Gandhi's criticism of their means demoralized her, 'And now, when all this trouble started and after Gandhi started fasting, I started feeling very distressed. So, to an extent, my heart was also broken, and I thought why should I carry on that movement (and) it was time for me to go to jail. I then started becoming careless.'[39]

After Kasturba Gandhi's death in 1944, Gandhi formed a trust 'to address the issues of women in rural India'.[40] After her release from prison, Sucheta went to meet Gandhi and he asked her to take on the work of the trust, which involved travelling across India and working in villages. She was reluctant as after a long time she and Kripalani were getting to spend time together; Kripalani had been in jail since 1942 and Sucheta was either underground or imprisoned. On the side, Gandhi pushed Kripalani into getting Sucheta to accept the offer, till she finally agreed. The trust's work brought her close to Gandhi again.[41]

In 1945–46, elections were held for the Central Legislative Assembly and provincial assemblies. Congress formed governments in eight provinces and was in majority at the Centre. The Muslim League formed governments in Bengal and Sindh and stepped up its demand for Pakistan, a separate nation for India's Muslims.

Muhammed Ali Jinnah, the leader of the Muslim League, declared 16 August as Direct Action Day and proclaimed, 'We will have either a divided India or a destroyed India.'[42] Direct Action Day was a call to arms, leading to large-scale riots in Bengal. Shortly, the violence spread around the country. In Noakhali in Bengal, organized violence broke out against Hindus who were in a minority. There were reports of mass killings, rape, and looting. The government was indifferent to the plight of the victims, claiming no conflict in the region.

Hearing of the devastation in Bengal, Gandhi announced that the Congress president would visit the area and prepare a report, adding, 'if need be he would die there'.[43] Kripalani, then the Congress president-elect, rushed to Noakhali, with Sucheta beside him. She had insisted on accompanying him as she feared he was in harm's way. They undertook a short survey of the violence-affected areas. The Hindu residents were scared for their lives and narrated harrowing tales of gruesome violence and forced marriages of young women. Kripalani returned to Delhi to submit his report to Gandhi, while Sucheta stayed back at the request of the residents. To help the survivors get back on their feet, Sucheta started relief and rehabilitation centres, setting up camps. She even patrolled villages to rescue families that were being held captive. In November, Gandhi visited Noakhali. He was distressed by the carnage he witnessed. He also instituted some changes in the relief work.

Gandhi wanted to do away with the camps. According to him, the need of the hour was to build amity between Hindus and Muslims. He argued that once the Congress workers left, the Hindus had to fend for themselves and the camps weren't going to be a long-term solution. Secondly, he asked Sucheta to not give away food without assigning work to people. Gandhi told her that by handing out doles, she was denying the poor their self-respect. When a stunned Sucheta argued that she cannot 'ask a poor woman, with a babe in her arms', to work, Gandhi replied,

'Put a stone on your heart and tell her to dig a hole, which may be filled afterwards. But never give the poor free doles!'[44]

Sucheta was in Noakhali doing relief work for around seven months. At around this time, she was elected to the Constituent Assembly from the United Provinces. In April 1947, she accompanied Kripalani on a visit to Kashmir to meet Sir Hari Singh, the Maharaja of Jammu and Kashmir. They travelled via Lahore and Rawalpindi and heard tales of great distress and communal unrest. Fearing the unknown, a mass migration was underway as Hindus and Sikhs were travelling towards the east and Muslims to the west of Punjab to find safety. Sometimes, these communities would be faced with violence, and often women and children would bear the brunt of it. On their way back, Sucheta decided to stay put at Rawalpindi. She toured the areas hit by communal violence, making detailed notes of the testimonies. On her return to Delhi, she informed Gandhi of the disturbing events. He was aghast and told her that he had no inkling 'of the intensity of the cruelty'. She forwarded her report to the press, in the process earning reprimand from Sardar Vallabhbhai Patel, the minister in charge of internal security, who felt that the publication was going to fuel conflict in Delhi.[45]

Delhi had become a centre for the refugees fleeing the communal frenzy in Punjab. Hindus and Sikhs from Pakistan arrived in Delhi in large numbers. As a result, the Congress formed a committee to oversee relief work for refugees. Dr Rajendra Prasad was appointed chair and Sucheta the general secretary. Sucheta brought immense energy to the task and mounted an effective relief operation within days. She became the voice of the refugees in Parliament, advocating for just compensation and rehabilitation. A few years later, she was at the forefront of the relief work during the arrival of the Tibetan refugees in 1959. In 1971, she helped raise funds and organize support for refugees fleeing East Pakistan (now Bangladesh).[46]

On the eve of Independence, Sucheta led the singing of the national anthem and the national song in the Constituent Assembly. This was followed by Nehru's 'Tryst with destiny' speech. Her involvement with relief work did not leave her with enough time for an active role in the Constituent Assembly. One major intervention she made was when the legislative assembly was discussing the Hindu Code Bill. She spoke in favour of the Bill, highlighting how it stood for equality.

The trajectory of her political career took a turn with Kripalani's changing equation with the Congress. Kripalani's tenure (1946–47) as the party president was marred by internal squabbling. Senior Congress leaders had assumed ministerial roles in the newly formed government. On this, Kripalani was frustrated at the lack of consultation vis-à-vis government policy. He felt that the 'members of the government ought to consult with Party leaders'. Patel, however, who served as deputy prime minister, was of the view that the government was 'responsible only to the elected legislature and not to the Party'.[47]

Kripalani commanded little influence even within the party and this may have been the trigger for his resignation as the president in November 1947. In 1950, he ran for the post of party president again and was defeated by Purushottamdas Tandon. Weeks later, he joined hands with Rafi Ahmad Kidwai to form the Democratic Front, a bloc within the Congress. Although, the Congress Working Committee disapproved the formation of the bloc, they found support from Congress dissidents across the country. In May 1951, Kripalani officially left Congress and formed KMPP a month later. The party's manifesto outlined socialist ideas, calling for 'land to the tiller, more reclamation projects, encouragement to cottage and decentralised industries, an equitable distribution of wealth'.[48]

Sucheta joined KMPP and contested the first Lok Sabha elections from the New Delhi and Gorakhpur District seats; she won the former. In Gorakhpur, she fared badly and could not even retain her deposit.[49]

Her choice of the New Delhi seat was influenced by her work amongst the refugees. In New Delhi, she was up against Manmohini Zutshi Sahgal, a member of the Nehru family. Sucheta and Sahgal had been classmates at Lahore's Kinnaird College. Sahgal noted that Sucheta was popular amongst the Congress office-bearers in New Delhi despite her decision to leave the party. She wrote that 'Congress leaders were determined to help Mrs Kripalani at every turn'.[50] Sucheta won the election in spite of the canvassing against her by the Nehru–Gandhi family. The victory was special because Sucheta had won despite a subdued campaign after she had sustained a spinal fracture caused by an accident.[51]

KMPP fared badly in the elections. It put up candidates in 145 seats and managed to win only nine contests. Sucheta was one of the nine KMPP candidates that won; in fact even Kripalani lost his seat. She led the party in the Lok Sabha. Congress had done exceedingly well in the first general elections. This compelled the detractors to come together. In June 1952, KMPP and the Socialist Party formed a 'parliamentary alliance based on adherence to a "minimum programme"'. Sucheta was elected leader of this group. In August that year, the two parties merged to form the Praja Socialist Party (PSP).[52]

In her first speech at Parliament, Sucheta castigated the government for its failures and lack of vision. She felt the government was being complacent and showed no urgency in dealing with the different challenges facing the nation: 'At the inauguration of the first Parliament of the Indian Republic we were looking forward with hope and expectation to the Presidential address… What was in that speech? It was the usual, formal speech meant for a ceremonial occasion, full of platitudes, beautiful words and high sounding and empty phrases. There were phrases of "national and social justice" and "pledging ourselves to the service of the nation". But the whole speech was marked by a tone of placid complacency. We missed the sense of urgency that should have been there to grapple with the serious problems that face the country, the serious problems corroding the very life of the nation.'[53]

In May 1955, the Hindu Marriage Bill was introduced in the Lok Sabha. The conservative leaders opposed the Bill. One criticism was that the Hindu laws were being drafted from a progressive standpoint when the Muslim personal laws were granted protection. Kripalani argued that the Muslim community was in favour of monogamy and the government must legislate on that. Sucheta spoke in favour of the Uniform Civil Code (UCC), a proposal for one law for all religious communities regarding marriage, inheritance, divorce, and adoption. But she pointed to communal divisions as the reason for the government not enacting a UCC. She supported the Hindu Marriage Bill but cautioned that a law alone was not going to alleviate the status of women. She said, 'We will get the emancipation of women only when women are economically able to stand on their own legs. These laws alone will not emancipate women.'[54] Sucheta was an effective opposition leader, keeping the government on its toes and raising the voice of the marginalized.

Her trenchant criticism of the Congress continued outside Parliament as well. Moving the political resolution at PSP's national conference in December 1955, Sucheta labelled the Congress government 'autocratic and totalitarian', accusing it of 'governing the country in a most undemocratic manner'. She added, 'The Congress ministers behave as though there is no difference between the government and their party.' She then turned her attention towards her former colleague and now prime minister, Nehru. 'The Congress Party itself has assumed a totalitarian form. It is controlled by one single person. The whole policy is guided by him alone. His wishes are carried out as law. Even the Union Cabinet is not a Cabinet in the true sense. There seems to be only one minister in the Central Cabinet. The rest are all yes-men. Thus, one single individual rules supreme in this country.'[55]

A staunch Gandhian, Sucheta believed that the government had veered away from Gandhi's teachings. She felt Nehru didn't understand Gandhi and derided his ideas while projecting Western thoughts.[56]

Sucheta's first term in the Lok Sabha came to an end when her election was annulled in 1955. This happened after Sahgal, her former opponent, filed a petition before the Election Commission claiming that Sucheta had filed conflicting return, an account of election expenditure, as a candidate.[57]

Oddly enough, in 1956, Sucheta returned to the Congress after her scathing attack on the party and its leadership. It is difficult to say what caused her change of heart, given that Nehru was still the prime minister and there was no drastic shift in governmental policies. Sucheta attributed the decision to return to Congress to her desire to do constructive work, not just criticism. She shared, 'After some time, somehow or other, I felt that our work was merely criticism. My own bent was for constructive work. So, I was a little dissatisfied.'[58]

Unsurprisingly, her return to the Congress earned her some uncharitable remarks. Her supporters were annoyed with her for going back to a party that she so strongly condemned in the past. They even accused her of turning into a lamb from a tigress. In the 1957 elections, she was the Congress candidate from the New Delhi seat. Sucheta once again won and represented the constituency till 1961, when she resigned her position to assume charge as a minister in the Uttar Pradesh government.

Sucheta's second innings in the Congress was mostly successful. In 1959, she assumed the role of general secretary (organization), once held by her husband, Kripalani. She was also general secretary when Indira Gandhi was elected president of the party. Initially Sucheta was unwilling to take on the role as she was senior to Indira Gandhi in the party machinery, but she eventually relented.[59]

A series of historic events were soon to take place. Kerala was formed in 1956, following the enactment of the State Reorganization Act when states were reorganized on linguistic lines. In Kerala's first election in 1957, a communist government came to power. In 1959, mass protests broke out against the government and the opposition parties staged Vimochana Samara, or liberation struggle.[60] The Congress played a significant role in mobilizing protests alongside other parties, civil society, and religious groups. Sucheta wrote that she witnessed the communist oppression first-hand and urged the governor to send a report to the Centre recommending the dismissal of the state government. She wrote, 'If I had not gone there, I don't think the Governor would have picked up the courage to report to the Centre that the people in the State were absolutely against the Ministry and they were ready to rise in rebellion against it.'[61] Eventually, the government was dismissed, and fresh elections were called. In the ensuing elections, the Congress, PSP, and the Indian Union Muslim League formed a pre-poll alliance that was successful in coming to power.

It is noteworthy as Sucheta had a special dislike for communists. Many years ago, her arrest in Bihar came about after a communist worker gave away her identity to the police. In addition, while organizing relief work in Delhi in the aftermath of the Partition, a few communist volunteers had even raised a banner of revolt against her.

In 1959, Sucheta played host to American civil rights activists Martin Luther King Jr and his wife, Coretta Scott King. She was then the vice-chair of the Gandhi National Memorial Fund. The Kings visited Sucheta and Kripalani for lunch.[62] A year later, the Kings joined Sucheta and Kripalani as they embarked on a lecture tour in the USA. The Indian couple led training camps organized by the Student Nonviolent Coordinating Committee (SNCC), a civil rights group. Their visit to the USA 'bridged generations of activists working to bring Gandhian non-violence into the struggle for American racial equality'. Their former colleague, Lohia, had a more eventful stay. In 1964, he had been turned away from a 'white's only' cafeteria. Unperturbed, Lohia arrived dressed in whites next day. The management asked him to leave but he wouldn't budge. He was arrested. The US State Department would later issue an apology.[63]

In 1961, Uttar Pradesh Chief Minister Chandra Bhanu Gupta (also known as C.B. Gupta) invited Sucheta to join his Cabinet. She was appointed minister for labour, industry, and community development. Two years later, Sucheta became the chief minister as a result of what is dubbed as palace intrigue.

The incumbent Gupta was asked to tender his resignation to the national leadership under the Kamaraj Plan. The Kamaraj Plan, devised by the then Tamil Nadu chief minister K. Kamaraj, proposed that senior Congress leaders should resign from ministerial positions and focus on the revitalization of the party. In Uttar Pradesh, there were two major factions within the Congress vying for the plum post. One was led by Gupta and the other by Kamala Pati Tripathi. Sucheta was put up as a candidate by the Gupta group. She prevailed upon Tripathi in the contest,[64] becoming the first woman to head a government in India.

As the first female chief minister in India, Sucheta proved to be an able administrator. She focused her energies on governance, paying special attention to improving the irrigation network in the state. She invited industrialists to invest in the development of Uttar Pradesh, offering them incentives. However, on the political front, she faced many challenges. Gupta turned on her when he realized she was not going to do her bidding. The other factions, too, wanted her out. Twice, Sucheta offered her resignation to the governor but was asked to continue as the chief minister. Kripalani noted that Sucheta was unhappy with the political machinations. Her health had suffered tremendously, and she felt unwanted by her colleagues as well as the party's central leadership. In the 1967 elections, Congress formed the government in Uttar Pradesh and Gupta became chief minister. Sucheta contested the Lok Sabha seat from Gonda, in Uttar Pradesh, and won.

Two years later, in 1969, Indira Gandhi was expelled from Congress and the party split in two – Congress (O) for organization and Congress (R) for requisition. Sucheta remained with Congress (O), the old guard, headed by Kamaraj and Morarji Desai, an Independence activist and a political rival of Indira Gandhi. She contested her last election in 1971 from Faizabad in Uttar Pradesh, losing by 78,000 votes.

Sucheta continued to be active in public life for as long as she lived. Sadly, her health deteriorated even more as the years passed. In 1974, she tragically died of a heart attack. She was survived by Kripalani who continued to lend support to democratic causes and lived long enough to see the first non-Congress government assume power in 1977 after the Emergency.

Sucheta ultimately joined the pantheon of selfless leaders that created history and dedicated their lives to striving for a progressive nation. The *New York Times* paid obeisance to her, 'a leading fighter in the struggle for Indian independence'.[65] Sucheta was admired for her idealism even by her political opponents. Prime Minister Indira Gandhi called her a 'person of rare courage and character. She brought credit to Indian womanhood.'[66]

VIJAYA LAKSHMI PANDIT

'When liberty is suppressed, evil flourishes and much of our degeneration today is due to our loss of liberty. It is all the more necessary for us to be alert and on the watch for every little defect and weakness.'

– On the importance of preserving liberty, in the book *So I Became a Minister* (1939)

The end of World War II heralded a new global order. The sun had all but set on the vast British Empire, independence had taken root in the global south, and the USA and the USSR emerged as superpowers. India joined other independent nations in striving to find its feet. Two hundred years of colonialism had battered the economy and deepened communal strife. India's ambitious nation-building programme required international support that wouldn't undermine its sovereignty. At this critical juncture, Vijaya Lakshmi Pandit was India's representative to the world. As ambassador to the USA, and the USSR, and the high commissioner to the UK, she helped implement and mould India's foreign policy agenda. She was a tireless freedom fighter and a feminist activist who donned many hats in the service of her country. Though often overshadowed by her sibling Jawaharlal Nehru, Vijaya broke many glass ceilings, both nationally and globally.

★★★

Born in Allahabad to Swarup Rani and Motilal Nehru on 18 August 1900, Vijaya was initially named Swarup Kumari. The first of two daughters, she was younger than Jawaharlal by eleven years and elder to her sister Krishna by seven. She was lovingly called 'Nanhi' (Hindi for little one), the nickname was shortened to 'Nan' by her European governess, a name that stuck.[1]

Motilal Nehru belonged to a Kashmiri family settled in Delhi since the early eighteenth century. In 1716, the family was granted a land near a canal (*nahar* in Hindustani) in Delhi by the Mughal emperor Farrukhsiyar. Residing near the *nahar*, the family came to be known as 'Nehru'.

Motilal's father, Gangadhar, was a police officer in the court of Bahadur Shah Zafar, the last Mughal emperor, when the Revolt of 1857 broke out. The insurrection was crushed by the British forces and a bloody retaliation followed. Like thousands of families, the Nehrus left Delhi 'in search of safety and shelter' and settled in Agra in the United Provinces (now Uttar Pradesh). Motilal was born in 1861, three months after Gangadhar's unfortunate death. For a while, the family fell into hard times but quickly overcame the odds. Motilal's mother, Indrani, was a remarkable woman who taught herself to read and write and raised the family in traditional Kashmiri customs. Motilal joined the legal profession and eventually shifted to Allahabad, the seat of the high court.[2] Within a decade, he was renowned for his intellect and hard work, and was amongst the highest-paid lawyers of the time.

As he ascended the legal profession, Motilal bought a bungalow in the elite Civil Lines area in Allahabad, then inhabited exclusively by European families. The lives of the Nehru clan were transformed. European governesses were recruited for the young children's education; knives and forks found their way to the dining table. It is believed that Motilal once decreed that only English was to be spoken in the house, resulting in silence as most of the women and children did not know the language.[3] His dress and mannerisms were increasingly Western and his outlook liberal.

Swarup was born at a time when her father Motilal was at the pinnacle of his legal career. In the same year Swarup was born, he bought another massive property in Allahabad. The property was opposite the Bhardwaj Ashram, a venerated spot mentioned in the Ramayana. Motilal named the building Anand Bhawan (abode of happiness). At the housewarming party, a high-ranking British official hoped that the house 'would become the cement holding together the British Empire'. Ironically, Anand Bhawan went on to become a central location in the struggle for India's independence after Motilal gifted it to the Congress.

Despite Motilal's affluence and progressive views, Swarup was not granted formal education. Even her homeschooling by private tutors invited taunts from orthodox people, outraged at the 'freedom' she had been given. Swarup yearned for a university degree, which, in her view, was 'a passport to opportunity', and was disappointed with her father when her brother was sent to London for higher education: 'A paradox about my father was his championship of women's rights but his disregard for his daughters' education.'[4] Swarup continued to receive tuition at Anand Bhawan and even helped her father as a 'compounder' when he practised homoeopathy in his spare time.[5]

The atmosphere at Anand Bhawan compensated for some of the disparity created by the gender divide in terms of education. Motilal was fond of the Western lifestyle and spent lavishly in maintaining the same. He fostered good relations with the British in Allahabad. Anand Bhawan became the venue for countless 'dinners and teas' for senior government officials.[6] Motilal was a product of 'late-Victorian free thinking rationalism' which professed its faith in 'human intellect and science'.[7] This trait defined the lives of his children. The Western lifestyle and the intermingling with the British initiated them into a cosmopolitan world, providing them with ready access to differing views and cultures. It was perhaps at these gatherings that both Jawaharlal and Swarup imbibed the crafts of diplomacy – Swarup more so, as she stayed on while Jawaharlal went to London for his studies. She was instilled with self-confidence, a quality which served her well when she was required to put across her views forcefully without being antagonistic. In her own words, she 'grew up without any sort of rancour toward or dislike of white people'.[8] Swarup's privileged childhood shielded her from such instincts, giving her an edge in diplomatic endeavours. Here she may also have imbibed lessons from her father's life. Motilal, who was one of the 1,400 delegates at the Allahabad session of the Congress in 1888 and 1892,[9] did not let his nationalist views stand in the way of cordial relations with the British.

With Motilal's growing involvement with the Congress, Anand Bhawan became prominent in the field of politics. This accorded Swarup the privilege of an enviable vantage point for national developments. From a young age, she knew of the affairs of the country. There was constant hustle and bustle in her household, with many people streaming in to discuss politics with her father. She was in close proximity to people who became India's greatest freedom fighters. Like her father, she greatly admired Gopal Krishna Gokhale, political activist and a social reformer. In fact, she received her 'first lesson in patriotism' when Gokhale, on a visit to Allahabad, asked if the dress she had on was Swadeshi, impressing upon young Swarup the value of promoting Indian textile industries. Gokhale was in Allahabad to garner public support over the treatment of Indian indentured labour in South Africa. Swarup attended a women's meeting in Allahabad to publicize the issue.[10] Years later, at the United Nations (UN), Swarup led India's fight against South Africa's denial of human rights to people of Indian origin.

Young Swarup's interest in politics was not restricted to domestic affairs. She 'followed with an emotional interest' the Easter Rising of 1916 and the Irish Home Rule Movement – a campaign for self-government in Ireland. The same year, she attended the Lucknow session of the Congress and was mesmerized by the oratory of Annie Besant and Sarojini Naidu. The Irish Home Rule Movement inspired Indian leaders to start a movement of their own (Home Rule League) under Annie Besant and Bal Gangadhar Tilak. Though Swarup was too young to join the League, she nevertheless volunteered at its Allahabad office.[11]

1916 was also the year that Swarup first saw Mahatma Gandhi, who would soon play a major role in Swarup's life – much to her displeasure.

In February 1919, Dr Syud Hossain was appointed the editor of *The Independent*, a newspaper founded by Motilal. An ardent follower of Gandhi, Syud belonged to an aristocratic family from Dhaka. The young editor took up residence in Anand Bhawan. This was where he first met Swarup and after a brief courtship, the couple secretly married.[12] The news shocked the Nehrus. For Swarup, it was 'perfectly natural to marry' outside her religion.[13] However, the marriage was annulled after Motilal refused to bless the union.

Within weeks of his informal marriage with Swarup being uncovered, Syud wrote his last editorial for *The Independent* – his 'independent' ways having cost him the job. Soon after, he left for England as a member of the Khilafat delegation and devoted his years abroad towards the freedom cause in an unofficial exile. Syud remained a bachelor. Almost two decades passed before Swarup and Syud met again, when the former, then known as Vijaya Lakshmi, was on a tour of the USA. They remained friends thereafter.[14]

While Syud left Allahabad for England, the Nehrus decided to send Swarup to Sabarmati Ashram in Ahmedabad. Gandhi chastised Swarup and Syud for entertaining the thought of a Hindu-Muslim marriage, and around this time even wrote in *Young India*, a newspaper he edited, how a marriage between Hindus and Muslims 'would seriously interfere with the growing unity' between the two communities. Swarup's strained relations with her father following the episode improved only after her return from Sabarmati.

Swarup, so far brought up in luxury, found Sabarmati to be 'austere beyond belief'. At the ashram, everyone was expected to partake in household activities and food was sparse and Swarup noted that no one 'was in danger of putting on weight'.[15] The spartan living conditions and an unduly strict moral code – Gandhi advised married couples to abstain from intercourse – left the young Swarup unimpressed. She joined the league of those who respected Gandhi for his ideals but were not keen on adopting his ways.

Satyagraha, Gandhi's philosophy of 'holding onto truth' and frugal living, eventually found its way into the Nehru household. The Jallianwala Bagh massacre, where a British general opened fire on an unarmed gathering, had shaken the country. In a remarkable step for one of the richest lawyers of the time, Motilal, also the Congress president in 1919–20, plunged into practising Satyagraha and boycotted the Western lifestyle. The lavish lifestyle at Anand Bhawan became a thing of the past.

Sometime in 1920, Gandhi's secretary, Mahadev Desai, showed Swarup an article on Jawaharlal by one Ranjit Pandit. The writer was a barrister from Gujarat who revered Gandhi. In November that year, he visited Allahabad to consult Motilal on a case – though Swarup felt it was a pretext to meet her.

On meeting, Swarup and Ranjit took a liking to each other. Ranjit was smitten and on his third day at Anand Bhawan, he proposed marriage. He asked her, 'Could you trust me enough to travel hand in hand with me through life?' Swarup replied, 'Let us always travel together.'[16] The family approved of the match and astrologers were consulted, who suggested 10 May 1921 as an auspicious date for the wedding. Incidentally, 10 May was also the anniversary of the Revolt of 1857. The wedding festivities went off smoothly. The only hiccup that arose was when Gandhi insisted that the bride wear a khadi sari and no jewellery, which was unthinkable for a wealthy Kashmiri Brahmin family. Swarup's mother strongly opposed the idea, but Gandhi's will triumphed in the end. When the couple went to him to get his blessings, he apprised them of their duty to the country and recommended abstinence as a way of life. A defiant Swarup, who wanted a 'normal married life', flatly refused. As was the custom, she changed her name after marriage, and became 'Vijaya Lakshmi Pandit'. [17]

Newlyweds Vijaya and Ranjit settled in Rajkot, Gujarat, with the groom's family. Vijaya's in-laws were not too pleased with the match as they felt that the association with the Nehrus was going to hinder Ranjit's career prospects. Ranjit belonged to an illustrious conservative family from the Saurashtra region in Gujarat. In 1920, after Gandhi's call for non-cooperation, many Indians withdrew from activities that sustained the British Empire. Following suit, Ranjit decided to give up his legal practice. The following year, both Motilal and Jawaharlal were arrested and sentenced to six-month prison terms for boycotting the Prince of Wales's visit to Allahabad.[18]

The Non-Cooperation Movement brought Swadeshi back in vogue, with people burning imported goods, a symbolism that Vijaya found inexplicable given the scale of poverty in the country. Nonetheless, she joined her husband in setting up spinning and weaving centres in villages around Rajkot. Their home became a centre for Congress's 'constructive program', where they founded schools and developed programmes for the Harijans and other under-privileged people.[19] Even after the movement was called off in 1922, Vijaya and Ranjit continued their work in Rajkot. In 1926, they moved to Allahabad. The couple had three daughters, Chandralekha, Nayantara, and Rita.

The latter half of the 1920s formalized the dominance of the Nehrus in the Congress. Motilal and Jawaharlal headed the party in 1928 and 1929 respectively; they remain the only father-son duo to preside over the party in consecutive years. During the same years, as part of an All-Party Committee against the Simon Commission, they authored the 'Nehru Report' – the first blueprint for independent India's Constitution. The 1929

Congress session, headed by Jawaharlal, called for 'Purna Swaraj' (complete independence) and set the date of 26 January 1930, to be celebrated as 'Independence Day'.

Vijaya was an enthusiastic participant in the Congress activities in Allahabad. She helped organize events, led processions, and delivered speeches against the British Raj. In 1930, the Congress launched the Civil Disobedience Movement and the authorities responded by detaining party leaders. This time, Ranjit was also put behind bars, along with her father and brother.

This detainment would be detrimental for the Nehrus. The prison term damaged Motilal's health and he died in 1931 after a bout of illness. A year later, Vijaya was arrested for leading an Allahabad City Congress Committee meeting. She was also sentenced to rigorous imprisonment for a year along with a fine of fifteen hundred rupees. Failure to pay the sum would attract an additional prison term of six months and a Congress policy forbade the payment of fines. At one point, the entire Nehru family was jailed except for Swarup Rani. After some time, Vijaya was moved to a jail in Lucknow, which was an eye-opening experience. While there, she was exposed to the milieu of caste and class barriers. It perplexed her that some inmates, jailed for participating in the freedom movement, chose to uphold 'conservative pattern of their homes' – perhaps an allusion to the practice of untouchability.[20]

In 1934, Vijaya contested the elections for the Allahabad Municipal Board, forging ahead in her political career. She was successful and was made the chair of the education committee.[21] Vijaya took to administration like a duck to water. She convened regular meetings with teachers, patiently hearing their grievances. In meetings with the Board, she called for greater funding for the 'milk scheme', which entailed providing 'sufficiently undernourished' children with 'diluted milk'. Vijaya called for expanding the scheme – one of the first recorded cases of a mid-day meal programme designed to improve the nutrition standards of children. Faced with low budgets, she decided to crowdfund the initiative and the milk scheme she envisioned eventually saw the light of day. At around the same time, Vijaya started exchanging correspondence with Margaret Sanger, a noted American birth-control activist. She even invited Sanger to Allahabad for a lecture in later years.[22] During Vijaya's time as chairperson of the education committee, a young, widowed teacher became pregnant. The Board rules called for the dismissal of the woman in question. Disturbed by the blatant misogyny, Vijaya raised her voice against such sexist rules, but in vain. She did, however, manage to help the woman get the baby adopted and find another job but was indignant over the double standards.[23]

After the enactment of the Government of India Act 1935 (GOI Act 1935), the British announced elections in the provinces. Congress registered handsome returns, winning 758 of the 1,500 seats, and was in a position to form government in seven provinces. There were differing views within the Congress on the question of accepting office. One group wanted to be part of the government whereas the other felt that it was a futile exercise since the prevailing constitutional scheme (GOI Act 1935) was against Congress's demands. At the 1937 Delhi session, a resolution was moved to allow Congress leaders to accept office. The socialist wing of the party opposed the resolution; Vijaya supported the socialists and was against joining the government. Eventually, the party agreed on the demand for office and Congress formed a government in seven provinces. Congress also passed a resolution that directed elected leaders to demand the formation of a Constituent Assembly in the legislatures.

In the 1936–37 provincial elections, Vijaya won a seat in the United Provinces Assembly from Kanpur. Although she was against joining the government, she was appointed minister and given charge of local self-government and health, becoming the first woman in India to be elected to a Cabinet position.[24] When she assumed office, healthcare services were in shambles; she noted that no minister wanted the health portfolio. She, however, gave her best to the task at hand, and increased the budget allocation for healthcare, laying emphasis on developing maternity and childcare services.[25]

The first order of business that came her way was moving a resolution demanding the repeal of the GOI Act 1935 and the formation of a Constituent Assembly.

Vijaya's anti-imperialist stance hardened further when, in 1939, Britain made India a participant in World War II. It caused an uproar in the provinces, with Congress governments condemning the unilateral decision. At the United Provinces Assembly, Vijaya denounced Britain's policies and urged Indians to come together to fight for freedom. She called out Britain's hypocrisy in subjugating India while claiming to fight a righteous war. Vijaya saw through the design of the British 'divide and rule' policy and exhorted others to put aside differences and work towards the common goal. She said, 'The interest of our country demands our unity in face of a common and growing danger. Let us not hold back, because remember: If India dies who lives? If India lives, who dies?'[26]

Vijaya's criticism of the British was not restricted to the affairs of the state. She did not mince words when calling out the press for its sexism. Despite her hard work and drive, it was often her appearance that elicited the first questions from journalists. She compared her press experience with that of her brother, which was dramatically different from hers. 'I think of the interviews I have seen my brother give. What straight, clear, and intelligent questions are put to him, and yet I, who also attempt to do public work, am treated as if my interests were confined to clothes and children and those petty social activities in which the lady of means and leisure engages in order to allay the prickings of her conscience,' she fumed.[27]

Vijaya had a perceptive mind regarding gender issues. She realized that the problems were structural, and a few interventions alone wouldn't change the status quo. She noted the deficiencies in the education system that reinforced gender stereotypes. 'We teach a boy to be manly, and we preach womanhood to our girls.'[28]

Vijaya was also actively involved in the women's movement, and her nationalist agenda complemented her goal of gender equality. She was a part of the AIWC and was elected as its vice president in 1938 and president in 1941–42. She used her position to urge women worldwide to unite on the platform of non-violence. In her AIWC presidential address, Vijaya attacked Britain's hypocrisy of fighting a war for liberty but denying the same to Indians. 'The authoritative nature of British rule in India contradicts Britain's announcements about her war aims. Unless the right of India to freedom is recognized how can the people of India fight to preserve the freedom of other nations.' She suggested that women's organizations work towards disarmament and the establishment of a just world. Vijaya made a remarkable pacifist appeal, calling on the women to denounce wars and ally with 'forces of life'. 'Are we going to join the group that by their acquiescence make wars possible? Shall we bear sons only that they may murder other women's sons and help to maintain a system which stands self-condemned?... The future, not for women only but for humanity as well, is what the women of today make of it.'[29]

The British government had paid no heed to India's protests regarding participation in the World War II. This resulted in Congress leaders resigning from the provincial governments. The party announced the launch of individual Satyagraha. Vijaya too joined the movement and was sentenced again, this time to four months imprisonment.

While she campaigned for freedom from British subjugation, Vijaya was acutely aware of the fact that women's rights depended on the larger political milieu. Keeping this in mind, she urged the AIWC to ally with other progressive movements in the country. She also stressed on codifying the Hindu laws to ensure equality of status between men and women.[30] In an ironic twist of fate, the outdated succession laws would leave her penniless.[31]

In August 1942, Congress launched the Quit India Movement. Shortly after the launch, Vijaya returned to prison on 12 August 1942. At 2 a.m. that night, 'seven truckloads of armed policemen' came to arrest her in Allahabad.[32] She immediately knew that the movement would mean multiple jail terms for the Congress leadership.

In 1943, Vijaya and Ranjit decided to send their children to USA as they felt the tense political situation in India was not conducive for their studies. She saw off her daughters in Bombay while she was on parole and headed straight to jail.[33] This must have been a testing time for the Pandit family. Both Vijaya and Ranjit, lodged in the same jail, found time for each other, exchanging notes, at times singing together. In her diary entry on 27 April 1943, she wrote, 'I hope Ranjit will not be transferred to Bareilly jail. In 1932 this place broke his health completely.'[34] Her worst fears came true when Ranjit was transferred to the Bareilly prison, and eventually died there after being denied timely medical attention.[35]

Ranjit's demise was not just a personal loss for Vijaya. The absence of a direct male heir and a will meant that Vijaya and her daughters had no claim on his property.[36] To make matters worse, Ranjit's family refused to provide Vijaya with a share; her brother-in-law went to the extent of freezing a joint bank account in the name of Ranjit and Vijaya.

The fighter that she was, Vijaya filed a case to claim a share, although senior lawyers told her that she stood no chance in a court of law. Gandhi came to her rescue and helped negotiate a compromise with her in-laws.[37] Her case was widely reported and gave impetus to the demands for the codification of Hindu laws based on equality between men and women. The conservative section resisted the move, calling it an interference in religious affairs. Ultimately, the Hindu

Succession Act was enacted in 1956 and gave the wife, mother, and direct descendants precedence in succession over other family members. The Act was amended in 2005 and now allows married daughters a share in ancestral property.

After Ranjit's death, Vijaya's workload increased. She headed for Calcutta to help with the famine relief effort and raise funds for children. Gandhi wanted her to travel to USA to inform the Americans of how the British were oppressing Indians.[38] Congress leaders were hopeful that USA would put pressure on Britain to allow independence for India. This was a morale boost for Vijaya, who had considered travelling there herself in the hope of earning an income through lecturing.

In January 1945, the Allied countries were scheduled to meet at the Conference of the Institute of Pacific Relations in Hot Springs, Virginia, to discuss Asia's future post the world war. Vijaya was to represent India at the conference but her passport had been confiscated and there was little hope of the government reissuing it. After some hectic back-channel discussions, the Americans came to her aid. She was offered a seat on a USA Army transport plane.[39] Her travel on an army plane sans passport was believed to have been facilitated by President Roosevelt himself.[40] Once in USA, she was reunited with her daughters who were studying there.

In USA, she met Dr Syud Hossain, who was the chair of the National Committee for India's Freedom (NCIF). It fell upon him and his Committee to organize 'platforms for Vijaya Lakshmi when she reached America to become the voice of independent India'.[41] Her calendar was packed with speaking engagements around the country, press interviews, and meeting the American public and officials. Vijaya criticized USA for not fully supporting India's cause of freedom. This elicited an official response from the USA government saying it was ready to help 'in any appropriate manner'.[42]

In meeting after meeting, she raised the subject of India's freedom, skilfully getting the American public on her side.[43]

Wherever she went she was greeted by huge crowds. Vijaya's tour was a success, but she wasn't done yet.

In 1944, the USA, the UK, the USSR, and China proposed the formation of an international organization – what is today the UN. Representatives of the four countries, along with several other nations, convened in San Francisco in April 1945 to work out the modalities of the proposed organization. The British government sent an official delegation from India with members sympathetic to the Empire. Vijaya declared that the official Indian delegation had no representative capacity and labelled the members 'British stooges'. The official Indian delegation was no match for Vijaya's oratory and passionate appeal, and her biting criticism even changed the mind of at least one of the members of the official delegation.[44]

Her successful tour of 1945 led Viceroy Lord Wavell to appoint her as head of the Indian delegation for the UN General Assembly session of 1946. She was the first woman to head a country's delegation.[45] At the UN, she led India's case against South Africa's mistreatment and denial of human rights to Indians residing there – an issue she had raised in Allahabad thirty years ago.[46] The General Assembly passed a resolution noting the mistreatment of Indians. While India won the vote by a two-thirds majority, it did not lead to any positive change for the residents in South Africa.

Her time in USA equipped Vijaya with the skills to become a diplomat-par-excellence. Soon after the UN session, she moved back to India, where she was elected to the Constituent Assembly. In her first and only speech, she recalled moving a resolution in 1937, demanding the formation of a Constituent Assembly: 'It was my privilege in 1937 to move the first resolution… in my Province, demanding a Constituent Assembly to draw up a constitution for an independent India. Today, ten years later, that Constituent Assembly is meeting here. This is a historic milestone in our progress toward freedom and yet, Sir, freedom remains just a little beyond our grasp.'[47]

In August 1947, Vijaya was appointed India's ambassador to the USSR and moved to Moscow. Her two-year stint there kept her away from many sessions of the Constituent Assembly. In her many successes, the USSR was perhaps the only exception. Envoys of Eastern European countries were favoured over others, and in her entire time Vijaya could not get a meeting with Stalin.[48] Not knowing the local language, and the inward-looking Stalin era, marred her performance in Moscow.

In 1949, she was appointed ambassador to USA. Her illustrious diplomatic career was to take off. She was, in fact, the first woman ambassador to USA.

Vijaya received a warm welcome in USA. She was a recognized face in Washington and Americans were hopeful of stitching a key partnership. She oversaw Nehru's first visit to the USA and negotiated a generous wheat loan when India was facing a famine. With the ongoing Cold War, USA was irked by India's non-alignment strategy. They saw it as India 'sitting on the fence'[49] and adopting neutrality towards Russia's transgressions. Vijaya had to work doubly hard at gaining the trust of the Americans.

Vijaya remained a believer of non-alignment, regarding it as 'the unjaundiced outlook [India chose] to apply to all international issues'.[50]

Vijaya also went on to become the high commissioner of the UK. She was at her diplomatic best in both the USA and the UK. Despite that, she was also at the receiving end of some off-colour comments. In London, British Prime Minister Winston Churchill once brusquely told her, 'Because I have accepted you doesn't mean my views of women have changed. I don't want you putting ideas into women's heads.'[51]

In 1953, she was elected president of the UN General Assembly, the first woman and the only Indian to occupy the office.[52] Vijaya's candidacy was supported by the unlikely troika of USA, USSR, and the British Commonwealth.[53] For nearly two decades, she was India's most recognizable face on global platforms. In 1965, after Pakistan attacked India, she was enlisted by Prime Minister Lal Bahadur Shastri to negotiate with France for arms, as USA's supply of weapons to Pakistan threatened to tip the scales against India. Vijaya went to Europe as the prime minister's personal envoy and returned successfully.[54]

After her assignment in the UK as the high commissioner, she returned home. Nehru told her he wanted to appoint her as India's vice president but changed his mind later. Instead, in 1962, she was appointed the governor of Maharashtra. The same year, she was conferred with the Padma Vibhushan in the civil service category.[55]

After Nehru's death in 1964, she won the by-election to the vacant Phulpur seat, her brother's constituency. She won again from Phulpur in 1967 but differences with her niece Indira Gandhi forced her into early retirement. The aunt and the niece once shared a strong bond, but it deteriorated after Indira became the prime minister in January 1966. In her memoir, Vijaya blamed the clique around Indira for creating a gulf between them. She described how distorted versions of events were carried to the prime minister, who willingly believed the fictitious tales. During one awkward conversation, Indira told Vijaya that she didn't trust her. Sometime after, Vijaya decided to retire from public life as she felt the distrust was also damaging her personal relationship with her niece.[56]

But she remained deeply concerned by the growing personality cult of Indira. When Indira imposed the Emergency in June 1975, her aunt became one of her fiercest critics and may have been put under surveillance.[57] When elections were held in 1977, she campaigned for the Janata Party.

Vijaya was a champion of liberty and self-determination for nations and their people. Blood relations did not come in her way of striving for causes she held dear. In February 1977, a *New York Times* headline read, 'Mrs. Gandhi's Aunt Is Joining Foes', referring to Vijaya Lakshmi's move to campaign against her niece.[58] In an interview in 1987, Vijaya rued the lack of opposition in India and remarked that 'democracy cannot function without dissent'.[59]

Several former colonies that gained independence following World War II could not sustain their democratic character. It is to the credit of leaders like Vijaya Lakshmi Pandit that India managed to survive challenges and thrive as a democracy. Her life is perhaps best described by the code word sent in the telegram to her father in Paris to announce her birth: 'Tempest'.[60]

Vijaya Lakshmi Pandit's tempestuous life tossed her into prison from the comforts of a luxurious home. The prison also took her father and then her husband away from her. After years of struggle for freedom, she charted India, a young democracy, to a stable course. She even came out of retirement to stand up to authoritarianism, doing her part in guiding the country back to the constitutional framework. In December 1990, at the ripe age of ninety, this illustrious leader breathed her last in Dehradun, at the foothills of the Himalayas.

ACKNOWLEDGEMENTS

ANGELLICA ARIBAM

The seed of this book was sown in late 2018 when I was in a dark phase and going through sections of the Constituent Assembly debates for leisure. The speeches by Begum Aizaz Rasul on separate electorates intrigued me. I wanted to learn more and write about these forgotten women leaders. A few months later, my friend Kirthi Jayakumar asked me to write the foreword of her book on Indian feminists and sent me the manuscript. Reading Ammu Swaminathan's story re-ignited my desire to highlight the women in India's Constituent Assembly and bring their stories in the mainstream discourse.

I'm super grateful to my close friend Akash Satyawali who listened to my half-baked pitch during a game of badminton and instantly agreed to come on board as my co-author. His confidence in the project ensured that we steered towards making it a possibility.

It was a pleasure to work with the team members at Hachette India who have helped put this book together since 2020. A special thanks to our first editor Rukmini Chawla who commissioned this book and believed in it. A shout-out to Aditi Sengupta and Ayushi Thapliyal for the editorial support. I am also grateful for Sonali Jindal's inexhaustible patience and nudges towards the right direction – applicable to both time and the written text.

I would like to thank my research associates Amritha Foustine and Innocentia Atchaya. Thanks also to Rakesh Kotti who translated resources from Telugu to English.

The writing process comes with multiple challenges, and I'm lucky to have friends whose enthusiasm and emotional support encouraged me throughout the process. Thanks to all my amazing friends, especially Chitra Ahanthem, Dhanya Ramachandran, Girish Chandra Singh, and Mansi Jain. I know I am forgetting many names, but all my real friends know I have a weak memory and I am certain they'll understand.

I want to thank my father, Aribam Manisana Sharma, for going through the drafts and urging me to simplify jargon so that he could fully understand the text. My mother, Aribam Thoibi Devi, who I lost during the pandemic, would have loved holding the final copy in her hands for she treasured all my writings although she couldn't read English. My regret remains that I couldn't complete the book sooner.

Lastly, seeing my four nieces – Likla & Leichal, Aria & Amaia – being unapologetically themselves motivated me every day. Though they're too young to comprehend this book for at least another decade, it was necessary for me to tell them about the women who came before them and the struggles endured to enable the basic freedoms that all four of them enjoy today. I hope history moulds their understanding of the future.

AKASH SATYAWALI

The journey of this book started on an evening in 2018. From the start, Angellica has been the driving force behind the book. She conceptualized it, did the heavy lifting during the lean phases, and believed in it when I doubted, giving me much needed confidence. To make this book a reality, she took on the role of my coach, cheerleader, and critic. Without her perseverance, this book would not exist. I am forever grateful she offered me a chance to come on board as a co-author.

In early 2020, we started working on this book with the team at Hachette India. I am thankful to our first editor, Rukmini Chawla, who commissioned this book and Poulomi Chatterjee for steering this book in the early days. It has been a pleasure working with our editor Sonali Jindal, whose thoughtful edits and comments have enriched the book. Her patience and insights have contributed to the final product. I am also grateful to Aditi Sengupta, Ayushi Thapliyal, Ananya Bhatia, and others at Hachette India for their painstaking editorial support.

My friends and family have been a vital source of encouragement. I am glad that my parents can finally hold the book, they have been waiting for this moment a long time. Tanika Chandna has been my biggest cheerleader and a pillar of strength. Her unstinted love and confidence have greatly helped my work. I am thankful to Kulisha Mishra, Aishwarya Mohapatra, Manisha Shastri, and many others whose enthusiasm was crucial. My apologies to anyone whose name I may have missed.

A special thanks to Prof. Rajeev Gowda, my co-author in several other published materials, from whose inspiring writing style and mentorship I have benefitted immensely over the years. My thanks to Amritha Foustine for her help with research.

Soon after we began work on this book, the COVID-19 pandemic halted normal life. As libraries and archives were shut during the lockdowns, we relied a lot on online resources. I am grateful that platforms like Internet Archive and National Archives exist, providing a centralized database for public documents and reports from decades ago that are not available otherwise. This book would be poorer without the access to knowledge these platforms provide. A shout-out to the Facebook community 'Ask for PDFs from People with Institutional Access'. The kindness of strangers helped me access articles and books which would not have been affordable in the normal course. My special thanks to my friends Soham Patel and Hamed Safwi who went out of their ways to arrange archival material and books in Ahmedabad and Kolkata respectively.

It takes a village to raise a child and also to write a book. I am grateful to everyone who has been part of this wonderful journey.

NOTES

INTRODUCTION

1. Data from Inter-Parliamentary Union.

2. Ray, Renuka, *My Reminiscences: Social Development During the Gandhian Era and After* p. 267.

AMMU SWAMINATHAN

1. Constituent Assembly debates, Volume 11, 24 November 1949 https://www.constitutionofindia.net/debates/24-nov-1949/.

2. Kirthi Jayakumar, *Game Changers: Untold Stories of Indian Feminists from the Past and the Present*, Hay House, 2020, p. 105.

3. Aparna Gopan, 'Ammu Swaminathan: The Strongest Advocate against Caste Discrimination, She Lived by Example,' *Indian Express*, 16 January 2018, https://indianexpress.com/article/gender/ammu-swaminathan-the-strongest-advocate-against-caste-discrimination-she-lived-by-example-5035766/.

4. Peter Ward Fay, *The Forgotten Army: India's Armed Struggle for Independence 1942–1945*, Raja Rammohun Roy Library Foundation, Rupa Co., 1995, p. 33.

5. Ibid.

6. Ibid, p. 34.

7. Ibid.

8. Ibid.

9. Ibid, p. 35.

10. Subhashini Ali, 'Education for Women,' *Seminar*, 540, 2004, https://www.india-seminar.com/2004/540/540%20subhashini%20ali.htm.

11. AM, 'Lakshmi Sahgal and Free Will,' *Economic and Political Weekly*, vol. 47, no. 33, 2012, pp. 26–28. *JSTOR*, www.jstor.org/stable/41720034. Accessed 24 June 2021.

12. Fay, *The Forgotten Army*, p. 35.

13. Ibid.

14. Gopan, 'Ammu Swaminathan'.

15. Fay, *The Forgotten Army*, p. 35.

16. Ibid.

17. Gopan, 'Ammu Swaminathan.'

18. Ibid.

19. Fay, *The Forgotten Army*, p. 35

20. Leela Gulati, 'Age of Marriage of Women and Population Growth: The Kerala Experience,' *Economic and Political Weekly*, vol. 11, no. 31/33, 1976, pp. 1225–1234. *JSTOR*, www.jstor.org/stable/4364831. Accessed 24 June 2021.

21. Ibid.

22. Gopan, 'Ammu Swaminathan'.

23. Fay, *The Forgotten Army*, p. 35.

24. Ibid, p. 36.

25. Ibid, p. 37.

26. Ibid, p. 38.

27. Ibid, p. 37.

28. Ibid, p. 38.

29. Ibid, p. 39.

30. Ibid, p. 37.

31. Ibid, p. 43.

32. Maulik Pathak, 'Mrinalini Sarabhai, Legendary Dancer, Dies at 97,' *Mint*, 21 January 2016, https://www.livemint.com/Consumer/EvJpffdSNrDKKqKdinH2pL/Mrinalini-Sarabhai-legendary-Indian-classical-dancer-dies.html.

33. Ali, 'Education for Women'; Gopan, 'Ammu Swaminathan'.

34. AM, 'Lakshmi Sahgal and Free Will.'

35. Fay, *The Forgotten Army*, p. 37.

36. AM, 'Lakshmi Sahgal and Free Will.'

37. Fay, *The Forgotten Army*, p. 37.

38. Gopan, 'Ammu Swaminathan'.

39. Jayakumar, *Game Changers* p. 107; Gopan, 'Ammu Swaminathan.'

40. Jayakumar, *Game Changers* p. 107; G. Gomathi, 'Social and Political Awakening of Women in Tamil Nadu 1917 to 1975,' Mother Teresa Women's University, 2007, p. 58, http://hdl.handle.net/10603/263805.

41. 'Women's Indian Association,' Encyclopedia.com, https://www.encyclopedia.com/international/encyclopedias-almanacs-transcripts-and-maps/womens-indian-association.

42. 'Copy of the Address presented by the All India Women's Deputation,' *Women's Franchise*, Vol. 5, Issue 1, 1998, https://journals.sagepub.com/doi/10.1177/097152159800500112.

43. Margaret Cousins, 'Franchise for Indian Women', *The Hindu*, 22 May 1919 https://www.thehindu.com/archives/franchise-for-indian-women/article27199593.ece

44. Gomathi, 'Social and Political Awakening of Women in Tamil Nadu.'

45. Smita Gupta, 'Comrade Lakshmi Sahgal (1914–2012): Revolutionary, a True Daughter of India,' *Social Scientist*, vol. 40, no. 9/10, 2012, pp. 85–89. *JSTOR*, www.jstor.org/stable/23338888. Accessed 25 June 2021.

46. AM, 'Lakshmi Sahgal and Free Will.'

47. Gupta, 'Comrade Lakshmi Sahgal.'

48. Fay, *The Forgotten Army*, p. 38.

49. Ibid, p. 40.

50. Ali, 'Education for Women.'

51. Fay, *The Forgotten Army*, p. 39.

52. Gomathi, 'Social and Political Awakening of Women;' Fay, *The Forgotten Army*, p. 40.

53. AM, 'Lakshmi Sahgal and Free Will.'

54. Fay, *The Forgotten Army*, p. 40.

55. Ibid, p. 41.

56. AM, 'Lakshmi Sahgal and Free Will.'

57. Gupta, 'Comrade Lakshmi Sahgal (1914–2012).'

58. Fay, *The Forgotten Army*, p. 42; Parvathi Menon, 'Captain Lakshmi Sahgal (1914–2012): A Life of Struggle,' *The Hindu*, 23 July 2012, https://www.thehindu.com/news/national/captain-lakshmi-sahgal-1914-2012-a-life-of-struggle/article3672666.ece.

59. Fay, *The Forgotten Army*, p. 42.

60. Rosalind Parr, 'Solving World Problems: The Indian Women's Movement, Global Governance, and "the Crisis of Empire", 1933–46,' *Journal of Global History, 16*(1), 122–40, doi:10.1017/S1740022820000169.

61. Gomathi, 'Social and Political Awakening of Women'; J Devika, *Her-self: Early Writings on Gender by Malayalee Women, 1898–1938*, Stree, 2005, p. 116.

62. Jayakumar, *Game Changers*, p. 108.

63. Ibid.

64. Jawaharlal Nehru, 'Letter to Ammu Swaminathan 2 September 1936,' *Selected Works of Jawaharlal Nehru*, Orient Longman, Vol. 7, 1972, p. 466.

65. Fay, *The Forgotten*, p. 43.

66. Gupta, 'Comrade Lakshmi Sahgal (1914–2012).'

67. Fay, *The Forgotten Army* p. 48.

68. A. Chandrasekaran, 'Women of Tamil Nadu and Indian National Movement During 1920–1947,' *Proceedings of the Indian History Congress*, 58, 536–42, 1997, http://www.jstor.org/stable/44143958. Retrieved 21 September 2020.

69. Gopan, 'Ammu Swaminathan.'

70. Jayakumar, *Game Changers*, p. 110; Gopan, 'Ammu Swaminathan.'

71. 'Mrs Ammu Swaminathan', *The Indian Review*, G.A. Natesan & Company, 1945, Vol. 46, p. 736, https://archive.org/details/in.ernet.dli.2015.144603/page/n1081/mode/2up?q=ammu+swaminathan&view=theater.

72. Maya Majumdar, *Encyclopaedia of Gender Equality Through Women Empowerment*, Sarup and Sons, 2005, p. 49.

73. Chitra Sinha, 'Images of Motherhood: the Hindu Code Bill Discourse', *Economic and Political Weekly*, Vol. 42, 43, 27 October 2007, https://www.epw.in/journal/2007/43/special-articles/images-motherhood-hindu-code-bill-discourse.html.

74. Jayakumar, *Game Changers*, p. 107.

75. Majumdar, *Encyclopaedia of Gender Equality*, p. 49.

76. Vasant Moon, *Dr Ambedkar: Speeches and Writings*, Dr Ambedkar Foundation, vol 14, part 1, pp. 4–12, https://www.mea.gov.in/Images/CPV/Volume14_Part_I.pdf.

77. Ibid, pp. 4–12.

78. Constituent Assembly Debates, Volume 11, 24 November 1949.

79. Parliamentary Debates, Vol. 2, Part I, 3 April 1950, p. 1267, https://eparlib.nic.in/bitstream/123456789/759949/1/ppd_03-04-1950.pdf.

80. 'List of Members,' Lok Sabha, https://sansad.in/ls/members.

81. 'Statistical Report on General Elections 1951 to the First Lok Sabha,' Election Commission of India, p. 97.

82. Parliamentary Debates, Vol. 4, Part 2, 3 August 1953, https://eparlib.nic.in/bitstream/123456789/55547/1/lsd_01_04_03-08-1953.pdf.

83. Rajya Sabha, https://rajyasabha.nic.in/rsnew/member_site/mpterms.aspx.

84. Jayakumar, *Game Changers*, p. 111.

85. Soumya Mathew, 'Ammu Swaminathan: The Strongest Advocate Against Caste Discrimination, She Lived by Example', *Indian Express*, 3 February 2018, https://indianexpress.com/article/gender/ammu-swaminathan-the-strongest-advocate-against-caste-discrimination-she-lived-by-example-5035766/.

86. Gopan, 'Ammu Swaminathan.'

ANNIE MASCARENE

1. Constituent Assembly Debates, Volume 8, 16 June 1949.

2. K.C. John, *Songs of Freedom: Kerala's Many Mutinies*, Frog Books, p. 98.

3. Manu S. Pillai, *The Ivory Throne: Chronicles of the House of Travancore*, Harper Collins, 2015, p. 9.

4. C. J. Fuller, 'Kerala Christians and the Caste System,' *Man*, vol. 11, no. 1, 1976, pp. 53–70, *JSTOR*, www.jstor.org/stable/2800388. Accessed 17 June 2021.

5. Philip Varghese, 'Introduction to Caste in Christianity: Case of Kerala,' Jawaharlal Nehru University, 12 March 2010, https://ssrn.com/abstract=2694487

6. 'Members Bio-Profile,' sansad.in.

7. J. Devika, *Engendering Individuals: The Language of Re-forming in Early Twentieth Century Keralam*, Orient BlackSwan, p. 331.

8. SA, 'Mixed Fortunes for the Daughters of Travancore,' *The Economist*, 28 March 2013, https://www.economist.com/banyan/2013/03/28/mixed-fortunes-for-the-daughters-of-travancore.

9. Pillai, *The Ivory Throne*, p. 279.

10. Shruti Jani, 'Annie Mascarene: Trailblazer From Travancore,' Feminism in India, 7 March 2018, https://feminisminindia.com/2018/03/07/annie-mascarene-constituent-assembly/.

11. Pillai, *The Ivory Throne*, p. 399.

12. Asha Nair, 'Universal Franchise, a Hard-earned Right,' *New Indian Express*, 17 May 2012, newindianexpress.com/cities/thiruvananthapuram/2011/apr/12/universal-franchise-a-hard-earned-right-243899.html.

13. Pillai, *The Ivory Throne*, p. 400.

14. PT Haridas, 'Genesis of the Travancore State Congress,' *Proceedings of the Indian History Congress*, vol. 38, 1977, pp. 398–404., www.jstor.org/stable/44139095. Accessed 17 June 2021.

15. Pillai, *The Ivory Throne*, p. 400.

16. Ibid, p. 401.

17. Ibid.

18. Ibid.

19. Ibid, p. 405.

20. M. Karunakaran, 'The Role of Annie Mascarene, the Freedom Fighter in the Travancore Princely State,' *Proceedings of the Indian History Congress*, vol. 69, 2008, pp. 1268–1269., www.jstor.org/stable/44147300. Accessed 16 June 2021.

21. Haridas, 'Genesis of the Travancore State Congress.'

22. Pillai, *The Ivory Throne*, p. 406.

23. Karunakaran, 'The Role of Annie Mascarene.'

24. Ibid.

25. Ibid

26. Ibid.

27. Priya Ravichandran, 'Annie Mascarene: Freedom Fighter, Nation Builder, Guardian of Democracy and Kerala's First MP,' *Indian Express*, 13 August 2022, https://indianexpress.com/article/gender/annie-mascarene-freedom-fighter-nation-builder-guardian-of-democracy-and-keralas-first-mp-5066085/.

28. Karunakaran, 'The Role of Annie Mascarene.'

29. Pillai, *The Ivory Throne*, p. 406.

30. https://cmsadmin.amritmahotsav.nic.in/district-reopsitory-detail.htm?2438

31. Karunakaran, 'The Role of Annie Mascarene.'

32. S. Jamasin Rajini, 'Trial and Punishment,' *Progress of Judiciary in Travancore 1800–1947*, Manonmaniam Sundaranar University, 2007, https://shodhganga.inflibnet.ac.in/bitstream/10603/56351/11/11_chapter%204.pdf.

33. M. K. Gandhi, *The Indian States' Problem*, Navjivan Press, 1941, p. 114, https://ia600607.us.archive.org/19/items/in.ernet.dli.2015.114358/2015.114358.The-Indian-States-Problem_text.pdf.

34. Karunakaran, 'The Role of Annie Mascarene.'

35. Rajini, 'Trial and Punishment.'

36. Gopika IS, 'Annie Mascarene: A Freedom Fighter Erased from History,' *New India Express*, 15 August 2019, https://www.newindianexpress.com/cities/thiruvananthapuram/2019/aug/15/annie-mascarene-a-freedom-fighter-erased-from-history-2019113.html.

37. Mahatma Gandhi, *The Collected Works of Mahatma Gandhi*, Vol. 88, Gandhi Sevagram Ashram, p. 229, http://www.gandhiashramsevagram.org/gandhi-literature/mahatma-gandhi-collected-works-volume-88.pdf.

38. Mahatma Gandhi, *The Collected Works of Mahatma Gandhi*, Vol. 89, Gandhi Sevagram Ashram, https://www.gandhiashramsevagram.org/gandhi-literature/mahatma-gandhi-collected-works-volume-89.pdf.

39. Gandhi, *The Collected Works of Mahatma Gandhi*, Vol. 89.

40. RT Anjana, 'Extremist Movement in Kerala During the Struggle for Responsible Government,' *Shanlax International Journal of Arts, Science and Humanities*, Vol. 5, No. 4, April 2018, http://www.shanlaxjournals.in/wp-content/uploads/ash_v5n4_015.pdf; Pillai, *The Ivory Throne*, p. 464.

41. Anjana, 'Extremist Movement in Kerala.'

42. Pillai, *The Ivory Throne*, p. 466.

43. Rajini, 'Trial and Punishment.'

44. Pillai, *The Ivory Throne*, pp. 468–71.

45. Pillai, *The Ivory Throne*, p. 472.

46. M.M. Kochuthressia, *Women and Political Change in Kerala since Independence*, Cochin University of Science and Technology, 1994, http://hdl.handle.net/10603/54234.

47. Ibid.

48. Constituent Assembly Debates, Volume 8, 16 June 1949.

49. Ibid.

50. Constituent Assembly Debates, Volume 11, 18 November 1949, https://www.constitutionofindia.net/debates/18-nov-1949/.

51. Ibid.

52. Ibid.

53. KC John, *Kerala, the Melting Pot*, Nunes Publishers, 1991, p. 231; *Ministers of Kerala: Down the Years*, http://www.niyamasabha.org/codes/Ministers%20Book%20Final.pdf.

54. John, *Songs of Freedom*, p. 99.

55. *Journal of Kerala Studies*. (2007) Volume 34: University of Kerala. p. 201, https://books.google.co.in/books?redir_esc=y&id=nzcWpENcaEEC&focus=searchwithinvolume&q=24+february+1951.

56. KK Jose, *The Relevance of Gandhism in the Post-independence Politics in Kerala*, Mahatma Gandhi University, 1995, p. 14, http://hdl.handle.net/10603/6137.

57. ECI, Statistical Report on General Elections 1951 to the First Lok Sabha, Volume 1.

58. 'Women: Poorly Represented Numerical Majority,' *The Hindu*, 26 March 2014, https://www.thehindu.com/news/national/kerala/women-poorly-represented-numerical-majority/article5830766.ece.

59. Archna Shukla, '60 years ago, in Parliament', *Indian Express*, 13 May 2012, http://archive.indianexpress.com/news/60-years-ago-in-parliament/948623/0.

60. B.L. Shankar and Velrian Rodrigues, *The Indian Parliament: A Democracy at Work*, Oxford University Press, 2011.

61. 'Only 42 More Women in Parliament since First Lok Sabha,' Business Standard, 14 April 2019, https://www.business-standard.com/article/news-ians/only-42-more-women-in-parliament-since-first-lok-sabha-119041400371_1.html.

62. Lok Sabha Debates, 2 August 1952, https://eparlib.nic.in/bitstream/123456789/55548/1/lsd_01_01_02-08-1952.pdf.

63. 'Second Lok Sabha: Members Bioprofile,' https://web.archive.org/web/20160304022508/http://164.100.47.132/LssNew/biodata_1_12/1168.htm.

64. Kaavya Pradeep Kumar, 'Gathering Nuggets of History,' *The Hindu*, 16 June 2014, https://www.thehindu.com/news/cities/Thiruvananthapuram/gathering-nuggets-of-history/article6119447.ece.

65. 'Vice-President Unveils Statue of Annie Mascarene,' Indian Express, 12 September 2013, https://www.newindianexpress.com/states/kerala/2013/sep/12/Vice-President-unveils-statue-of-Annie-Mascarene-515950.html.

BEGUM QUDSIA AIZAZ RASUL

1. Karl Marx, 'The Revolt In The Indian Army,' *New York Daily Tribune*, 15 July 1857, https://www.marxists.org/archive/marx/works/1857/07/15.htm

2. Neil Stewart, 'Divide and Rule: British Policy in Indian History,' *Science & Society*, Guilford Press, Vol. 15, No. 1 (Winter, 1951), pp. 49–57.

3. Address presented to Lord Minto, Viceroy and Governor General of India, By A Deputation of the Muslim Community of India on 1st October 1906 at Shimla; and Reply thereto https://web.archive.org/web/20200628200558/http://www.columbia.edu:80/itc/mealac/pritchett/00ambedkar/ambedkar_partition/appendices/12app.html#n01

4. Barbara D. Metcalf and Thomas R. Metcalf, *A Concise History of Modern India*, Second Edition, Cambridge University Press, 2006, p. 161.

5. Lok Sabha Proceedings, 14 August 2001, https://web.archive.org/web/20050324175906/http:/parliamentofindia.nic.in/lsdeb/ls13/ses7/140801.html.

6. Rajmohan Gandhi, *Punjab: A History from Aurangzeb to Mountbatten*, Aleph Book Company, 2013, Chapter 6.

7. 'Malerkotla,' The Royal Ark, https://www.royalark.net/India/malerk7.htm.

8. Asma Rasheed, *Imposing Identities Interface of Self and Nation in Autobiographical Narratives*, Maharaja Sayajirao University of Baroda, 2006, p. 179, http://hdl.handle.net/10603/59348.

9. 'Loharu,' The Royal Ark, https://www.royalark.net/India/loharu3.htm.

10. 'Malerkotla,' Sikhi Wiki, https://www.sikhiwiki.org/index.php/Malerkotla; Maneesh Chhibber, 'Where Peace Reigns Supreme,' *Tribune*, 19 August 2006, https://www.tribuneindia.com/2006/20060819/saturday/main1.htm.

11. Somerset Playne, R.V. Solomon, J.W. Bond, and Arnold Wright, *Indian States: A Biographical, Historical, And Administrative Survey*, Foreign and Colonial Compiling and Publishing Co., 1922.

12. 'Loharu State,' Imperial Gazetteer of India, Digital South Asia Library https://dsal.uchicago.edu/reference/gazetteer/pager.html?objectid=DS405.1.I34_V16_175.gif; 'Loharu,' The Royal Ark, https://www.royalark.net/India/loharu.htm.

13. Census of India, 2011.

14. Karin A. Deutsch, *Muslim Women in Colonial North India Circa 1920-1947: Politics, Law, and Community Identity*, University of Cambridge, 1998, p. 49.

15. Rasheed, *Imposing Identities*, p. 180.

16. Geraldine Forbes, *Women in Modern India*, Cambridge University Press, 1996, p. 198.

17. Rasheed, *Imposing Identities*, p. 181.

18. Forbes, *Women in Modern India*, p. 198.

19. Rasheed, *Imposing Identities*, p. 179.

20. Deutsch, *Muslim Women in Colonial North India*, p. 116.

21. Gail Minault, *Secluded Scholars, Women's Education and Muslim Social Reform in Colonial India*, Oxford University Press, 1998, p. 295.

22. Simmi Kapoor Mehta, 'Punjab Politics 1922–1934,' *Proceedings of the Indian History Congress*, Vol. 75, Platinum Jubilee, 2014, pp. 536–45 https://www.jstor.org/stable/44158428.

23. Deutsch, *Muslim Women in Colonial North India*, p. 65.

24. Rasheed, *Imposing Identities*, pp. 182–83.

25. Deutsch, *Muslim Women in Colonial North India*, p. 102.

26. *The Indian Annual Register*, July–December 1931, Vol. II.

27. Venkat Dhulipala, *Creating a New Medina, State Power, Islam, and the Quest for Pakistan in Late Colonial North India*, Cambridge University Press, 2015, p. 29.

28. *The Indian Year Book*, Bennett Coleman, 1937–38, Vol. XXIV.

29. Deutsch, *Muslim Women in Colonial North India*, p. 187.

30. Forbes, *Women in Modern India*, pp. 198–99.

31. Rasheed, *Imposing Identities*, p. 185.

32. Humaira Choudhury, 'The Life and Times of Begum Qudsia Aizaz Rasul: An Exploration of Muslim Women's Self-Fashioning in Post-Colonial India,' *South Asia: Journal of South Asian Studies*, Volume 44, 2021, Issue 2.

33. *Women Members of Rajya Sabha*, Rajya Sabha Secretariat, New Delhi, 2003.

34. Deutsch, *Muslim Women in Colonial North India*, p. 187.

35. Forbes, *Women in Modern India*, p. 199.

36. Deutsch, *Muslim Women in Colonial North India*, p. 190.

37. Ibid, p. 267.

38. Christina George, 'Begum Aizaz Rasul: The Only Muslim Woman to Oppose Minority Reservations in the Constituent Assembly,' *Indian Express*, 14 February 2018, https://indianexpress.com/article/gender/begum-aizaz-rasul-the-only-muslim-woman-to-oppose-minority-reservations-in-the-constituent-assembly-5057096/.

39. *The Indian Annual Register*, July–December 1939, Vol. II.

40. *Report of the United Provinces Zamindari Abolition Committee*, 1948, Vol I, Part 2 https://charansingh.org/books/1986.

41. *Constituent Assembly Debates*, Volume IX, 12 September 1949

42. Syed Sharifuddin Peerzada, *Foundations of Pakistan: All-India Muslim League Documents, 1906–1947*, Volume II, National Publication House Limited, 1970, p. 318.

43. *Quaid-I-Azam Mohammad Ali Jinnah Papers: Quest for Political Settlement in India, 1 October 1943–31 July 1944*, Second Series, Volume X, Government of Pakistan, 2004, p. 457.

44. Begum Rasul, *From Purdah to Parliament*, Ajanta Publications, 2001, p. 66.

45. Report of the 12th Session of All India Women's Conference.

46. Deutsch, *Muslim Women in Colonial North India*, p. 200.

47. Report of the 14th Session of All India Women's Conference.

48. Aruna Asaf Ali, G.N.S. Raghavan, *The Resurgence of Indian Women*, Radiant, p. 131.

49. 'Lahore Resolution,' Republic of Rumi, https://pakistanspace.tripod.com/archives/40lahore.htm.

50. 'Presidential Address by Muhammad Ali Jinnah to the Muslim League Lahore, 1940,' Frances Pritchett, http://www.columbia.edu/itc/mealac/pritchett/00islamlinks/txt_jinnah_lahore_1940.html.

51. *Quaid-I-Azam Mohammad Ali Jinnah Papers, Jinnah: Call for Unity, Faith and Discipline, 1 August 1941–31 March 1942*, Third Series, Volume XVII, Government of Pakistan, 2009, pp. 325–26.

52. Resolutions of the All India Muslim League from April 1942 to May 1943, Published by Liaquat Ali Khan, All India Muslim League.

53. Peerzada, *Foundations of Pakistan*, p. 520.

54. *Quaid-I-Azam Mohammad Ali Jinnah Papers: League-Congress Deadlock, 1 August 1946–19 February 1947*, Second Series, Volume XIV, Government of Pakistan, 2006, p. 541.

55. Rasheed, *Imposing Identities,* p. 186.

56. Andrew Whitehead, 'Interview with Begum Aizaz Rasul,' SOAS, https://digital.soas.ac.uk/OA30000086/00001/video.

57. Ibid.

58. Dhulipala, *Creating a New Medina*, p. 474.

59. Granville Austin, *The Indian Constitution: Cornerstone of a Nation*, Clarendon Press, 1966, p. 44.

60. Ibid, p. 154.

61. *Constituent Assembly Debates*, Volume VIII, 25 May 1949.

62. Dhulipala, *Creating a New Medina*, p. 478.

63. *Constituent Assembly Debates*, Volume VIII, 25 May 1949.

64. Ibid.

65. Ibid.

66. *Constituent Assembly Debates*, Volume VII, 3 January 1949.

67. *Constituent Assembly Debates*, Volume VII, 8 December 1948.

68. Whitehead, 'Interview with Begum Aizaz Rasul'.

69. *Constituent Assembly Debates*, Volume VII, 8 November 1948.

70. *Constituent Assembly Debates*, Volume IX, 22 November 1949.

71. *Women Members of Rajya Sabha*, Rajya Sabha Secretariat, New Delhi, 2003

72. Radhika Bordia, 'From Purdah to Parliament: Begum Aizaz Rasul,' NDTV, 26 January 2017, https://www.ndtv.com/people/from-purdah-to-parliament-begum-aizaz-rasul-1652956.

73. Christina George, 'Begum Aizaz Rasul: The Only Muslim Woman to Oppose Minority Reservations in the Constituent Assembly,'

Indian Express, 14 February 2018, https://indianexpress.com/article/gender/begum-aizaz-rasul-the-only-muslim-woman-to-oppose-minority-reservations-in-the-constituent-assembly-5057096/.

74. Padma Awards, https://padmaawards.gov.in/.

DAKSHAYANI VELAYUDHAN

1. Constitution Assembly Debates, Volume 1, 19 December 1946, https://www.constitutionofindia.net/debates/19-dec-1946/.

2. Saritha S. Balan, 'Remembering Dakshayani Velayudhan, the Lone Dalit Woman in the Constituent Assembly,' News Minute, 26 November 2018, https://www.thenewsminute.com/article/remembering-dakshayani-velayudhan-lone-dalit-woman-constituent-assembly-92265.

3. M.A. Valsa, 'Dalit Women Empowerment Struggles in Pre-Independent Kerala,' *Proceedings of the Indian History Congress*, vol. 79, Indian History Congress, 2018, pp. 583–90, https://www.jstor.org/stable/26906295.

4. Ashly Mathew, 'Labour Participation and Social Mobility among the Pulaya Women of Rural Kerala,' Mahatma Gandhi University, 1995, p. 11, http://hdl.handle.net/10603/399.

5. Ibid, 12.

6. Ibid, p. 13; K. C. Alexander, 'Changing Status of Pulaya Harijans of Kerala,' *Economic and Political Weekly*, vol. 3, no. 26/28, *Economic and Political Weekly*, 1968, pp. 1071–74, http://www.jstor.org/stable/4358815.

7. Alexander, 'Changing Status of Pulaya Harijans'.

8. Divya Kannan, 'Socio-religious Reform in Twentieth Century Kerala: Vagbhadananda and the Atma Vidya Sangham, 1900–40,' *Proceedings of the Indian History Congress*, vol. 73, Indian History Congress, 2012, p. 1006, http://www.jstor.org/stable/44156300.

9. Mathew, 'Labour Participation and Social Mobility,' p. 14.

10. Alexander, 'Changing Status of Pulaya Harijans.'

11. Mathew, 'Labour Participation and Social Mobility,' 15.

12. Meera Velayudhan, 'Changing Roles and Women's Narratives,' *Social Scientist*, vol. 22, no. 1/2, 1994, p. 65, https://doi.org/10.2307/3517852.

13. Mathew, 'Labour Participation and Social Mobility,' 15.

14. Ibid, p. 18.

15. Ibid.

16. Divya Kannan, 'Socio-religious Reform'.

17. Meera Velayudhan, 'Linking Radical Traditions and the Contemporary Dalit Women's Movement: An Intergenerational Lens,' *Feminist Review*, no. 119, Sage Publications, Inc., 2018, p. 111, https://www.jstor.org/stable/26776504; Mathew, 'Labour Participation and Social Mobility,' p. 19.

18. Mathew, 'Labour Participation and Social Mobility,' p. 19.

19. Rajsekhar Basu, 'A Page from Dalit History in Kerala: The Pulaya Movement in Travancore–Cochin in the Pre-Communist Phase,' *Studies in People's History*, vol. 3, no. 1, June 2016, p. 50, doi:10.1177/2348448916636699.

20. Velayudhan, 'Linking Radical Traditions'.

21. Article 16 Focus Group, 'Dr. Meera Velayudhan: Key Note Speech (Webinar on Dakshayani Velayudhan),' YouTube video, 1:12:05, 25 July 2012, https://youtu.be/DUbsMJ69R7k.

22. Ishita Sengupta, 'Dakshayani Velayudhan, the First and Only Dalit Woman in the Constituent Assembly,' *Indian Express*, 19 January 2018, https://indianexpress.com/article/gender/dakshayani-velayudhan-the-first-and-only-dalit-woman-in-the-constituent-assembly-5030932/.

23. Velayudhan, 'Linking Radical Traditions'.

24. Alexander, 'Changing Status of Pulaya Harijans'.

25. Velayudhan, 'Linking Radical Traditions'.

26. Ibid.

27. Article 16 Focus Group, 'Dr. Meera Velayudhan,' 10:13.

28. Ibid, 8:56.

29. Ibid, 10:55.

30. Ibid, 11:53.

31. Velayudhan, 'Linking Radical Traditions.'

32. Ibid.

33. Article 16 Focus Group, 'Dr. Meera Velayudhan,' 14:29.

34. Ibid, 19:26.

35. Ibid, 17:06.

36. Ibid, 19:19.

37. Ibid, 21:21; Saritha S Balan, 'Remembering Dakshayani Velayudhan, the lone Dalit woman in the Constituent Assembly',

The News Minute, 26 November 2018, https://www.thenewsminute.com/kerala/remembering-dakshayani-velayudhan-lone-dalit-woman-constituent-assembly-92265.

38. Article 16 Focus Group, 'Dr. Meera Velayudhan'.

39. Ibid, 21:18; Charmy Harikrishnan, 'How Dakshayani Velayudhan Broke the Iron Ceiling of Caste to Become the Only Dalit Woman in Constituent Assembly', *Economic Times*, 15 August 2017, https://economictimes.indiatimes.com/news/politics-and-nation/how-dakshayani-velayudhan-broke-the-iron-ceiling-of-caste-to-become-the-first-dalit-woman-graduate-of-india/articleshow/60037034.cms?from=mdr.

40. Article 16 Focus Group, 'Dr. Meera Velayudhan,' 22:21.

41. Ibid, 22:24.

42. Velayudhan, 'Linking Radical Traditions.'

43. Article 16 Focus Group, 'Dr. Meera Velayudhan,' 26:40.

44. Velayudhan, 'Linking Radical Traditions.'

45. Dakshayani Velayudhan and Meera Velayudhan, 'I Graduated with High Second Class Despite the Teachers' Hesitance to Teach Me,' Indian Cultural Forum, 15 August 2019, https://indianculturalforum.in/2019/08/15/dakshayani-velayudhan-fragments-from-her-life/.

46. Article 16 Focus Group, 'Dr. Meera Velayudhan,' 29:07.

47. Velayudhan, 'Linking Radical Traditions.'

48. Article 16 Focus Group, 'Dr. Meera Velayudhan,' 30:45.

49. Ibid.

50. Ibid, 32:00.

51. Ibid, 32:10.

52. A. Valsalan, 'Formation of Kerala: Problems and Perspectives,' University of Calicut, 2010, p. 82, http://hdl.handle.net/10603/211017.

53. Article 16 Focus Group, 'Dr. Meera Velayudhan,' 33:57.

54. Ibid, 36:44.

55. Ibid 37:00.

56. Meera Velayudhan, 'History Headline: Remembering Dakshayani – A Remarkable Dalit Life,' *Indian Express*, 28 April 2019, https://indianexpress.com/article/opinion/columns/history-headline-remembering-dakshayani-a-remarkable-dalit-life-5698513/.

57. Ibid.

58. 'List of Members,' Lok Sabha, https://sansad.in/ls/members.

59. Charmy Harikrishnan 'How Dakshayani Velayudhan Broke the Iron Ceiling of Caste to Become the Only Dalit Woman in Constituent Assembly'.

60. Article 16 Focus Group, 'Dr. Meera Velayudhan,' 41:08.

61. Harikrishnan, 'How Dakshayani Velayudhan Broke.'

62. Article 16 Focus Group, 'Dr. Meera Velayudhan,' 40:50.

63. Ibid, 41:00.

64. Ibid, 40:53.

65. Meera Velayudhan, 'History Headline: Remembering Dakshayani– A Remarkable Dalit Life'.

66. *Cochin Legislative Council Proceedings*, Cochin Government Press, Sixth Series, Vol. 1, Part 4, http://www.klaproceedings.niyamasabha.org/pdf/CLC-006-00001-00005.pdf.

67. Ibid.

68. Ibid.

69. Harikrishnan, 'How Dakshayani Velayudhan Broke.'

70. Article 16 Focus Group, 'Dr. Meera Velayudhan,' 44:45.

71. Constituent Assembly Debates, Volume 1, 19 December 1946, https://www.constitutionofindia.net/debates/19-dec-1946/.

72. Ibid.

73. Ibid.

74. Ibid.

75. Ibid.

76. Constituent Assembly Debates, Volume 2, 24 January 1947, https://www.constitutionofindia.net/debates/24-jan-1947/.

77. Ibid.

78. Constituent Assembly Debates, Volume 3, 1 May 1947, https://www.constitutionofindia.net/debates/01-may-1947/.

79. Ibid.

80. Constituent Assembly Debates, Volume 5, 28 August 1947, https://www.constitutionofindia.net/debates/28-aug-1947/.

81. Ibid.

82. Ibid.

83. Ibid.

84. Constituent Assembly debates, volume 7, 29 November 1948, https://www.constitutionofindia.net/debates/29-nov-1948/.

85. Ibid.

86. Constituent Assembly debates, volume 7, 8 November 1948, https://www.constitutionofindia.net/debates/08-nov-1948/.

87. Ibid

88. Article 16 Focus Group, 'Dr. Meera Velayudhan,' 53:46.

89. 52:46.

90. 53:26.

91. Chakshu Roy, 'The Early Years of India's Parliament', Hindustan Times, https://www.hindustantimes.com/75th-independence-day/politics/the-early-years-of-india-s-parliament.

92. 'Rajya Sabha,' Digital Sansad, https://rajyasabha.nic.in/rsnew/constituent_assembly/constituent_assembly_mem.asp.

93. Article 16 Focus Group, 'Dr. Meera Velayudhan,' 1:00:30.

94. Sengupta, 'Dakshayani Velayudhan.'

95. Article 16 Focus Group, 'Dr. Meera Velayudhan,' 59:20.

96. Ibid. 59:30.

97. Ibid, 59:35.

98, 'List of Members,' Lok Sabha, https://sansad.in/ls/members.

99. Article 16 Focus Group, 'Dr. Meera Velayudhan,' 1:01:50; Velayudhan, 'Linking Radical Traditions.'

100. Article 16 Focus Group, 'Dr. Meera Velayudhan,' 1:02:00.

101. Ibid.

102. 'Lok Sabha / 1957 / Kerala / Kottayam,' India Votes, https://www.indiavotes.com/lok-sabha-details/1957/kerala/kottayam/555/28/2.

103. Article 16 Focus Group, 'Dr. Meera Velayudhan,' 1:04:51.

104. 'All IND Candidates Contested in Lok Sabha / Parliamentary Election in 1971,' India Votes, https://www.indiavotes.com/pc/allcandidates/28/5/7.

105. 'IndiaVotes.com | Lok Sabha / 1971 / Kerala / Adoor,' India Votes, https://www.indiavotes.com/lok-sabha-details/1971/kerala/adoor/1981/28/5.

106. Velayudhan, 'Linking Radical Traditions.'

107. Ibid.

108. Velayudhan, 'History Headline.'

109. Velayudhan, 'Linking Radical Traditions.'

110. Article 16 Focus Group, 'Dr. Meera Velayudhan,' 1:07:00.

111. Ibid, 1:08:07.

112. Ibid, 1:09:15.

113. Ibid.

114. Ibid, 1:09:53; Velayudhan, 'History Headline.'

115. Sanjay Paswan and Paramanshi Jaideva, *Encyclopaedia of Dalits in India: Leaders*, Kalpaz Publications, 2002.

116. Article 16 Focus Group, 'Dr. Meera Velayudhan,' 1:07:17.

117. PTI, 'Kerala Announces "Dakshayani Velayudhan Award" for Women Empowerment,' *The Economic Times,* 25 January 2021, https://economictimes.indiatimes.com/news/politics-and-nation/kerala-announces-dakshayani-velayudhan-award-for-women-empowerment/articleshow/80449182.cms?from=mdr.

DURGABAI DESHMUKH

1. Durgabai Deshmukh, *Chintaman and I*, Allied Publishers, p. 117.

2. Forbes, *Women in Modern India*, p. 64.

3. Ibid, p. 70.

4. Jayakumar, *Game Changers* p. 107; Gopan, 'Ammu Swaminathan.'

5. Forbes, *Women in Modern India*, p. 73.

6. P. Rajeswar Rao, *The Great Indian Patriots*, Mittal Publications, p. 133; B.G. Smith, *The Oxford Encyclopedia of Women in World History*, Oxford University Press, p. 42.

7. Ibid.

8. 'Durgabai Deshmukh', All India Radio, Hyderabad, 15 July 2009, https://archive.org/details/DurgabaiDeshmukh.

9. Deshmukh, *Chintaman and I,* p. 1.

10. Ibid.

11. 'Durgabai Deshmukh', All India Radio.

12. Deshmukh, *Chintaman and I*, p. 2.

13. 'Durgabai Deshmukh', All India Radio.

14. Deshmukh, *Chintaman and I*, pp. 5–12; 'Durgabai Deshmukh', All India Radio.

15. Deshmukh, *Chintaman and I*, p. 5.

16. Ibid, p. 3.

17. Ibid.

18. Ibid.

19. 'Durgabai Deshmukh', All India Radio.

20. Deshmukh, *Chintaman and I*, p. 4.
21. Ibid.
22. Ibid.
23. Ibid, p. 5.
24. Ibid.
25. Ibid.
26. Ibid, p. 6.
27. Ibid, p. 7.
28. Ibid.
29. Ibid, p. 5.
30. Ibid, p. 7.
31. Ibid.
32. Ibid, p. 8.
33. Ibid.
34. Ibid, p. 9.
35. Ibid, p. 10.
36. Ibid, p. 11.
37. 'Durgabai Deshmukh', All India Radio.
38. Deshmukh, *Chintaman and I*, p. 11.
39. Ibid.
40. Ibid, p. 12.
41. Ibid, p. 13.
42. Ibid, p. 14.
43. Ibid.
44. Ibid, p. 24.
45. Ibid, p. 19.
46. Ibid, p. 22.
47. Andhra Education Society, http://www.andhraeducationsociety.com/Cmspage.aspx?Cid=Our250.
48. Deshmukh, *Chintaman and I*, p. 24.
49. Ibid, p. 25.
50. Ibid.
51. Constituent Assembly Debates, Vol. VIII, Lok Sabha Secretariat, 18 May 1949, https://www.constitutionofindia.net/debates/18-may-1949/.
52. 'Discussion on New Part XIV-A Regarding Language of the Draft Constitution,' Constituent Assembly Debates, Vol. IX,

Lok Sabha Secretariat, 14 September 1949, pp. 1426–29. http://loksabhaph.nic.in/writereaddata/cadebatefiles/C14091949.html.

53. 'Consideration of Report of the Union Constitution Committee Pertaining Federal Judiciary'.

Constituent Assembly Debates, Vol. IV, Lok Sabha Secretariat, 29 July 1947, pp. 894, 900–01, http://164.100.47.194/loksabha/writereaddata/cadebatefiles/C29071947.html.

54. 'Discussion on the Article 25 of the Draft Constitution Regarding Guarantees for Fundamental Rights,' Constituent Assembly Debates, Vol. VII, Lok Sabha Secretariat, 9 December 1948, pp. 937–38, http://164.100.47.194/loksabha/writereaddata/cadebatefiles/C09121948.html.

55. 'In Support of the Motion to Pass the Constitution by Dr. B.R. Ambedkar,' Constituent Assembly Debates, Vol. XI, Lok Sabha Secretariat, 24 November 1949, pp. 887–89, http://loksabhaph.nic.in/writereaddata/cadebatefiles/C24111949.html.

56. 'Discussion on Article 15A of the Draft Constitution Regarding Protection against Certain Arrests,' Constituent Assembly Debates, Vol. IX, Lok Sabha Secretariat, 16 September 1949, pp. 1554–56, http://loksabhaph.nic.in/writereaddata/cadebatefiles/C16091949.html.

57. Discussion on Entry 6 of the Concurrent List of the Draft Constitution, Constituent Assembly Debates, Vol. IX, Lok Sabha Secretariat, 3 September 1949, pp. 933–37, http://loksabhaph.nic.in/writereaddata/cadebatefiles/C03091949.html.

58. Ibid.

59. Deshmukh, *Chintaman and I*, p. 25.

60. Vasant Moon (ed.), *Dr Babasaheb Ambedkar: Writings and Speeches*, Vol. 14, Part 1, Dr Ambedkar Foundation, 2014, https://mea.gov.in/Images/attach/amb/Volume_14_01.pdf.

61. Ibid, p. 400.

62. Ibid, p. 403.

63. Renuka Ray, *My Reminiscences: Social Development During the Gandhian Era and After*, Stree, 2005, p. 149.

64. Ibid, p. 194.

65. Deshmukh, *Chintaman and I*, p. x.

66. Ibid, p. 32.

67. Ibid, p. 33.

68. Ibid, p. 34.

69. Ibid, p. 35.

70. Ibid, p. 36.

71. Ibid, p. 39.

72. Ibid, p. x.

73. Ibid, p. 40.

74. 'Durgabai,' *India International Centre Quarterly*, vol. 22, no. 4, 1995, p. 83, http://www.jstor.org/stable/23003866. Accessed 17 Apr. 2022.

75. Deshmukh, *Chintaman and I*, p. 67.

76. Ibid, p. 71.

77. Ibid, preface.

78. Ibid, p. 76.

79. Ibid, p. 52.

80. Ibid, p. 63.

81. 'Durgabai Deshmukh', All India Radio.

82. Devaki Jain, 'Understanding Leadership: Lessons from the Women's Movement,' *India International Centre Quarterly*, vol. 39, no. 3/4, 2012, p. 6, http://www.jstor.org/stable/24394271. Accessed 17 April 2022.

83. Deshmukh, *Chintaman and I*, p. 78.

84. Ibid, p. 79.

85. Ibid.

86. Ibid, p. 80.

87. Ibid, p. 95.

88. Ibid, p. 98.

89. 'Commemorative postage stamp on C.D. Deshmukh', Press Information Bureau, Government of India, Ministry of Communications, 13 January 2004, https://pib.gov.in/newsite/printrelease.aspx?relid=679#:~:text=He%20received%20the%20Magsaysay%20award,on%20him%20and%20his%20wife.

90. 'Durgabai,' *India International Centre Quarterly*.

91. Ibid.

92. Seline Augustine, 'She Blazed a Trail,' *The Hindu*, 13 April 2017, https://www.thehindu.com/children/she-blazed-a-trail/article17892868.ece.

93. *Report of The National Committee on Women's Education*, Ministry of Education, 1959, http://14.139.60.153/bitstream/123456789/132/3/Report-Report%20of%20the%20National%20Committee%20on%20Women%27s%20Education_G2766.pdf.

94. 'Durgabai Deshmukh started National Council for Women,' India Today, 16 October 2018, https://www.indiatoday.in/education-today/gk-current-affairs/story/durgabai-deshmukh-started-national-council-for-women-know-about-its-aims-and-functions-1368951-2018-10-16.

95. 'Durgabai Deshmukh', All India Radio.

96. 'Durgabai,' *India International Centre Quarterly*.

HANSA MEHTA

1. 'Universal Declaration of Human Rights at 70: 30 Articles on 30 Articles – Article 1,' United Nations Office of the High Commissioner for Human Rights, 10 November 2018, https://www.ohchr.org/EN/NewsEvents/Pages/DisplayNews.aspx?NewsID=23857&LangID=E.

2. Nandkishor Mehta according to some records.

3. Tulsi Vatsal and Aban Mukherji, '"Karan Ghelo": Translating a Gujarati Classic of Love and Passion, Revenge and Remorse,' Scroll, 25 October 2015, https://scroll.in/article/764549/karan-ghelo-translating-a-gujarati-classic-of-love-and-passion-revenge-and-remorse; Radhika Herzberger, 'A Fine Balance: Nandshankar's Karan Ghelo and the Downfall of Gujarat's Last Rajput Ruler,' Caravan, 19 July 2015, https://caravanmagazine.in/vantage/fine-balance-nandshankar-karan-ghelo-downfall-gujarat-last-rajput-ruler.

4. Alastair Lawson, 'Indian Maharajah's Daring Act of Anti-colonial Dissent,' BBC News, 10 December 2011, https://www.bbc.com/news/world-asia-16051168.

5. Hansa Mehta, *Oral History Transcript*, Nehru Memorial Museum and Library, 1967.

6. A.K. Trivedi, *The Baroda College Golden Jubilee Commemoration Volume*, The Times of India Press, 1933, pp. 58–60.

7. Aditi Shah, 'Hansa Mehta: India's First Woman Vice-Chancellor,' Peepul Tree, 8 July 2020, https://www.livehistoryindia.com/story/herstory/hansa-mehta/.

8. Mehta, *Oral History Transcript*.

9. Shah, 'Hansa Mehta'.

10. '19th Amendment: Women's Right to Vote,' National Constitution Center, https://constitutioncenter.org/interactive-constitution/amendment/amendment-xix.

11. 'H.J. Res. 75, Proposing an Equal Rights Amendment to the Constitution,' National Archives Catalog, 13 December 1923, https://catalog.archives.gov/id/7452156

12. 'Copy of the Address presented by the All India Women's Deputation,' *Women's Franchise*, Vol. 5, Issue 1, 1998, https://journals.sagepub.com/doi/10.1177/097152159800500112.

13. Tushar Tere, 'In India, Bapu Detained First in Vadodara,' Times of India, 3 October 2018, https://timesofindia.indiatimes.com/city/vadodara/in-india-bapu-detained-first-in-vadodara/articleshow/66046330.cms.

14. Hansa Mehta, *Indian Woman*, Butalia, 1981, pp. 190–91

15. 'Jivraj Narayan Mehta,' https://www.constitutionofindia.net/members/jivraj-narayan-mehta/.

16. Mehta, *Oral History Transcript*; Mehta, *Indian Woman*.

17. 'Jivraj Narayan Mehta,' https://www.constitutionofindia.net/members/jivraj-narayan-mehta/.

18. Mrinalini Sinha, *Spectres of Mother India: The Global Restructuring of an Empire*, Duke University Press, 2006, pp. 162–63.

19. Ibid, p. 164.

20. Ibid, pp. 175–78.

21. Mehta, *Indian Woman*, pp. 175–78.

22. Mehta, *Oral History Transcript*.

23. Uma Shanker, 'Interview with Hansa Mehta,' The Centre of South Asian Studies, University of Cambridge, 1969, https://www.s-asian.cam.ac.uk/archive/audio/collection/hansa-mehta/.

24. The Collected Works of Mahatma Gandhi, Vol. 43, Ministry of Information and Broadcasting, Government of India, 1999, p. 244.

25. Mehta, *Oral History Transcript*; Shanker, 'Interview with Hansa Mehta.'

26. Ibid.

27. *Constituent Assembly Debates*, Volume XI, 22 November 1949.

28. 'Mrs. Hansa Mehta Resigns J.P. Ship', The Bombay Chronicle, 9 May 1930.

29. *The Indian Annual Register, July–Dec 1930*, Volume II, Annual Register Office, p. 13.

30. Shanker, 'Interview with Hansa Mehta.'

31. 'Working Committee Outlawed Again', The Bombay Chronicle, 26 August 1930.

32. Visalakshi Menon, *Indian Women and Nationalism: The UP Story*, Shakti Books, 2003, p. 88; Manmohan Kaur, *Women in India's Freedom Struggle*, Sterling, 1985, p. 215.

33. 'Bombay's Sixth War Council of Trial', The Bombay Chronicle, 2 September 1930.

34. Sanjoy Ghose, 'Rights For "Human Beings", Not Just for "Men": The Amazing Life of Hansa Mehta,' Wire, 28 December 2020, https://thewire.in/history/hansa-mehta-jivraj-sarojini-naidu-mahatma-gandhi-united-nations; Sonakshi Awasthi, 'Hansa Jivraj Mehta: Freedom Fighter, Reformer; India Has a lot to Thank Her For,' Indian Express, 24 January 2018, https://indianexpress.com/article/gender/hansa-jivraj-mehta-freedom-fighter-reformer-india-has-a-lot-to-thank-her-for-5034322/.

35. 'Remember February 11', The Bombay Chronicle, 11 January 1937; Susan Muaddi Darraj, *The Universal Declaration of Human Rights*, 2010, Chelsea House, p. 53.

36. Report of the 12th Session of All India Women's Conference.

37. Shah, 'Hansa Mehta.'

38. Nripendra Nath Mitra (ed.), *The Annual Register*, Vol. II, July to December 1932, Annual Register Office, 1933, p. 358.

39. Annie Devenish, *Debating Women's Citizenship in India, 1930–1960*, Bloomsbury, 2019, Chapter 2.

40. *Constituent Assembly Debates*, Vol I, 19 December 1946.

41. Shanker, 'Interview with Hansa Mehta.'

42. Ibid.

43. Ibid.

44. Rohit De, *A People's Constitution: The Everyday Life of Law in the Indian Republic*, 2018, Princeton University Press

45. Report of the 18th Session of the All India Women's Conference.

46. Ibid.

47. De, *A People's Constitution*, p. 173.

48. 'Rajya Sabha,' Digital Sansad, https://rajyasabha.nic.in/rsnew/constituent_assembly/constituent_assembly_mem.asp.

49. *Constituent Assembly Debates*, Vol V, 14 August 1947.

50. 'United Nations Charter: Preamble,' United Nations, https://www.un.org/en/about-us/un-charter/preamble.

51. 'E/38,' United Nations, https://undocs.org/E/38; 'Document A/2929,' United Nations General Assembly Official Records, https://www2.ohchr.org/english/issues/opinion/articles1920_iccpr/docs/A-2929.pdf.

52. 'Report of the Sub-Commission on the Status of Women to the Commission on Human Rights,' United Nations Digital Library, https://digitallibrary.un.org/record/623145?ln=en.

53. 'Summary Record of the First Meeting,' Human Rights Commission, https://documents.un.org/doc/undoc/gen/gl9/902/29/pdf/gl990229.pdf?token=7JovPqVUvc2nbkIPM6&fe= true.

54. 'Summary Record of the Second Meeting,' Commission on Human Rights, https://documents.un.org/doc/undoc/gen/gl9/902/31/pdf/gl990231.pdf?token=0YswraCTYNApL2yKm0&fe=true.

55. 'Summary Record of the Twenty Seventh Meeting', Commission on Human Rights, https://documents.un.org/doc/undoc/gen/gl9/902/57/pdf/gl990257.pdf?token=ISqvM9xUrhoeUWvvMZ&fe=true.

56. Roger Normand and Sarah Zaidi, *Human Rights at the UN: The Political History of Universal Justice*, Indiana University Press, 2008, p. 210.

57. 'Summary Record of the Thirty Fourth Meeting', Commission on Human Rights, https://documents.un.org/doc/undoc/gen/gl9/902/64/pdf/gl990264.pdf?token=J1kR9MGkELGxv4o3tC&fe=true.

58. Susan Darraj, *The Universal Declaration of Human Rights*, Chelsea House, 2001; Rebecca Adami, *Women and the Universal Declaration of Human Rights*, Routledge, 2018.

59. B. Shiva Rao, *The Framing of the Indian Constitution, Select Documents*, Volume II, The Indian Institute of Public Administration, 1968, p. 146.

60. Ibid.

61. Ibid, pp. 162–63.

62. *Constituent Assembly Debates*, Vol XI, 22 November 1949.

63. *Constituent Assembly Debates*, Vol I, 19 December 1946.

64. Vasant Moon, *Dr. Babasaheb Ambedkar, Writings and Speeches*, Vol. 14, Ministry of Social Justice & Empowerment, Govt. of India, 1995, p. 27.

65. *Constituent Assembly Debates*, Vol XI, 22 November 1949.

66. Ibid.

67. 'Hansa Jivraj Mehta: 1897–1995,' Constitution of India, https://www.constitutionofindia.net/constituent_assembly_members/hansa_jivraj_mehta.

68. Nidhi Chaudhary, 'Hansa Mehta: Reformer In Gender Justice And Education,' Feminism in India, 30 May 2018, https://feminisminindia.com/2018/05/30/hansa-mehta-gender-parity-education/.

69. Ramachandra Guha, 'The Fear of Freedom in Gujarat,' Telegraph, 16 February 2018, https://www.telegraphindia.com/opinion/the-fear-of-freedom-in-gujarat/cid/1684614.

70. Allison B. Horrocks, 'Good Will Ambassador with a Cookbook: Flemmie Kittrell and the International Politics of Home Economics,' University of Connecticut, 2016, https://opencommons.uconn.edu/cgi/viewcontent.cgi?article=7325&context=dissertations.

71. 'Election of Members of the Executive Board,' https://unesdoc.unesco.org/ark:/48223/pf0000131544#:~:text=Evans%201953%2D1954%20Mr%20John,1958%2D1963%20Mr%20George%20N.

72. Neera Desai and Usha Thakkar, *Women in Indian Society*, National Book Trust, India, 2001.

KAMALA CHAUDHRI

1. Moon (ed.), *Dr Babasaheb Ambedkar* p. 659; *The Constituent Assembly of India (Legislative) Debates*, Part 1, Volume 4, 1949, p. 535, https://eparlib.nic.in/bitstream/123456789/761574/1/cald_06_13-12-1949.pdf.

2. Lok Sabha records, Government of India https://sansad.in/ls/members

3. Disha Experts, *Amazing Uttar Pradesh: General Knowledge for UPPSC, UPSSSC & other Competitive Exams*, Disha Publications, 2020, p. 86

4. Susie Tharu and K. Lalita, *Women Writing in India: 600 B.C. to the Early Twentieth Century*, Feminist Press, 1991, p. 472.

5. Lok Sabha records, Government of India https://sansad.in/ls/members

6. Ira Saxena and Nilima Saxena, *India's Freedom Story*, HarperCollins, 2021, personal tributes

7. Tharu and Lalita, *Women Writing in India*, p. 472.

8. Tharu and Lalita, *Women Writing in India*, p. 472.

9. Kamala Chaudhri, *Bel Patra*, Shiv Books, 2016, p. 12.

10. Tharu and Lalita, *Women Writing in India*, p. 472.

11. Ibid, p. 474.

12. Ibid, p. 475.

13. *Who's Who 1950*, Parliament of India, 1950, p. 20, https://eparlib.nic.in/bitstream/123456789/782468/1/publication_whoswho_eng_pp_1950.pdf.

14. Ira Saxena and Nilima Saxena, *India's Freedom Story*.

15. Disha Experts, *Amazing Uttar Pradesh*, p. 86

16. Ibid.

17. Constituent Assembly Debates, Vol. 1, Lok Sabha Secretariat, 1949, https://eparlib.nic.in/bitstream/123456789/762978/1/cad_09-12-1946.pdf.

18. E. Newbigin, *The Hindu Code Bill: Creating the Modern Hindu Legal Subject*; In *The Hindu Family and the Emergence of Modern India: Law, Citizenship and Community* (Cambridge Studies in Indian History and Society, Cambridge University Press, 2013, p. 158, doi:10.1017/CBO9781139795364.006.

19. Moon (ed.), *Dr Babasaheb Ambedkar* p. 656.

20. Ibid, p. 657.

21. Ibid, p. 658.

22. Ibid, p. 656.

23. *The Constituent Assembly of India (Legislative) Debates*, Part 1, Volume 4,. 539.

24. Moon (ed.), *Dr Babasaheb Ambedkar* p. 663.

25. Lok Sabha records, Government of India https://sansad.in/ls/members

26. 'Lok Sabha / 1962 / Uttar Pradesh [1947–1999] / Hapur,' India Votes, https://www.indiavotes.com/lok-sabha-details/1962/uttar-pradesh-[1947–1999]/hapur/1243/8/3.

27. Ira Saxena and Nilima Saxena, *India's Freedom Story*.

LEELA ROY

1. A. Lahiri and Bijoy Nag, *Flaming Leela Roy*, Jayashree Patrika Trust, 2007, p. 5.

2. P.C. Chakravarti, 'Genesis of the Partition of Bengal (1905),' *Proceedings of the Indian History Congress*, vol. 21, 1958, p. 551, JSTOR, www.jstor.org/stable/44145253. Accessed 16 August 2021.

3. Ibid; Anil Baran Ray, 'Communal Attitudes to British Policy: The Case of the Partition of Bengal 1905,' *Social Scientist*, vol. 6, no. 5, 1977, p. 39, *JSTOR*, www.jstor.org/stable/3520087. Accessed 16 August 2021.

4. Ibid, pp. 38–39.

5. David M. Laushey, 'The Terrorist and Marxist Challenges to Gandhian Leadership of the Indian Nationalist Movement in Bengal,' *Journal of Third World Studies*, vol. 3, no. 2, 1986, p. 33, *JSTOR*, www.jstor.org/stable/45197219. Accessed 15 August 2021; Sukla Sanyal, 'Legitimizing Violence: Seditious Propaganda and Revolutionary Pamphlets in Bengal, 1908–1918,' *The Journal of Asian Studies*, vol. 67, no. 3, 2008, p. 761, *JSTOR*, www.jstor.org/stable/20203424. Accessed 15 August 2021.

6. Ray, 'Communal Attitudes to British Policy,' p. 41.

7. Sanyal, 'Legitimizing Violence.'

8. Laushey, 'The Terrorist and Marxist Challenges,' p. 35.

9. D.A. Low, 'The Government of India and the First Non-Cooperation Movement: 1920–1922,' *Journal of Asian Studies*, vol. 25, no. 2, 1966, p. 252, *JSTOR*, www.jstor.org/stable/2051326. Accessed 15 August 2021.

10. Laushey, 'The Terrorist and Marxist Challenges,' p. 35.

11. Palash Mondal, 'From Militant Nationalism to Democratic Socialism (The Case-Study of a Revolutionary Group Oof Bengal, India, 1920–1970),' 23rd International Conference of Historians of Asia 2014, 23–27 August 2014, Alor Setar, Kedah, Malaysia, p. 486, https://repo.uum.edu.my/id/eprint/14482/

12. Shubhra Dey, 'Gender Assymetry: Brief Remarks on Its Conceptual Aspects and the Social Experiences of Women Revolutionaries of Bengal,' *Proceedings of the Indian History Congress*, vol. 55, 1994, p. 670, www.jstor.org/stable/44143424. Accessed 16 August 2021.

13. Ibid, p. 669.

14. Ibid, p. 670.

15. Ibid.

16. Sarmistha Dutta Gupta, 'Death and Desire in Times of Revolution,' *Economic and Political Weekly*, vol. 48, no. 37, 2013, p. 62, *JSTOR*, www.jstor.org/stable/23528276. Accessed 22 August 2021.

17. T. Mandal, *The Women Revolutionaries of Bengal, 1905–1939*, Minerva Associates, p. 68.

18. N. Sanjiva Reddy, *Speeches of President Sanjiva Reddy: January 1, 1980–July 24, 1982*, Publications Division, Ministry of Information and Broadcasting, Government of India, 1982, p. 181

19. Lahiri and Nag, *Flaming Leela Roy*, p. 1, 2.

20. Ibid. p. 1.

21. Datta-Ray, *Assam Secretariat, 1874–1947: An Administrative History of North-East India*, K.P. Bagchi, 1978, p. 122.

22. Lahiri and Nag, *Flaming Leela Roy*, p. 2.

23. Suparna Roy, 'Swadeshi and Boycott in Barak Valley,' *Proceedings of the Indian History Congress*, vol. 71, 2010, p. 616., www.jstor.org/stable/44147528. Accessed 22 August 2021.

24. Mandal, *The Women Revolutionaries of Bengal*, p. 28; M. Kar, *Evolution of Constitutional Government and Assam Legislatures*, Akansha Publishing House, 2005, p. 251.

25. Nagendra K. Singh (ed.), *Encyclopaedia of Women Biography: India, Pakistan, Bangladesh*, vol. 3, A.P.H. Publishing Corporation, 2001, p. 140.

26. Barbara Southard, 'Colonial Politics and Women's Rights: Woman Suffrage Campaigns in Bengal, British India in the 1920s,' *Modern Asian Studies*, vol. 27, no. 2, 1993, p. 403, *JSTOR*, www.jstor.org/stable/312775. Accessed 23 August 2021.

27. *The Oracle*, Netaji Research Bureau, n.d., p. 4.

28. Lahiri and Nag, *Flaming Leela Roy*, p. 2; Southard, 'Colonial Politics and Women's Rights,' p. 402.

29. Lahiri and Nag, *Flaming Leela Roy*, p. 3.

30. G.H. Forbes, *Indian Women and the Freedom Movement: A Historian's Perspective*, Research Centre for Women's Studies, S.N.D.T. Women's University, 1997, p. 117.

31. Lahiri and Nag, *Flaming Leela Roy*, p. 3.

32. Forbes, *Indian Women and the Freedom Movement*, p. 117.

33. *Sylhet: History and Heritage*, Bangladesh Itihas Samiti, 1999, p. 833.

34. Lahiri and Nag, *Flaming Leela Roy*, p. 3.

35. Sharmistha Dutta Gupta, 'Jayashree and the National Feminist Movement,' *Pakistan Journal of Women's Studies*, 1 January 2010, https://www.thefreelibrary.com/Jayashree+and+the+nationalist-feminist+women.-a0240185781.

36. Lahiri and Nag, *Flaming Leela Roy*, p. 3.

37. University of Dhaka, https://www.du.ac.bd/.

38. Gupta, 'Jayashree and the National Feminist Movement.'

39. Farizaa Sabreen, 'Leela Nag: First female student of Dhaka University,' Daily Asian Age, 20 August 2019, https://dailyasianage.com/news/193211/leela-nag-first-female-student-of-dhaka-university; Lahiri and Nag, *Flaming Leela Roy*, p. 4.

40. *Sylhet: History and Heritage*, p. 834.

41. Southard, 'Colonial Politics and Women's Rights,' p. 404.

42. Ibid, p. 405.

43. Lahiri and Nag, *Flaming Leela Roy*, p. 4; Gupta, 'Jayashree and the National Feminist Movement.'

44. Southard, 'Colonial Politics and Women's Rights,' p. 422.

45. *Sylhet: History and Heritage*, p. 835.

46. Gupta, 'Jayashree and the National Feminist Movement.'

47. Lahiri and Nag, *Flaming Leela Roy*, p. 5.

48. Gupta, 'Jayashree and the National Feminist Movement.'

49. Lahiri and Nag, *Flaming Leela Roy*, p. 6.

50. Ibid, p. 5.

51. Ibid.

52. Ibid, p. 10.

53. Ibid, p. 20.

54. Ibid, p. 15.

55. Gupta, 'Jayashree and the National Feminist Movement.'

56. Ibid.

57. Lahiri and Nag, *Flaming Leela Roy*, p. 2.

58. Forbes, *Indian Women and the Freedom Movement*, p. 118; Gupta, 'Jayashree and the National Feminist Movement.'

59. Ibid.

60. Laushey, 'The Terrorist and Marxist Challenges,' p. 37.

61. Gupta, 'Jayashree and the National Feminist Movement.'

62. Lahiri and Nag, *Flaming Leela Roy*, p. 21.

63. Gupta, 'Jayashree and the National Feminist Movement.

64. Lahiri and Nag, *Flaming Leela Roy*, p. 17; Gupta, 'Jayashree and the National Feminist Movement.'

65. Gupta, 'Jayashree and the National Feminist Movement'.

66. Lahiri and Nag, *Flaming Leela Roy*, p. 29.

67. Ibid, p. 30.

68. Ibid, p. 32.

69. Lahiri and Nag, *Flaming Leela Roy*, p. 34; Gupta, 'Jayashree and the National Feminist Movement.'

70. Sagar Simlandy and Sharmila Datta Banik, *The Legacy of Mahatma Gandhi*, PS Opus Publications, 2021, p. 267.

71. Ratna Ghosh, *Netaji Subhas Chandra Bose and Indian Freedom Struggle: Subhas Chandra Bose—His Ideas and Vision*, Deep & Deep, p. 140; Gupta, 'Jayashree and the National Feminist Movement.'

72. Ghosh, *Netaji Subhas Chandra Bose*, p. 141.

73. Lahiri and Nag, *Flaming Leela Roy*, p. 34.

74. Gupta, 'Jayashree and the National Feminist Movement.'

75. Ibid.

76. Ibid.

77. Ghosh, *Netaji Subhas Chandra Bose*, p. 141.

78. Gupta, 'Jayashree and the National Feminist Movement.'

79. Ibid.

80. Lahiri and Nag, *Flaming Leela Roy*, p. 35.

81. Ibid, p. 38.

82. Ibid, p. 35.

83. Ibid, p. 39.

84. Ibid, p. 40; Ghosh, *Netaji Subhas Chandra Bose*, p. 143.

85. Lahiri and Nag, *Flaming Leela Roy*, p. 42.

86. Ibid, p. 48.

87. Umesh Raghuvanshi, 'Now, Netaji Associate's Son Questions Panel Report on Gumnami Baba,' Hindustan Times, 5 January 2020, https://www.hindustantimes.com/lucknow/now-netaji-associate-s-son-questions-panel-report-on-gumnami-baba/story-aCcmrC7hKwVliz8PBGGu7K.html.

88. Ibid, p. 48.

89. Ghosh, *Netaji Subhas Chandra Bose*, p. 143.

90. Lahiri and Nag, *Flaming Leela Roy*, p. 48.

91. Ibid, p. 47.

92. Ibid, p. 49.

93. Ibid, p. 50.

94. Lahiri and Nag, *Flaming Leela Roy*, p. 50.

95. Ibid.

96. Ibid, p. 52.

97. Ibid, p. 55.

98. Ibid, p. 56.

99. Ibid, p. 58.

100. Ibid, p. 56.

101. Ibid, p. 9.

102. Ibid, p. 59.

103. Ibid, p. 60.

104. Ibid, p. 60.

105. Ibid, p. 61.

106. Ibid, p. 62.

107. Ibid, p. 69.

108. Ibid, p. 70.

109. Ibid, p. 71.

110. Prime Minister's Office Archive, Government of India, https://archivepmo.nic.in/drmanmohansingh/photogallery_next.php?pageid=1127.

111. 'Obituary References,' *Lok Sabha Debates*, Fourth Series, Lok Sabha Secretariat, 1970, p. 6, https://eparlib.nic.in/bitstream/123456789/2593/1/lsd_04_11_27-07-1970.pdf.

MALATI CHOUDHURY

1. Krushna Mohanty, 'From the pages of Malati Devi's Diary 1971', *The Tribal Tribune*, Volume 1, Issue 11, 26 July 2005.

2. Biswaroop Ghosh, 'Religion and Politics in Bengal: The Noakhali Carnage 1946–47,' *Proceedings of the Indian History Congress*, vol. 72, 2011, pp. 936–46, www.jstor.org/stable/44146785. Accessed 14 July 2021.

3. Chandni Saxena, 'Dimensions and Dynamics of Violence During Partition of India,' *Proceedings of the Indian History Congress*, vol. 74, 2013, pp. 909–20, www.jstor.org/stable/44158892. Accessed 13 July 2021.

4. Ibid

5. Ghosh, 'Religion and Politics in Bengal.'

6. Asok Mitra, 'The Great Calcutta Killings of 1946: What Went before and After,' *Economic and Political Weekly*, vol. 25, no. 5, 1990, pp. 273–85, *JSTOR*, www.jstor.org/stable/4395903. Accessed 14 July 2021.

7. Ghosh, 'Religion and Politics in Bengal.'

8. Mitra, 'The Great Calcutta Killings of 1946.'

9. *The Collected Works of Mahatma Gandhi*, Vol. 93: 7 November, 1946–16 February, 1947, Gandhi Ashram Sevagram, p. 46, https://www.gandhiashramsevagram.org/gandhi-literature/mahatma-gandhi-collected-works-volume-93.pdf.

10. 'Malati Chaudhary,' Constitution of India, https://www.constitutionofindia.net/members/malati-chaudhary/.

11. 'From the pages of Malati Devi's Diary 1971', *The Tribal Tribune*, Volume 1, Issue 11, 26 July 2005.

12. *Orissa Society of Americas 35th Annual Convention Souvenir: For Annual Convention Held in 2004 at Dallas, Texas*, Odisha Society of the Americas, n.d., p. 52. Accessed at https://www.google.co.in/books/edition/Orissa_Society_of_Americas_35th_Annual_C/U_aADwAAQBAJ?hl=en&gbpv=1.

13. *Freedom Fighters Remember*, Publications Division, Ministry of Information and Broadcasting, Government of India, 1997, p. 84.

14. Meenakshi Mukherjee, *An Indian for All Seasons: The Many Lives of R.C. Dutt*, Penguin Books India, 2009, p. 76.

15. Ibid, p. 75.

16. Ibid, p. 72.

17. Ibid, pp. 72–77.

18. Manjushree Pradhan, *Role of Malati Devi Choudhury in the Promotion of Basic Education in Orissa 1946–1984*, Utkal University, p. 58, http://hdl.handle.net/10603/281589.

19. Snehlata Sen, *Nehal the Musician and Other Tales*, S. Ganesa, 1923, https://ia801608.us.archive.org/29/items/in.ernet.dli.2015.92190/2015.92190.Nehal-The-Musician-And-Other-Tales_text.pdf; Rajananda Chatterjee (ed.), *The Modern Review*, p. 381, https://ia902800.us.archive.org/24/items/dli.bengal.10689.4296/10689.4296_text.pdf.

20. *Freedom Fighters Remember*, Publications Division, p. 84.

21. *Orissa Society of Americas*, p. 48.

22. *Freedom Fighters Remember*, Publications Division, p. 84.

23. Ibid.

24. Pradhan, *Role of Malati Devi Choudhury*, p. 58.

25. *Freedom Fighters Remember*, Publications Division, p. 84.

26. Ibid.

27. S. Kar Chaudhuri, and C. Chakravarty, *Tagore's Ideas of the New Woman: The Making and Unmaking of Female Subjectivity*, SAGE Publications, 2017.

28. Kathleen M. O'Connell, 'Education at Santiniketan: 1902–1920,' *India International Centre Quarterly*, vol. 38, no. 1, 2011, pp. 18–31, *JSTOR*, www.jstor.org/stable/44733614. Accessed 17 July 2021.

29. Swati Lal, 'Rabindranath Tagore's Ideals of Aesthetic Education,' *Journal of Aesthetic Education*, vol. 18, no. 2, 1984, pp. 31–39, *JSTOR*, www.jstor.org/stable/3332497. Accessed 17 July 2021.

30. O'Connell, 'Education at Santiniketan.'

31. Pradhan, *Role of Malati Devi Choudhury*, p. 59.

32. Ibid, p. 60.

33. *The Modern Review*, Prabasi Press Private Limited, 1959 p. 192.

34. *Freedom Fighters Remember*, Publications Division, p. 84.

35. Manas Kumar Das, *Nationalist Movement in Odisha*, Lulu Press, 2019, p. 61.

36. Justice Harihar Mahapatra, *My Life, My Work*, Allied Publishers, 2011, p. 152.

37. Pradhan, *Role of Malati Devi Choudhury*, p. 60.

38. Mahapatra, *My Life, My Work*, p. 152.

39. Ramadevi Choudhury and Supriya Kar, 'Journey of Life,' *Indian Literature*, vol. 59, no. 3 (287), 2015, pp. 39–51, *JSTOR*, www.jstor.org/stable/44478661. Accessed 17 July 2021.

40. Diptimayee Jena, *The Educational Philosophy and Contribution of Sri Nabakrushna Choudhury in the Field of Education: An In-depth Analysis*, Utkal University, 2011, p. 87, http://hdl.handle.net/10603/282173.

41. Mahapatra, *My Life, My Work*, p. 152.

42. Das, *Nationalist Movement in Odisha*, p. 67.

43. Pradhan, *Role of Malati Devi Choudhury*, p. 62.

44. Ibid, p. 63.

45. Harekrushna Mahtab (ed.), *History of the Freedom Movement in Orissa*, Vol. 3, State Committee for Compilation of History of the Freedom Movement in Orissa, 1957, p. 84, https://ia801405.

us.archive.org/21/items/history-of-the-freedom-movement-in-orissa-vol-3-1957/history-of-the-freedom-movement-in-orissa-vol-3-1957_text.pdf.

46. *Freedom Fighters Remember*, Publications Division, p. 85.

47. Pradhan, *Role of Malati Devi Choudhury*, p. 64.

48. Das, *Nationalist Movement in Odisha*.

49. Mahtab (ed.), *History of the Freedom Movement in Orissa*, p. 87.

50. Ibid, p. 86.

51. Mahtab (ed.), *History of the Freedom Movement in Orissa*, p. 90.

52. Ibid, pp. 88–90.

53. *Freedom Fighters Remember*, Publications Division, p. 85.

54. Kenneth Pletcher, 'Gandhi-Irwin Pact,' Britannica, 27 February 2024, https://www.britannica.com/event/Gandhi-Irwin-Pact#ref1173233.

55. Pradhan, *Role of Malati Devi Choudhury*, p. 67.

56. Pradhan, *Role of Malati Devi Choudhury*, p. 68.

57. *Freedom Fighters Remember*, Publications Division, p. 85.

58. D. N., 'Gandhi, Ambedkar and Separate Electorates Issue,' *Economic and Political Weekly*, vol. 26, no. 21, 1991, pp. 1328–30, *JSTOR*, www.jstor.org/stable/4398052. Accessed 19 July 2021.

59. Dhrubo Jyoti, 'Gandhi, Ambedkar and the 1932 Poona Pact,' *Hindustan Times*, 1 October 2023, https://www.hindustantimes.com/india-news/gandhi-ambedkar-and-the-1932-poona-pact/story-5WuyrphB8OwtRp5lC9XQGP.html; 'To Ramsay Macdonald,' MKGandhi.org, https://www.mkgandhi.org/selectedletters/67ramsay_macdonald.html.

60. Jyoti, 'Gandhi, Ambedkar and the 1932 Poona Pact.'

61. Uday Balakrishnan, 'Ambedkar and the Poona Pact,' *The Hindu*, 14 April 2020, https://www.thehindu.com/opinion/op-ed/ambedkar-and-the-poona-pact/article31333684.ece.

62. Jyoti, 'Gandhi, Ambedkar and the 1932 Poona Pact.'

63. Janmejay Choudhury, 'Gandhi's Padayatra in Orissa and Upliftment of Harijans,' *Orissa Review*, 2011, http://magazines.odisha.gov.in/Orissareview/2011/Jan/engpdf/51-54.pdf.

64. Pradhan, *Role of Malati Devi Choudhury*, p. 69.

65. Jugal Kishore Hota, 'Parliamentary Activities of Surendranath Dwivedy,' *Orissa Review*, 2015, http://magazines.odisha.gov.in/Orissareview/2015/Dec/engpdf/23-28.pdf.

66. Pradhan, *Role of Malati Devi Choudhury*, p. 71.

67.

68. S.C. Padhy, 'Peasant Movement in Coastal Orissa (1936–39): Mobilisation and Participation,' *Proceedings of the Indian History Congress*, vol. 73, 2012, pp. 774–81, www.jstor.org/stable/44156273. Accessed 20 July 2021.

69. Biswamoy Pati, 'Of Movements, Compromises and Retreats: Orissa, 1936–1939,' *Social Scientist*, vol. 20, no. 5/6, 1992, pp. 64–88, *JSTOR*, www.jstor.org/stable/3517932. Accessed 20 July 2021.

70. Pradhan, *Role of Malati Devi Choudhury*, p. 74.

71. Ibid, p. 75.

72. Ibid, p. 78; Akshaya Kumar Patra, 'Socialist Movement and Sarangadhar Das,' *Orrisa Review,* 2012, p. 3, http://magazines.odisha.gov.in/Orissareview/2012/April/engpdf/25–29.pdf.

73. Pradhan, *Role of Malati Devi Choudhury*, p. 78.

74. Ibid.

75. Sarat Parida, 'The Praja Mandal Movement and the Birth of Greater Orissa,' *Orrisa Review*, 2009, p. 3, http://magazines.odisha.gov.in/Orissareview/2009/Jan/engpdf/17–19.pdf.

76. Pradhan, *Role of Malati Devi Choudhury*, p. 82.

77. *Freedom Fighters Remember*, Publications Division, p. 85.

78. Ibid.

79. Pradhan, *Role of Malati Devi Choudhury*, p. 84.

80. Ibid.

81. Ibid, p. 85.

82. Ibid, p. 111.

83. Ibid.

84. *Orissa Society of Americas 35th Annual Convention Souvenir*, p. 51.

85. Pradhan, *Role of Malati Devi Choudhury*, p. 111.

86. Ibid, p. 118.

87. 'From the Pages of Malati Devi's Diary 1971', *The Tribal Tribune*, Volume 1, Issue 11, 26 July 2005

88. Pradhan, *Role of Malati Devi Choudhury*, 30.

89. Sanghamitra Behera, 'A Brief Biographical Study of Nabakrushna Choudhury', *Social Development in Orissa: A Study of the Contributions of Sri Nabakrushna Choudhury*, Utkal University, 30 January 2019, p. 100, https://shodhganga.inflibnet.ac.in:8443/jspui/handle/10603/227639.

90. S. Dwivedy, *Quest for Socialism: Fifty Years of Struggle in India*, Radiant, 1984, p. 158; J.K. Mohapatra, *Factional Politics in India*, Chugh Publication, 1985, p. 119.

91. Anadi Naik, *A Man of Humility: Life and Times of Sarat Chandra Maharana*, Ketaki Foundation Trust, 2021, p. 125.

92. Ibid, p. 127.

93. *Freedom Fighters Remember*, Publications Division, p. 86.

94. Pradhan, *Role of Malati Devi Choudhury*, p. 87.

95. Ibid, p. 88.

96. Ibid, p. 87.

97. Ibid, p. 89.

98. Krushna Mohanty, 'From the Pages of Malati Devi's Diary 1971.'

99. Ibid

100. Pradhan, *Role of Malati Devi Choudhury*, p. 89.

101. Ibid.

102. *Orissa Society of Americas 35th Annual Convention Souvenir*, p. 49.

103. Das, *Nationalist Movement in Odisha*, p. 66.

104. *Orissa Society of Americas 35th Annual Convention Souvenir*, p. 49.

105. Das, *Nationalist Movement in Odisha*, p. 66.

106. Subranshu Patnaik, *A Study on Naba Krushna Choudhury as a Legislator 1937–56*, Utkal University, p. 14, https://shodhganga.inflibnet.ac.in:8443/jspui/handle/10603/281596.

107. Ibid, p. 287.

108. Pradhan, *Role of Malati Devi Choudhury*, p. 98.

109. Ibid.

110. *Orissa Society of Americas 35th Annual Convention Souvenir*, p. 52.

111. Pradhan, *Role of Malati Devi Choudhury*, p. 100.

112. *Orissa Society of Americas 35th Annual Convention Souvenir*, p. 52.

113. Pradhan, *Role of Malati Devi Choudhury*, p. 100.

114. Ibid, p. 99.

115. Ibid, p. 100.

116. Swaraj Mishra, 'Fight Between Two Generations of Women Leaders: Malati Vs Nandini,' Sambad English, 17 April 2019, https://sambadenglish.com/fight-between-two-generations-of-women-leaders-malati-vs-nandini/.

117. 'Malati Chaudhury – A Biographical Sketch,' *The Tribal Tribune*, Volume 1, Issue 11, 26 January 2005.

118. *Orissa Society of Americas 35th Annual Convention Souvenir*, p. 48.

119. 'Sarvodaya Leader Malati Choudhury Passes Away,' Times of India, 16 March 1998.

120. E. Linton, *Fragments of a Vision: A Journey Through India's Gramdan Villages*, Prithvi Raj, 1972, p. 57.

PURNIMA BANERJI

1. Upasana Goswami, 'Purnima Banerji: The Backstage Feminist of The Indian Constituent Assembly,' Feminism in India, 27 June 2019, https://feminisminindia.com/2019/06/27/purnima-banerji-indian-constituent-assembly/; Priya Ravichandran, 'Purnima Banerji (1911–1951),' Women Architects of the Indian Republic, 1 April 2016, https://15fortherepublic.wordpress.com/2016/04/01/purnima-banerji-1911-1951/.

2. David Kopf, *The Brahmo Samaj and the Shaping of the Modern Indian Mind*, Princeton University Press, 1979, p. 238.

3. Abeek Barman, 'My Arunapishi: A Personal Look at the Life of Aruna Asaf Ali,' The Quint 29 July 2022, https://www.thequint.com/voices/opinion/arunapishi-a-personal-look-at-the-life-of-aruna-asaf-ali.

4. 'Mira Devi (1892–1962); Daughter of Rabindranath,' The Scottish Centre of Tagore Studies, https://scotstagore.org/mira-devi-1892-1962-daughter-of-rabindranath-by-christine-kupfer/.

5. Sucheta Kripalani, *Sucheta: An Unfinished Autobiography*, Navjivan Publishing House, 1978, p. 27.

6. Jawaharlal Nehru, *A Bunch of Old Letters*, Oxford University Press, 1988, p. 457.

7. G N S Raghavan, *M. Asaf Ali Memoirs: The Emergence of Modern India*, Ajanta Publications, 1994, p. 203.

8. Sri Kedar Nath Sinha, 'Mr. Pearey Lal Banerji,' http://www.allahabadhighcourt.in/event/MrPeareyLBanerjiKNSinha.pdf.

9. P.D. Tandon, *The Unforgettable Nehru*, National Book Trust, 2017, p. 198.

10. Report of the 14th Session of All India Women's Conference.

11. D.R. Mankekar, *Lal Bahadur Shastri*, Publications Division, Ministry of Information and Broadcasting, Government of India, 1973, pp. 85–86.

12. 'Nehru Report', 1928, https://www.constitutionofindia.net/historical-constitution/nehru-report-motilal-nehru1928/.

13. Jawaharlal Nehru, *Soviet Russia: Some Random Sketches and Impressions*, Allahabad Law Journal Press, 1928, p. 5.

14. Ajit Bhattacharjea, *Jayaprakash Narayan: A Political Biography*, Vikas Publishing House, 1978, p. 56.

15. Vijaya Lakshmi Pandit, *The Scope of Happiness: A Personal Memoir*, Weidenfeld and Nicolson, 1979, p. 102.

16. Visalakshi Menon, *Indian Women and Nationalism: The U. P. Story*, Shakti Books, 2003, p. 20.

17. Uma Rao, 'Women in the Frontline: Case of U.P.', in Leela Kasturi and Vina Mazumdar (ed.), *Women and Indian Nationalism*, Vikas Publishing, 1994, p. 47.

18. Menon, *Indian Women and Nationalism*, p. 139.

19. Pandit, *Scope of Happiness*, p. 165.

20. Sonia Gandhi (ed.), *Two Alone, Two Together: Letters Between Indira Gandhi and Jawaharlal Nehru, 1940–1964*, Hodder & Stoughton, 1992, p. 235.

21. Ibid, p. 242.

22. Ibid, p. 501.

23. Jayaprakash Narayan, *In the Lahore Fort*, Sahityalaya, 1947, p. vi.

24. United Provinces Legislative Assembly Records

25. *Constituent Assembly Debates*, Vol V, 30 August 1947.

26. Ibid.

27. Ibid.

28. T.M.A. Pai Foundation & Ors vs State of Karnataka & Ors https://main.sci.gov.in/jonew/judis/18770.pdf.

29. *Constituent Assembly Debates*, Vol VIII, 2 June 1949.

30. *Constituent Assembly Debates*, Vol IX, 30 July 1949.

31. *Constituent Assembly Debates*, Vol IX, 19 August 1949.

32. *Constituent Assembly Debates*, Vol IX, 9 August 1949.

33. *Constituent Assembly Debates*, Vol IX, 10 September 1949.

34. Ibid.

35. 'Draft Constitution of the Republic of India (Socialist Party, 1948),' Constitution of India, https://www.constitutionofindia.net/historical_constitutions/draft_constitution_of_the_republic_of_india__socialist_party__1948__1st%20January%201948.

36. B. Shiva Rao, *The Framing of the Indian Constitution: A Study*, Indian Institute of Public Administration, 1968, p. 231–36.

37. Ibid, p. 238.

38. *Constituent Assembly Debates*, Vol IX, 15 September 1949.

39. Ibid.

40. Jagjeet Singh and Ors vs Ashish Mishra @ Monu and Ors.

41. *Constituent Assembly Debates*, Vol X, 11 October 1949.

42. *Constituent Assembly Debates*, Vol XI, 24 November 1949.

43. Ibid.

44. Ibid.

45. Ibid.

RAJKUMARI AMRIT KAUR

1. 'List of Member,' Lok Sabha, https://sansad.in/ls/members.

2. 'Jassa Singh Ahluwalia: Remembering the Forgotten Hero,' Tribune, 19 May 2021, https://www.tribuneindia.com/news/amritsar/jassa-singh-ahluwalia-remembering-the-forgotten-hero-255110; 'Jassa Singh Ahluwalia,' https://www.sikhiwiki.org/index.php/Jassa_Singh_Ahluwalia;; 'History,' Kapurthala, https://kapurthala.gov.in/history/.

3. 'Kapurthala,' Royal Ark, https://www.royalark.net/India/kapurth3.htm.

4. Granville Austin, *Working a Democratic Constitution: The Indian Experience*, Oxford University Press, 1999, p. 196.

5. G.A. Natesan, *Indian Christians: Biographical and Critical Sketches of Poets, Educationists, Publicists, Reformers, Ministers of the Church in India*, G.A. Natesan & Company, 1928, p. 225–239; 'Kapurthala,' Royal Ark.

6. Natesan, *Indian Christians.*

7. Dr. Sushila Nayar, 'Rajkumari Amrit Kaur', *Eminent Parliamentarians Monograph Series*, Lok Sabha Secretariat, 1992, p. 27.

8. Rajmata Gayatri Devi, 'A Tribute to Rajkumari Amrit Kaur', *Eminent Parliamentarians Monograph Series*, p. 41; 'Indian Womanhood,' The Northam Advertiser, 3 December 1954.

9. Padmini Sen Gupta, *Pioneer Women of India*, Thacker, 1944, p. 69.

10. Indian Womanhood,' The Northam Advertiser.

11. Sidin Vadukut, 'The Remarkable Life of Leela Row Dayal,' Mint, 30 June 2018, https://www.livemint.com/Leisure/

hL3EjZctOHVopSB5TCOQUK/The-remarkable-life-of-Leela-Row-Dayal.html.

12. 'Rajkumari Amrit Kaur: A Profile,' *Eminent Parliamentarians Monograph Series*, p. 2.

13. Prof Anima Bose, 'A Profile in Courage', *Eminent Parliamentarians Monograph Series*, p. 55.

14. G.A. Natesan, *The Indian Demand*, G.A. Natesan and Co., 1917, pp. 52–53.

15. M.K. Gandhi, *Letters to Rajkumari Amrit Kaur*, Navajivan Publishing House, 1961, p. vi.

16. Chandrashekhar Shukla (ed.), *Incidents of Gandhiji's Life*, Vora and Co. Publishers Ltd, 1949, pp. 7–8.

17. Ibid.

18. Bose, 'A Profile in Courage'.

19. Shukla, *Incidents of Gandhiji's Life*, pp. 7–8.

20. Gandhi, *Letters to Rajkumari Amrit Kaur*, p. vi.

21. Renuka Ray, 'India's First Woman Cabinet Minister,' *Eminent Parliamentarians Monograph Series*, p. 47.

22. Sumita Mukherjee, *Indian Suffragettes: Female Identities and Transnational Networks*, Oxford University Press, 2018, Chapter 3.

23. R. Parr, 'Solving World Problems: The Indian Women's Movement, Global Governance, and 'the Crisis of Empire,' 1933–46. *Journal of Global History*, 16(1), pp. 122–40. doi:10.1017/S1740022820000169.

24. Mukherjee, *Indian* Suffragettes, Chapter 3.

25. Parr, 'Solving World Problems.'

26. Report of the Indian Franchise Committee, Vol I, Government of India, 1932, p. 8.

27. Report of the Fourteenth Session of All India Women's Conference.

28. Nehru Report', 1928, https://www.constitutionofindia.net/historical-constitution/nehru-report-motilal-nehru1928/.

29. Report of the Indian Franchise Committee, Vol I, Government of India, 1932, p. 177.

30. The Marquess of Lothian, 'India and the Franchise Problem,' International *Affairs* (Royal Institute of International Affairs 1931–1939,) Vol. 11, No. 5 (Sep., 1932), pp. 593–617.

31. 'Poona Pact 1932', B.R. Ambedkar and M.K. Gandhi, https://www.constitutionofindia.net/historical-constitution/poona-pact-1932-b-r-ambedkar-and-m-k-gandhi/.

32. Nripendra Nath Mitra (ed.), *The Annual Register*, Vol. II, July to December 1932, The Annual Register Office, 1933, p. 357.

33. Meera Dhanda (ed.), *Reservation for Women*, Women Unlimited, 2008, pp. 40–41.

34. Mitra (ed.), *The Annual Register*, p. 358.

35. Annie Devenish, *Debating Women's Citizenship in India, 1930–1960*, Bloomsbury, 2019, Chapter 2.

36. Dhanda (ed.), *Reservation for Women*, pp. 40–41.

37. Mitra (ed.), *The Annual Register*, p. 358.

38. Geraldine H. Forbes, 'Votes for Women: The Demand for Women's Franchise in India 1917–1937: Symbols of Power', in Vina Mazumdar (Ed.), *Symbols of Power, Studies on the Political Status of Women in India*, Allied Publishers Private Limited, 1979, p. 15

39. Vasant Moon, *Dr. Babasaheb Ambedkar, Writings and Speeches*, Vol. 2, Ministry of Social Justice & Empowerment, Govt. of India, 1995, p. 700–01.

40. Minutes of Evidence, *Joint Committee on Indian Constitutional Reforms [Session 1932–33]*, His Majesty's Stationery Office, 1934, pp. 1617–20.

41. Ibid.

42. *Constituent Assembly Debates*, Vol. IV, 18 July 1947.

43. Shukla, *Incidents of Gandhiji's Life*, p. 9.

44. Nayar, 'Rajkumari Amrit Kaur', p. 29.

45. Aruna Asaf Ali, 'A Woman Dedicated to Gandhian Ideas', *Eminent Parliamentarians Monograph Series*, p. 34.

46. Shukla, *Incidents of Gandhiji's Life*, p. 13.

47. M. K. Gandhi, *The Indian States' Problem*, Navjivan Press, 1941, p. 114.

48. 'Amrit Kaur's Propaganda Tour', Bombay Chronicle, 11 October 1938.

49. Shukla, *Incidents of Gandhiji's Life*, p. 9.

50. Aruna Asaf Ali, 'A Woman Dedicated to Gandhian Ideas', p. 35.

51. All India Congress Committee Records.

52. 'Rajkumari Amrit Kaur: A Profile,' *Eminent Parliamentarians Monograph Series*, p. 2.; Manmohan Kaur, *Role of Women in the Freedom Movement, 1857–1947*, Sterling Publishers, p. 218.

53. Report of the 12th Session of the All India Women's Conference.

54. Kaur, *Role of Women in the Freedom* Movement, p. 219; Rajkumari Amrit Kaur: A Profile,' Eminent Parliamentarians Monograph Series, pp. 2–3.

55. Amrit Kaur, *To Women*, Navjivan Publishing House, 1945.

56. Selected Works of Jawaharlal Nehru Series 1, Vol. 15, p. 260. https://nehruselectedworks.com/.

57. M.K. Gandhi, *Letters to Rajkumari Amrit Kaur*, Navjivan Publishing House, 1961, pp. 245–46.

58. Rao, *The Framing of the Indian Constitution: A Study*, p. 185.

59. B. Shiva Rao, *The Framing of the Indian Constitution: Select Documents*, Volume II, Indian Institute of Public Administration, 1968, p. 146.

60. Ibid, p. 146.

61. Ibid, pp. 162–63.

62. Ibid, p. 178.

63. Ibid, pp. 309–12.

64. Ibid, pp. 401–02

65. Renuka Ray, 'India's First Woman Cabinet Minister', *Eminent Parliamentarians Monograph Series*, p. 45.

66. Rajkumari Amrit Kaur: A Profile,' Eminent Parliamentarians Monograph Series, p. 6.

67. https://www.aiims.edu/aiims/ritact/aboutaiimsintro.htm

68. Subhash Kashyap (ed.), *100 Best Parliamentary Speeches*, Harper Collins Publishers India, 1999, p. 427.

69. Second Five-Year Plan, Planning Commission.

70. macrotrends.net.

71. Matthew Connelly, 'Population Control in India: Prologue to the Emergency Period', Population and Development Review, Vol. 32, No. 4 (Dec. 2006), pp. 629–67, https://www.jstor.org/stable/20058922.

72. Kashyap (ed.), *100 Best Parliamentary Speeches*, p. 383.

73. 'List of Members,' Lok Sabha, https://sansad.in/ls/members.

74. Rajkumari Amrit Kaur: A Profile,' Eminent Parliamentarians Monograph Series, p. 10.

75. Ibid, p. 11.

76. 'Rajkumari Amrit Kaur, 75, Dies; India's First Minister of Health; Gandhi's Secretary 17 Years, a Princess, Led Campaign to Eradicate Malaria,' New York Times, 7 February 1964, https://www.nytimes.

com/1964/02/07/archives/rajkumari-amrit-kaur-75-dies-indias-first-minister-of-health.html.

77. Margaret Cousins, *Indian Womanhood Today*, Kitabistan, 1941, p. 153.

RENUKA RAY

1. Constituent Assembly Debates, Vol. XI, 19 November 1949 https://www.constitutionofindia.net/debates/19-nov-1949/.

2. Renuka Ray, *My Reminiscences: Social Development During the Gandhian Era and After*, Stree, 2005, p. 2.

3. Ibid, pp. 3–7.

4. D. Banerjee, *Boundaries of the Self: Gender, Culture and Spaces*, Cambridge Scholars Publisher, 2014, p. 62.

5. Ray, *My Reminiscences*, pp. 1–12.

6. Ibid, p. 4.

7. Nalini Bhushan Jay L. Garfield, *Minds Without Fear: Philosophy in the Indian Renaissance*, Oxford University Press, p. 213; Ray, *My Reminiscences*, p. 36.

8. Bhushan Jay L. Garfield, *Minds Without Fear*, p. 213.

9. Ray, *My Reminiscences*, p. 6.

10. Past Presidents,' All India Women's Conference, 'http://aiwc.org.in/past_president.html

11. Supriya Roy, 'Sarala Ray's daughter Kanaklata was a true modern woman', *Get Bengal*, 6 June 2019. https://www.getbengal.com/details/sarala-ray-s-daughter-kanaklata-was-a-true-modern-woman

12. Ray, *My Reminiscences*, p. 11.

13. Ibid, p. 11.

14. Ibid, p. 10.

15. Ibid, p. 19.

16. Ibid, p. 27.

17. Ibid.

18. Ibid, p. 30.

19. Ibid.

20. Ibid, p. 31.

21. Ibid, p. 33.

22. Ibid, p. 43.

23. Ibid, p. 14.

24. Ibid, p. 41.

25. Ibid. p. 41.

26. Ibid, p. 34.

27. Ibid, p. 39.

28. Ibid, p. 43.

29. Ibid, p. 44.

30. Ibid.

31. Ibid, p. 1, 265; 'List of Members,' Lok Sabha, https://sansad.in/ls/members.

32. Ray, *My Reminiscences*, p. 45.

33. Ibid, p. 47.

34. Ibid, p. 81. *1*

35. Ibid, p. 82.*2*

36. Barbara Southard, 'Bengal Women's Education League: Pressure Group and Professional Association,' *Modern Asian Studies*, vol. 18, no. 1, Cambridge University Press, 1984, pp. 67, http://www.jstor.org/stable/312383.

37. Ray, *My Reminiscences*, p. 82.

38. Ibid.

39. Ibid, p. 83.

40. Renuka Ray, *Legal Disabilities of Indian Women: A Plea for a Commission of Enquiry*, Reprinted from *The Modern Review*, November 1934, p. 2, https://lse-atom.arkivum.net/uploads/r/the-womens-library/2/7/6/276f20533f97aa1dbf7f59fd7e84a602ca0480d6ed23f60d523d7d5cb1e79e04/3d3f9fe6-9664-4bdd-9e9e-6923477d77a5-UKLSE_DL1_IF01_003_001_0506_0001.pdf.

41. Ibid, p. 12.

42. Ray, *My Reminiscences*, p. 173.

43. Ibid, p. 178.

44. Ibid, p. 49.

45. Ibid, p. 51.

46. Ibid, p. 54.

47. Ibid, p. 56.

48. Reba Som, 'Jawaharlal Nehru and the Hindu Code: A Victory of Symbol over Substance?,' *Modern Asian Studies*, vol. 28, no. 1, Cambridge University Press, 1994, pp. 170, http://www.jstor.org/stable/312925.

49. Ray, *My Reminiscences*, p. 58.

50. Ibid, p. 58.

51. Ibid, p. 59.

52. Ibid, p. 60.

53. Som, 'Jawaharlal Nehru and the Hindu Code.'

54. Ray, *My Reminiscences*, p. 61.

55. Ibid.

56. 'List of Members,' Lok Sabha, https://sansad.in/ls/members.

57. Ray, *My Reminiscences*, p. 62.

58. Ibid, p. 63.

59. Ibid, p. 64–66.

60. Ibid, p. 68.

61. Ibid, p. 107.

62. Ibid, p. 116.

63. Ibid, p. 117.

64. Ibid, p. 119.

65. Constituent Assembly debates, volume 4, 18 July 1947, https://www.constitutionofindia.net/debates/18-jul-1947/.

66. Ibid.

67. Constituent Assembly debates, volume 7, 9 November 1948 https://www.constitutionofindia.net/debates/09-nov-1948/

68. Ray, *My Reminiscences*, p. 143.

69. Ibid, p. 146.

70. Gopal Sankaranarayanan, 'The Fading Right to Property in India,' *Verfassung Und Recht in Übersee/Law and Politics in Africa, Asia and Latin America*, vol. 44, no. 2, 2011, pp. 229, http://www.jstor.org/stable/43239608.

71. Constituent Assembly debates, Volume 7, 6 January 1949, https://www.constitutionofindia.net/debates/06-jan-1949/.

72. Ibid.

73. Ray, *My Reminiscences*, p. 148.

74. Ibid.

75. Ibid, p. 149.

76. Ibid, p. 193.

77. 'Lok Sabha / 1952 / West Bengal / Hooghly,' India Votes, https://www.indiavotes.com/lok-sabha-details/1952/west-bengal/hooghly/291/9/1.

78. Ray, *My Reminiscences*, p. 194.

79. Ibid, p. 158.

80. Ibid, p. 159.

81. Ibid.

82. Ibid, p. 207.

83. Ibid, p. 203.

84. Ibid, p. 159.

85. Ibid, p. 168.

86. 'Lok Sabha / 1957 / West Bengal / Malda,' India Votes, https://www.indiavotes.com/lok-sabha-details/1957/west-bengal/malda/770/9/2.

87. Ray, *My Reminiscences*, p. 168.

88. Prakash Chandra Mehta (ed.), Development of Indian Tribes, Discovery Publishing House, 2006, p. 85.

89. Ibid, p. 86.

90. Ray, *My Reminiscences*, p. 227.

91. Ibid, p. 287.

92. Ibid, p. 288.

93. 'Past Presidents,' All India Women's Conference, http://aiwc.org.in/past_president.html.

94. Ray, *My Reminiscences*, p. 245.

95. Ibid, p. 246–47.

96. Padma Awards Directory (1954-2011), Ministry of Home Affairs (Public Section), Government of India, 23 February 2012, p. 86, https://web.archive.org/web/20130510095705/http:/www.mha.nic.in/pdfs/LST-PDAWD.pdf.

97. Lok Sabha Debates, Volume 15, Issue 1, 23 July 1997, https://eparlib.nic.in/bitstream/123456789/5365/1/11_V_23071997_p19_p20_t2.pdf.

98. Ray, *My Reminiscences*, p. 264.

SAROJINI NAIDU

1. 'Macaulay's Minute on Education, 2 February 1835, http://home.iitk.ac.in/~hcverma/Article/Macaulay-Minutes.pdf.

2. Padmini Sengupta, *Sarojini Naidu: A Biography*, Asia Publishing House, 1966, p. 12.

3. Ibid, p. 13.

4. Ibid.

5. Ibid, p. 14; Uttara Rangarajan, 'Aghorenath Chattopadhyay,' https://www.ed.ac.uk/global/uncovered/1800-1859/aghorenath-chattopadhyay.

6. Tara Ali Baig, *Builders of Modern India*, Publications Division, Ministry of Information and Broadcasting, Government of India, 1974, p. 7

7. 'College Profile', https://web.archive.org/web/20220921075219/https://www.nizamcollege.ac.in/college-profile.html.

8. Sengupta, *Sarojini Naidu*, p. 15.

9. Sengupta, *Sarojini Naidu*, pp. 13–16; Baig, *Builders of Modern India*, pp. 8-10.

10. Sengupta, *Sarojini Naidu*, pp. 10–11.

11. Sarojini Naidu, *The Golden Threshold*, William Heinemann, 1905, p. 14.

12. Baig, *Builders of Modern India*, p. 12.

13. Ibid; 'Virendranath Chattopadhyaya,' The Open University, https://encyclopedia.1914-1918-online.net/article/chattopadhyaya_virendranath/; Heike Leibau, 'Chattopadhyaya, Virendranath,' 1914–1918 Online, https://encyclopedia.1914-1918-online.net/article/chattopadhyaya_virendranath/.

14. Naidu, *The Golden Threshold*, p. 11.

15. Ibid, p. 12.

16. Ibid, p. 13.

17. Sengupta, *Sarojini Naidu*, p. 27.

18. Ibid, p. 13.

19. Baig, *Builders of Modern India*, p. 18.

20. Sengupta, *Sarojini Naidu*, p. 31.

21. Ibid, p. 34.

22. Ibid, p. 37.

23. Baig, *Builders of Modern India*, p. 23.

24. Sengupta, *Sarojini Naidu*, p. 36.

25. Ray, *My Reminiscences*, p. 95.

26. G.N.S. Raghavan, *M. Asaf Ali's Memoirs: The Emergence of Modern India*, Ajanta Publications, 1994, pp. 98–99.

27. Ibid.

28. Elleke Boehmer, *Indian Arrivals, 1870-1915: Networks of British Empire*, Oxford University Press, 2015, p. 169.

29. Sarojini Naidu, *The Bird of Time: Songs of Life, Death & the Spring*, William Heinemann, 1912.

30. Baig, *Builders of Modern India*, p. 31.

31. *Speeches and Writings of Sarojini Naidu*, Third Edition, G.A. Natesan and Co., p. 7.

32. *Speeches and Writings of Sarojini Naidu*, pp. 12–13.

33. Sengupta, *Sarojini Naidu*, p. 68.

34. *Speeches and Writings of Sarojini Naidu*, p. 20.

35. Raghavan, *M. Asaf Ali's Memoir, p.* 102.

36. Sarojini Naidu, *Mohomed Ali Jinnah, an Ambassador of Unity: His Speeches & Writings 1912–1917*, Ganesh, 1918, p. 20.

37. Sengupta, *Sarojini Naidu*, pp. 86–88.

38. Sarojini Naidu, 'Foreword' in H.S.L. Polak, H.N. Brailsford, Lord Pethick-Lawrence, *Mahatma Gandhi*, Odhams Press, 1949, p. 7.

39. Mushirul Hasan, 'No Laughing Matter,' Hindustan Times, 1 June 2012, https://www.hindustantimes.com/books/no-laughing-matter/story-ykt7iT2IIS04HYhR9Ldm6K.html.

40. Vijaya Lakshmi Pandit, *The Scope of Happiness: A Personal Memoir*, Weidenfeld and Nicolson, 1979, p. 67.

41. Nayantara Sehgal, 'Iconic Songbird Sarojini Naidu Who Called Gandhi a Chocolate-coloured Mickey Mouse,' India Today, 15 September 2017, https://www.indiatoday.in/magazine/news-makers/story/20170925-sarojini-naidu-nightingale-of-india-music-poet-mimic-indian-independence-role-1045309-2017-09-15.

42. Pandit, *The Scope of Happiness*, p. 59.

43. Ray, *My Reminiscences*, p. 25.

44. Hansa Mehta, *Indian Woman*, Butala and Company, 1981, p. 188.

45. Cousins, *Indian Womanhood Today*, p. 157.

46. Ibid, p. 64.

47. *Speeches and Writings of Sarojini Naidu*, p. 152.

48. Cousins, *Indian Womanhood Today*, pp. 32–33.

49. *Speeches and Writings of Sarojini Naidu*, pp. 194–97.

50. Ibid, p. 198.

51. Ibid, p. 207.

52. Ibid, pp. 208–12.

53. Ibid, pp. 247–49.

54. Ibid, pp. 249–52.

55. John Last, 'The Prince of Wales' 1921 Trip to India Was a Royal Disaster,' JSTOR Daily, 2 February 2022, https://daily.jstor.org/the-prince-of-wales-1921-trip-to-india-was-a-royal-disaster/.

56. Krishna Das, Seven Months with Mahatma Gandhi: Being an Inside View of the Indian Non-Co-Operation Movement of 1921–22, S. Ganesan, 1928, p. 146.

57. *Speeches and Writings of Sarojini Naidu*, pp. 256–57.

58. 'Republic of Dissent: Gandhi's Sedition Trial,' Mint, 25 January 2019, https://www.livemint.com/politics/news/republic-of-dissent-gandhi-s-sedition-trial-1548352744498.html.

59. Nitya Menon, 'When Madras' Women Won the Vote,' The Hindu, 8 March 2015, https://www.thehindu.com/news/cities/chennai/when-madras-women-won-the-vote/article6969753.ece.

60. Anupama Roy, *Gendered Citizenship: Historical and Conceptual Explorations*, Orient Blackswan, E-edition, 2013, Chapter 4.

61. 'History,' All India Women's Conference, http://www.aiwc.org.in/history.html.

62. Report of the 4th Session Proceedings of All India Women's Conference.

63. *Constituent Assembly Debates*, Vol IV, 18 July 1947.

64. Ray, *My Reminiscences*, p. 60.

65. Margaret Cousins, *The Awakening of Asian Womanhood*, Ganesh & Co., 1922, p. 118.

66. Sengupta, *Sarojini Naidu*, pp. 158–59.

67. Report of the 40th Session of Indian National Congress.

68. Baig, *Builders of Modern India*, p. 96.

69. Ibid, p. 97.

70. Sengupta, *Sarojini Naidu*, pp. 268–72.

71. Baig, *Builders of Modern India*, p. 99.

72. 'Letter from Sarojini Naidu to Gandhiji, November 19, 1928,' MKGandhi.org, https://www.mkgandhi.org/Selected%20Letters/Sarojini/letter44.htm.

73. *Constituent Assembly Debates*, Vol. IV, 22 July 1947.

74. Sengupta, *Sarojini Naidu*, pp. 107–09.

75. Ibid, p. 244.

76. Ibid, pp. 130–41.

77. *Constituent Assembly Debates*, Vol. I, 11 December 1946.

78. Sengupta, *Sarojini Naidu*, p. 151.

79. Ibid, p. 305.

80. 'My Father, Do Not Rest', Broadcast on All India Radio, 1 February 1948, https://www.mkgandhi.org/Selected%20Letters/Sarojini/broadcast.htm.

81. *Selected Works of Jawaharlal Nehru*, Series 2, Volume 10, p. 488–89, https://nehruselectedworks.com/.

SUCHETA KRIPALANI

1. Surendra Gopal, *Mapping Bihar, From Medieval to Modern Times*, Routledge, 2018, p. 120.

2. Kripalani, *Sucheta: An Unfinished Autobiography*, p. 4.

3. Bibek Debroy, 'Manmatha Nath Dutt-I,' Open, 13 May 2019, https://openthemagazine.com/columns/guest-column/manmatha-nath-dutt-i/

4. Ibid.

5. Kripalani, *Sucheta: An Unfinished Autobiography*, p. 5.

6. Ibid, pp. 5–6.

7. 'Pindi Lull,' Royal Collection Trust, https://www.rct.uk/collection/2702649/prince-edward-of-wales-saluting-at-the-kitchener-college-delhi-edward-prince-of.

8. Kripalani, *Sucheta: An Unfinished Autobiography*, p. 7.

9. Ibid, p. 8.

10. Ibid, p. 10.

11. Ibid, p. 13.

12. Ibid.

13. 'Nehru Report (Motilal Nehru, 1928),' Constitution of India, https://www.constitutionofindia.net/historical_constitutions/nehru_report__motilal_nehru_1928__1st%20January%201928.

14. Kripalani, *Sucheta: An Unfinished Autobiography,* p. 15.

15. Ibid, p. 17.

16. Ibid, p. 20.

17. J.B. Kripalani, 'Introduction,' in *Sucheta: An Unfinished Autobiography*, p. xv.

18. Kripalani, *Sucheta: An Unfinished Autobiography*, pp. 21–22.

19. J.B. Kripalani, *Gandhi: His Life and Thought*, Publications Division, Ministry of Information and Broadcasting, Government of India, 1970, p. 473.

20. Kripalani, *Sucheta: An Unfinished Autobiography*, pp. 20–22.

21. Usha Thakkar and Jayshree Mehta (eds), *Understanding Gandhi: Gandhians in Conversation with Fred J. Blum*, Sage Publications, 2011, p. 438.

22. J.B. Kripalani, 'Introduction,' in *Sucheta: An Unfinished Autobiography*, p. xvi.

23. Ibid, pp. xvi–xvii.

24. 'Members Bioprofile,' Sansad.in https://sansad.in/ls/members

25. Forbes, *Women in Modern India*, p. 208.

26. 'Archive / Audio / S. Kripalani,' Interview number 196, Centre of South Asian Studies, University of Cambridge, https://www.s-asian.cam.ac.uk/archive/audio/collection/s-kripalani/.

27. Forbes, *Women in Modern India*, p. 208.

28. Kripalani, *Gandhi*, p. 206; 'Archive / Audio / S. Kripalani,' Interview number 196.

29. Kripalani, *Sucheta: An Unfinished Autobiography*, p. 32.

30. Arun Chandra Bhuyan, *The Quit India Movement: The Second World War and Indian Nationalism*, 1975, Manas Publications, 1975, pp. 104–05.

31. 'Archive / Audio / S. Kripalani,' Interview number 196.

32. Aanchal Malhotra, 'The Underground Congress Radio During Freedom Struggle and 22-yr-old Woman Behind Its Voice,' ThePrint, 26 January 2021, https://theprint.in/pageturner/excerpt/underground-congress-radio-during-freedom-struggle-and-usha-mehta/591863/.

33. Usha Thakkar, *Congress Radio: Usha Mehta and the Underground Radio Station of 1942*, Penguin Books, 2021, p. 119.

34. 'Archive / Audio / S. Kripalani,' Interview number 196.

35. Kripalani, *Sucheta: An Unfinished Autobiography*, pp. 33–35.

36. Ibid, p. 37.

37. Paul R. Greenough, *Political Mobilization and the Underground Literature of the Quit India Movement, 1942–44*, *Social Scientist*, Jul–Aug, 1999, Vol. 27, No. 7/8.

38. Bhuyan, *The Quit India Movement*, pp. 134–37.

39. 'Archive / Audio / S. Kripalani,' Interview number 196.

40. Kasturba Gandhi National Memorial Trust, http://kasturbatrust.org/.

41. Kripalani, *Sucheta: An Unfinished Autobiography,* p. 41.

42. Alex von Tunzelmann, *Indian Summer: The Secret History of the End of an Empire*, Simon & Schuster, 2012, Chapter 9.

43. Kripalani, *Gandhi*, p. 254.

44. Kripalani, *Sucheta: An Unfinished Autobiography*, pp. 43–52.

45. 'Archive / Audio / S. Kripalani,' Interview number 196.

46. Kripalani, *Sucheta: An Unfinished Autobiography*, pp. 70–71.

47. Myron Weiner, *Party Politics in India: The Development of a Multi-Party System*, Princeton University Press, p. 67.

48. Weiner, *Party Politics in India*, pp. 66–74.

49. 'Statistical Report on General Elections, 1951 to the First Lok Sabha Election, Vol. I', Election Commission of India.

50. Manmohini Zutshi Sahgal, *An Indian Freedom Fighter Recalls Her Life*, M. E. Sharp, 1994, pp. 136–40.

51. 'Archive / Audio / S. Kripalani,' Interview number 196.

52. Hari Kishor Singh, *A History of the Praja Socialist Party*, Narendran Prakashan, 1959, pp. 171–72.

53. Lok Sabha Debates, 19 May 1952, https://eparlib.nic.in/.

54. Lok Sabha Debates, 2 May 1955, https://eparlib.nic.in/.

55. Y.B.R. Murthy, Report of the Second National Conference of the Praja Socialist Party, 1955, p. 33.

56. Thakkar and Mehta (eds), *Understanding Gandhi*, p. 518.

57. 'Sucheta Kripalani vs Shri S.S. Dulat, I.C.S., Chairman of the Election Tribunal, on 6 September, 1955,' Indian Kanoon, https://indiankanoon.org/doc/573454/.

58. 'Archive / Audio / S. Kripalani,' Interview number 196.

59. Ibid.

60. N.R. Visalakshi, *President's Rule in Kerala*, The Indian Journal of Political Science, January–March, 1966, Vol. 27, No. 1 (January – March, 1966), pp. 55-68, https://www.jstor.org/stable/41854147.

61. 'Archive / Audio / S. Kripalani,' Interview number 196.

62. 'With the Kings in India, A Souvenir of Dr Martin Luther King's Visit to India, February–March 1959,' Gandhi Memorial Centre, 1959,

https://artsandculture.google.com/asset/with-the-kings-in-india-a-souvenir-of-dr-martin-luther-king-s-visit-to-india-february-march-1959/4gFmkvrY1HK22Q.

63. Nico Slate, *Lord Cornwallis is Dead*, Harvard University Press, 2019, p. 184.

64. Paul R. Brass, *An Indian Political Life: Charan Singh and Congress Politics, 1957 to 1967*, Sage Publications, 2013, Chapter 7.

65. 'Sucheta Kripalani, Indian Aide And Independence Fighter, Dies,' New York Times, 2 December 1974, https://www.nytimes.com/1974/12/02/archives/sucheta-kripalani-indian-aide-and-independence-fighter-dies-an.html.

66. Kripalani, *Sucheta: An Unfinished Autobiography*, pp. 43–52.

VIJAYA LAKSHMI PANDIT

1. B.R. Nanda, *The Nehrus: Motilal and Jawaharlal*, The John Day Company, 1963, p. 42.

2. Nanda, *The Nehrus*, pp. 21–25; Pandit, *The Scope of Happiness*, pp. 27–28.

3. Nanda, *The Nehrus*, p. 34.

4. Pandit, *The Scope of Happiness*, p. 57.

5. Ibid, p. 37.

6. Nanda, *The Nehrus*, p. 40.

7. Ibid, p. 43.

8. Pandit, *The Scope of Happiness*, p. 54.

9. Nanda, *The Nehrus*, p. 51.

10. Pandit, *The Scope of Happiness*, p. 61.

11. Ibid, pp. 60–62.

12. Sheela Reddy, *Mr and Mrs Jinnah: The Marriage That Shook India*, Penguin Random House India, 2017, Chapter 4.

13. Pandit, *The Scope of Happiness*, p. 65.

14. N.S. Vinodh, *A Forgotten Ambassador in Cairo*, Simon and Schuster India, 2021, Chapter 26.

15. Pandit, *The Scope of Happiness*, p. 65.

16. Ibid, p. 26.

17. Ibid, pp. 71–74.

18. Nanda, *The Nehrus*, p. 197.

19. Pandit, *The Scope of Happiness*, pp. 75–86.

20. Pandit, *The Scope of Happiness*, pp. 103–13.

21. 'List of Members,' Lok Sabha, https://sansad.in/ls/members.

22. Pandit, *The Scope of Happiness*, p. 117.

23. Ibid, p. 123.

24. 'Members Bioprofile,' Sansad.in https://sansad.in/ls/members.

25. R.L. Khipple, *The Woman Who Swayed America*, Lion Press, 1946, pp. 51–55.

26. Khipple, *The Woman Who Swayed America*, pp. 63–64.

27. Vijaya Lakshmi Pandit, *So I Became a Minister*, Kitabistan, 1939, p. 32.

28. Pandit, *So I Became a Minister*, p. 84.

29. Report of the 16th Session of All India Women's Conference.

30. Ibid.

31. 'In Conversation – Vijaya Lakshmi Pandit,' Rajiv Mehrotra, 27:13, https://www.youtube.com/watch?v=LmFZoGSPi6o&feature=youtu.be&t=18m36s.

32. Nayantara Sahgal, *Prison and Chocolate Cake*, Alfred A Knopf, 1954, p. 25.

33. Vijaya Lakshmi Pandit, *Prison Days*, The Signet Press, 1945, p. 97.

34. Pandit, *Prison Days*, p. 100.

35. Pandit, *Scope of Happiness*, p. 175.

36. 'In Conversation – Vijaya Lakshmi Pandit,' Rajiv Mehrotra.

37. Pandit, *Scope of Happiness*, pp. 176–181.

38. Ibid, p. 185.

39. Ibid, p. 186; Vera Brittain, *Envoy Extraordinary, A Study of Vijaya Lakshmi Pandit and Her Contribution to Modern India*, Routledge Revivals, 1965, p. 65.

40. Vinodh, *A Forgotten Ambassador*, Chapter 25.

41. Brittain, *Envoy Extraordinary*, p. 66.

42. Manu Bhagavan, *India and the Quest for One World: The Peacemakers*, Palgrave Macmillan, 2013, p. 29.

43. Khipple, *The Woman Who Swayed America*, p. 102.

44. Bhagavan, *India and the Quest for One World*, p. 40–42.

45. Brittain, *Envoy Extraordinary*, p. 76.

46. Pandit, *Scope of Happiness*, pp. 209–10.

47. *Constituent Assembly Debates*, Vol. II, 20 January 1947.

48. Pandit, *Scope of Happiness*, p. 245.

49. Ibid, p. 254.

50. Vijaya Lakshmi Pandit, 'India's Foreign Policy,' Foreign Affairs, 1 April 1956, https://www.foreignaffairs.com/articles/india/ 1956-04-01/indias-foreign-policy.

51. 'In Conversation - Vijaya Lakshmi Pandit,' Rajiv Mehrotra.

52. 'Past Presidents,' General Assembly of the United Nations, https://www.un.org/pga/73/about/past-presidents/

53. Kathleen Teltsch, '*MME. Pandit Mutes Status As Woman; New U. N. Assembly President Hopes Her Sex and Origin Will Not Be Stressed*,' New York Times, 16 September 1953, https://www.nytimes.com/1953/09/16/archives/mme-pandit-mutes-status-as-woman-new-u-n-assembly-president-hopes.html.

54. Robert Hardy Andrews, *A Lamp for India: The Story of Madam Pandit*, Arthur Barker Limited, p. 21.

55. 'Padma Awards', https://dashboard-padmaawards.gov.in/.

56. Pandit, *Scope of Happiness*, pp. 5–6.

57. Ibid, pp. 9–10.

58. William Borders, 'Mrs. Gandhi's Aunt Is Joining Foes,' New York Times, 14 February 1977, https://www.nytimes.com/1977/02/14/archives/mrs-gandhis-aunt-is-joining-foes.html.

59. 'In Conversation - Vijaya Lakshmi Pandit,' Rajiv Mehrotra.

60. Pandit, *Scope of Happiness*, p. 24.